Between Ocean and Bay

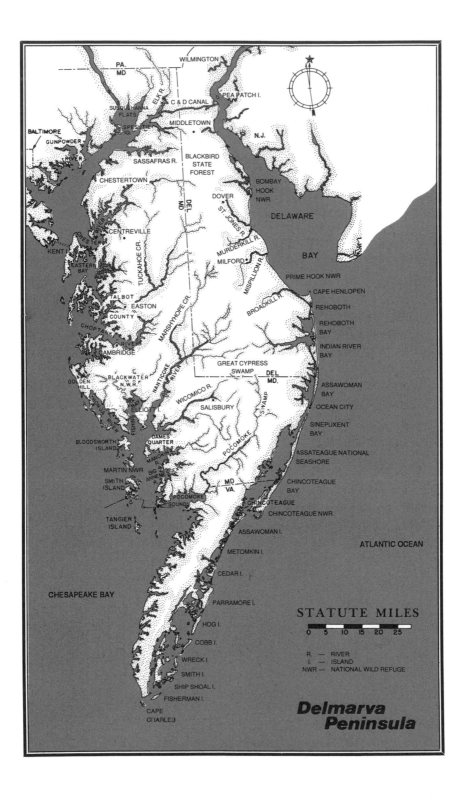

Delmarva Peninsula

Between Ocean and Bay

A Natural History of Delmarva

By Jane Scott

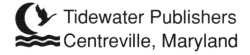 Tidewater Publishers
Centreville, Maryland

Library of Congress Cataloging-in-Publication Data

Scott, Jane
    Between ocean and bay : a natural history of Delmarva / by Jane
Scott.—1st ed.
       p.   cm.
    Includes bibliographical references and index.
    ISBN 0-87033-412-3 (paper) :
    1. Natural history—Delmarva Peninsula. 2. Geology—Delmarva
Peninsula.   I.Title.
QH104.5.D46S36 1991
508.752'1—dc20   90-50374
                                              CIP

Cover photo © Chesapeake Bay Foundation.

Manufactured in the United States of America
First edition, 1991; second printing, 1994

For Tony, with my love and thanks

Contents

Acknowledgments

This book could not have been written without the help and support of the members and staff of the Delaware Nature Society, particularly Michael Riska, Executive Director, and Lorraine Fleming, Manager of Conservation and Preservation. Lorraine, particularly, put me in touch with valuable contacts and helped me find pertinent books and papers. Nancy Frederick, vice president of the society, was responsible for the idea in the first place; Elton Woodberry, Mary Watkins, Darwin Palmer, Charles Gant, and Jim and Amy White all gave freely of their expertise.

Robert Ringler of the Maryland Ornithological Society sent me an annotated list of the birds of the Eastern Shore of Maryland and Janis Thomas, formerly of Delaware's Department of Natural Resources and Control, provided information about the Delaware Bay marshes. Peter Martin of Delaware Wildlands led me through the Great Cypress Swamp and Barry Truitt, Manager of the Virginia Coast Reserve, took me to see nesting birds on the barrier islands. Both were invaluable sources of information and lore.

Parts of the manuscript were read and commented on by Norman Wilder, Director Emeritus of the Delaware Nature Society; Dr. Jay R. Custer, Professor of Anthropology and Director of the Center for Archaeological Research at the University of Delaware; Dr. Thomas E. Pickett, Associate Director, Delaware Geological Survey; and Daniel R. Griffith, Acting Director of the Division of Historical and Cultural Affairs, Delaware Department of State. Dr. Franklin C. Daiber, Professor Emeritus, University of Delaware College of Marine Studies, read the section on wetlands, and Dr. John A. Munroe, Professor of History, University of Delaware, the chapters on the settlement and early farming practices of the peninsula. I am grateful to them all.

The Peninsula

Viewed from the western side . . . the map presents a most
appropriate resemblance to the head of a duck, the neck . . . [is].
constricted between the mouths of the Susquehanna and the
Delaware, while the bill seems puddling about among the
grass-flats and oyster-beds of the lower Chesapeake.
                                        —*Robert Wilson, 1876*

What is it about the Delmarva Peninsula that so many people love so much? It cannot be said to have spectacular scenery. Many a casual traveler has found the landscape boring, the summers humid, the waters murky, and the mosquitoes terrible. The roads, they say, run straight to the horizon between endless corn and soybean fields. The woods, for the most part, are but distant patches and there is little shade.

Yet, roots run deep on the peninsula. The towns are full of old brick and boxwood, ancient trees, neighborly porches, and hospitable people. The skies are soft and the rivers quiet. The pace is slow, the winters kind, and despite the dust of summer, there is always a salty smell of marshes. Most of all, there is a sense of space.

On the Eastern Shore they say that if you stay five years you will stay forever. Consider the epitaph of one Honorable John Custis, Esq., who was, incidentally, the father of Martha Washington's first husband. It ends:

Aged 71 years and yet lived but seven years Which was the space of time he kept A bachelor's house at Arlington On the Eastern Shore of Virginia.

Between Ocean and Bay

The Delmarva Peninsula lies between the Chesapeake and Delaware bays along the Middle Atlantic Coast, projecting southward like a fat thumb from the southern border of Pennsylvania to Cape Charles, Virginia, about two hundred miles to the south. It is called Delmarva because it contains the entire state of Delaware and the easternmost parts of Maryland and Virginia.

Most of the peninsula lies in the Atlantic coastal plain, and the low fields, woods, and marshes that the casual traveler finds so boring are, in fact, a typical coastal plain landscape where the level land and fertile soil have been intensively farmed since the earliest days of settlement. Yet Delmarva also has a strip of hilly piedmont country on its northern neck and between the piedmont and the coastal plain is a low ridge, known as the fall line, that crosses the peninsula from the mouth of the Susquehanna River to the city of Wilmington, Delaware. Wilmington, which sits on a rocky outcrop where the Brandywine and Christina rivers empty into the Delaware, is one of a string of East Coast

cities that grew up along the fall line at the point where waterfalls or rapids blocked the passage of ships coming upriver from the coast.

Broad coastal marshes line the shore of Delaware Bay from Wilmington to Cape Henlopen on the eastern side of the peninsula. South of Henlopen, Delmarva faces directly on the Atlantic Ocean behind a string of barrier islands, and narrows at its southern tip to the neck of land only a few miles wide that is known as the Eastern Shore of Virginia.

The entire peninsula tilts slightly to the southeast, and the land is noticeably higher on the western side along Maryland's upper Eastern Shore (so called because it is on the eastern shore of the Chesapeake Bay). Here, instead of broad marshes, there are low, sandy cliffs along the river banks, but they disappear south of Cambridge, Maryland, where the land again becomes low and marshy.

The peninsula's natural communities reflect this geographic diversity. Delmarva has both hilly landscapes and level fields, fast-flowing rocky streams and somnolent cypress swamps, ocean beaches, salt, fresh, and brackish tidal marshes, and so-called Delmarva bays. The "murky" waters of the Chesapeake and Delaware estuaries are, in fact, valuable nurseries for fish and shellfish, as well as important resting stations on the Atlantic Flyway, attracting huge flocks of migrating waterfowl and shorebirds. In fact, it is not unreasonable to view the Delmarva Peninsula as a microcosm of natural life as it is found along a major part of the eastern seaboard.

Climate

Spleen and vapours are as absolute Rarities here as a Winter's Sun or a Publick Spirit in England. A man may eat Beef, be as lazy as Captain Hardy or even marry in this Clymate, without having the least inclination to hang himself.
— *William Byrd, 1600s*

It is true that the summers are hot and humid; there are also frequent droughts as well as fierce local squalls and thunderstorms. The temperature often changes by several degrees at the Chesapeake and Delaware Canal which, in winter, causes snow above the canal to fall as rain below, and occasionally vice versa. The snow is normally short-lived, however. Winter temperatures are moderated by the surrounding bays and the Gulf Stream offshore to the east, which allow many southern plants and animals to thrive on the peninsula at the northern limit of their range, often within a few miles of northern species at the southern limit of theirs.

Between Ocean and Bay

It is a land of serenity and dignity, but . . . it must ever be a nook. It has no imperial possibilities.

—*George Alfred Townsend, 1872*

Perhaps, but the citizens of Delmarva have witnessed their share of history. According to archaeological evidence, man first came to the peninsula at the end of the Ice Age, sometime around 10,000 B.C. When early Swedish, Dutch, and English settlers arrived in the seventeenth century, they found a complex network of Indian tribes living peacefully, for the most part, in a land of rich natural resources.

During the Revolution, the British army under General Howe sailed up the Chesapeake in 1777 and disembarked at the head of the Elk. There was a skirmish on the way to Philadelphia at Cooch's Bridge in New Castle County, Delaware, where, it is said, the "Stars and Stripes" was carried into battle for the first time. In the summer of 1787, five representatives from the peninsula attended the Constitutional Convention in Philadelphia, and Delaware became the first state in the young nation to ratify the new document.

During the Civil War, the peninsula, like the nation, was divided. Virginia joined the Confederacy, while both Maryland and Delaware stayed in the Union. During those years, hundreds of fugitive slaves secretly crossed Delmarva on the Underground Railway and so many captured Confederate soldiers were confined at Fort Delaware that it became known as the "Andersonville of the North."

Profits generated by the demand for explosives during the First World War transformed the fledgling DuPont Company into a giant corporation and brought modern industrial development to the northern peninsula, yet the rural life and population of southern Delmarva remained essentially the same from the end of the nineteenth century until after World War II.

Today's Delmarva has both urban sophistication and rural seclusion. It is a land of cleared fields and lonely farmhouses, busy highways and beach resorts, where historic brick and clapboard towns are hidden behind an ever-increasing circle of commercial development. In many ways, the peninsula's human communities of watermen, farmers, military personnel, factory workers, corporate executives, doctors, lawyers, businessmen, and land developers could also be said to reflect contemporary America in microcosm.

Unfortunately, Delmarva also has all the pervasive environmental problems of the twentieth century. On the peninsula as elsewhere, the settlers who built our nation were not good stewards of the land. Faced with the need to survive and surrounded by a seemingly inexhaustible supply of resources, they embarked on a program of exploitation that destroyed the original forest, drained many of the wetlands, exterminated much of the wildlife, and polluted the waters. Today, in spite of a heartening new spirit of concern, these destructive attitudes continue to put much of the peninsula's environment under stress. Reversing the trend may be, as a director of the Chesapeake Bay Foundation once put it, "like rowing three knots against a four-knot current," but in the profound belief that knowledge of the natural world is our best weapon and greatest joy, I offer this book.

The History

. . . doe give, grant and confirme . . . all that part of a Peninsula, lying in the parts of America, betweene the Ocean on the East, and the Bay of Chesopeack on the West . . . unto that part of the Delaware Bay on the North, which lieth under the fortieth degree of Northerly Latitude.

—Charter of Maryland, 1632

Delmarva in the Dawn of Time

> *That shells should be found in this country, many feet under*
> *ground is not much to be wondered at since the strata of those*
> *shells might formerly have been the shores or bottom of the sea,*
> *upon which a crust of earth was superinduced in progress of time*
> *after the sea had retired.*
>
> *—A Citizen of Delaware, 1797*

Figuratively speaking, all of the Delmarva Peninsula south of Elkton, Maryland, and Newark, Delaware, is a sandbar, built from sediment left by the sea or eroded off the ancient Appalachian continent over the past 150-200 million years. It lies in the *Atlantic coastal plain*, itself a relatively recent emergence of the continental shelf. The coastal plain is the physiographic province that stretches from northeastern New Jersey, through the tidewater country of the Old South and around the southern tip of the Appalachians into eastern Texas, a land of broad salt marshes, slow-moving rivers, pine forest, and cypress swamps.

While ancient sediments constitute 90 percent of Delmarva's land area, the landscape changes on the narrow neck of the northern peninsula. This is piedmont country. The word (which means "foot of the mountain") represents, for geologists, the area bounded by the coastal plain on the east and the Appalachian Mountains on the west. The piedmont's clay soil, rocky streams, and rolling hills and valleys are underlaid with ancient rocks formed over vast stretches of time. Between the mouth of the Susquehanna River and Wilmington, Delaware, is the low ridge known as the fall line that marks the visible edge of the ancient Appalachian continent. Here, where the piedmont's bedrock dips seaward, it is not uncommon to find eroded hills with "young" sandy coastal plain soil at their tops and weathered crystalline rocks at their base.

Piedmont rocks are so ancient and the stretches of time involved in their formation so immense, that we find ourselves talking of geologic eras that cover hundreds of millions of years as if they were simple, orderly blocks of time: the Precambrian, from more than a billion years ago to 500 million, the Paleozoic, from 600 million to 220 million years ago, the Mesozoic, from 220 million to 63 million, and finally, the Cenozoic, from 63 million until now. In fact, the building of Delmarva's piedmont was far from orderly. Like the building of the North American continent itself, it was erratic, chaotic, and violent, and it took an inordinately long time.

The basic character of any landscape is profoundly influenced by the rock that lies beneath it. In the narrow slice of the piedmont province that can be included on Delmarva, there are distinctive rock formations, called "terranes." Each was formed by separate geologic events, perhaps occurring hundreds of millions of years apart. The oldest, called the Glenarm Terrane, was originally washed south as sandstone in Precambrian times, over a billion years ago, when the North American continent was but a pile of cooled magma in what is now eastern Canada. Five hundred million years ago, subsequent volcanic up-heavals transformed the sandstone into a banded, blue-grey metamorphic rock called gneiss. It is now the main component of a strata ten miles thick below the Delmarva piedmont.

Between the building of this basic terrane and the next lay a span of more than one hundred million years. A sea, already full of primitive living organisms covered much of the world, including Delmarva. It rose and fell repeatedly, first advancing to deposit layers of shale and sandstone hundreds of feet deep and then withdrawing to a position several hundred miles to the east of our present-day coastline. To the west, beyond what are now the piedmont hills, lay a great inland bay that covered the interior of the continent all the way from Labrador to the Gulf of Mexico.

On northern Delmarva, as elsewhere along the coast, sporadic volcanic activity split the ancient gneiss, intruding a layer of molten magma that would later cool into igneous rock. Several hundred million years later, this layer and the seaborne sediments that surrounded it would be metamorphosed into the schists and amphibolites that now form the second terrane, known as the "Wilmington Complex."

Before that happened, however, mountains would rise at intervals along the East Coast until the end of the Paleozoic era. Between upheavals, the incessant action of frost and rain leveled their craggy tops and washed untold tons of

4

sediment onto the continental shelf to the east and into the Appalachian trough to the west.

Meanwhile, vast chunks of the earth's crust were slowly rearranging themselves, like pieces of a jigsaw puzzle, across the surface of the globe. Even now neither the earth beneath our feet, nor the floor beneath the sea, is as solid as it appears. Great cracks, or faults, divide the earth's crust into giant plates that drift about on a sea of molten magma at the rate of roughly one mile in thirty thousand years. Earthquakes occur when two such plates attempt to slide past one another; mountain ranges are built where they collide head on; and, should they drift apart, the resulting fissure allows magma to boil up from the center of the earth in great volcanic explosions.

Something of the sort occurred late in the Paleozoic era when the Appalachian Mountains were born. Geologists know that the pieces that now compose the continents of Europe, Africa, and North America came together to form the great supercontinent they call Pangaea. Perhaps Africa pushed against our East Coast, buckling and cracking the earth's crust so that heat, steam, and molten magma spewed from the depths. The mighty force of such an upheaval would have forced the underlying rock of the Delmarva piedmont to break and fold over on itself, and, indeed, there is evidence of just such a cataclysmic mixing of strata in old quarries and railroad cuts near Rockland, Delaware. In fact, the mixing at this site is so severe that some geologists think it marked a major axis of thrust during the Appalachian upheaval.

The birth of the Appalachians was not an easy one. Chaotic volcanic activity continued for millennia to follow, building a range of craggy mountains up to five miles high. On Delmarva's piedmont, fire-born igneous rock spewed from the depths of the earth and intruded into existing foundations, forming the veins of granite, granodiorite, and gabbro that make up the fourth terrane of the Delmarva piedmont.

All during the geologic violence, living organisms were evolving, adapting, and spreading over the earth. The first organic compounds appeared over three billion years ago, as soon as the earth's temperature dropped low enough for clouds to form and rain to fall. Next came the first living cells, thought to have been a type of anaerobic bacteria. However, it was not until cells with chlorophyll appeared that the stage was truly set for evolution to begin. With chlorophyll came photosynthesis, or the ability to manufacture carbohydrates and oxygen from carbon dioxide. Photosynthesis, in effect, meant that life now could sustain itself indefinitely.

Again, in an attempt to clarify mysterious and complicated events, we tend to compress the long evolutionary night that followed into a sort of time-lapse photography in which the simplest invertebrate changes before our eyes into ever more complex organisms and ecosystems. Yet the road was not straight. Evolution traveled down many false paths and arrived at many dead ends; it has been estimated that up to 85 percent of all the species that ever existed on earth are now extinct.

Plant life was here from the beginning, yet the world's first great flush of vegetative growth did not appear until the Devonian period of the Paleozoic era, about four hundred million years ago, when ferns twenty to forty feet tall and forests of scale trees, *Lepidophyta*, spread across the land. (Today, these scale trees have evolved downward, so to speak, into the running ground pines, *Lycopodium*, of Delmarva woods.)

Paleozoic seas swarmed with primitive arthropods, called trilobites, while clams, snails, and early crinoids already inhabited shallow waters. So did the ancestors of Delmarva's familiar horseshoe crab, *Limulus polyphemus*, looking remarkably like it does today. The first vertebrate fish evolved: one, called a *Crossopterygian*, had lobed fins containing both gills and lungs. It is thought to have been the first creature to emerge from the sea.

During the Mississippian and Pennsylvanian epochs (one hundred million years before the Appalachian upheaval), the climate was tropical, the landscape swampy, and life-forms came in very large sizes. Varieties of scale trees towered two hundred feet high and seventy-foot ferns covered the landscape. Dragonflies with twenty-nine-inch wingspans soared over the swamps; there were cockroaches four inches long and spiders as big as saucers. The swamps already crawled with frogs, as well as a wide variety of small reptiles, some of which would evolve into the dinosaurs of the next great geologic era, the Mesozoic.

The Mesozoic era, which began after the Appalachian upheaval about two hundred million years ago, is divided into three periods: the Triassic, Jurassic, and Cretaceous. Dinosaurs walked the earth, on Delmarva as elsewhere. Fragments of a *Pterosaurus*, a flying reptile that took to the air in Jurassic times, have been found on the peninsula and a semiaquatic dinosaur from the Cretaceous period called the duck-billed *Hadrosaurus* unearthed near the Chesapeake and Delaware Canal.

The Mesozoic climate was still tropical, but the Paleozoic scale trees were replaced by primitive conifers, tree ferns, and cycads. Huge fishlike reptiles, up to forty feet long, swam in the seas. (Their image persists in old sailors' tales of monstrous sea serpents that once lurked beyond the horizon and perhaps do still in the depths of Loch Ness!) Sea creatures more familiar to us today included sharks, lungfish, and squids, as well as early clams and crustaceans. Grasshoppers, flies, and ants also existed before the first small catlike mammals appeared.

At this time, the Appalachians were huge craggy mountains to the west of Delmarva, and there was a line of volcanic islands across a shallow bay to the east. This bay dried by the end of the Jurassic period, exposing a level plain that extended up to two hundred miles to the east of the present coastline. This plain now forms the bedrock of the Delmarva Peninsula south of the piedmont. It laid exposed well into Cretaceous time, about one hundred thirty-five million years ago.

The story of Delmarva's coastal-plain sediments begins in Cretaceous times, the last great period of the Mesozoic era. This was also the period when flowering plants, or angiosperms, first became widespread, although some botanists now think they may have originated much earlier. The seeds of angiosperms, are enclosed in a pod and consequently can be saved for future germination. This was such a successful evolutionary step that within a short twenty million years, 70 percent of all the vegetation on earth was angiosperms. Some plants of today, notably those in the magnolia family, Magnoliaceae, are thought to have changed little since that time. Two conspicuous Delmarva magnolias are the sweet bay, *Magnolia virginiana*, of the coastal plain, and the tulip poplar, *Liriodendron tulipifera*, of the piedmont woods.

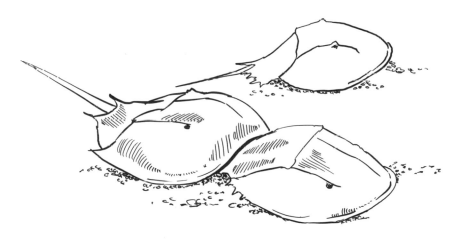

The Cretaceous period lasted about seventy million years. Sometime near its beginning, the sand, clays, and gravels that geologists now call the Potomac Formation were washed down from the Appalachian Mountains by fast-moving rivers and deposited in great deltas up to four thousand feet thick on the exposed bedrock of the coastal plain. Tens of millions of years later a second layer of sand and silt called the "Magothy Formation," was deposited by other streams that apparently originated within the coastal plain itself. Magothy sediments are studded with pieces of woody peat and coal, called lignite. They are deposited in a wedge, like a piece of pie lying on its edge, in depths ranging from a few feet in the northern peninsula to over five thousand feet farther south. In some places, these early layers of sediment have been pressed into a dense aggregate by the weight of later ones.

The first seaborne sediments to cover the Delmarva Peninsula were deposited later. The sea flooded Delmarva at least twice, and probably covered the peninsula off and on from the late Cretaceous period until the Eocene epoch, about forty million years later. Geologists can tell how far inland it reached by the size of the pieces it left behind. Fine particles of clay and silt can remain suspended in water for a long time, but heavier pebbles and sand grains are immediately rolled and dropped by breaking waves. Therefore, it is reasoned, the larger the size of particles in a marine formation, the closer to shore they were originally deposited.

These seaborne Cretaceous deposits, which are called the Matawan and Monmouth groups by geologists, contain quantities of fossilized bits of fish and shellfish. The best place to see them is along the Chesapeake and Delaware Canal where the original hand-dug channel cuts across the peninsula's drainage divide, exposing ancient sediment formations in multicolored layers. While much of the site has been degraded by later excavation, and many of the fossils removed or reburied, the canal cut was once one of the choicest spots for fossil collecting on the entire East Coast. In fact, the early collection of fossils in Philadelphia's Academy of Natural Science was collected here in the 1820s and 1830s.

A fossil is preserved evidence of an ancient animal or plant. It may be an actual piece of the animal—a shark's tooth or crab claw—or a petrified "model" of the original piece created by a process in which the shell pore spaces of the animal are replaced, molecule by molecule, with minerals. More often it is a cast or mold of the original piece that has been imprinted in sedimentary rock. The fossils most frequently found along the canal cut are a type of internal mold known as a "steinkern." Such molds occur when a buried shell is left undisturbed long enough for the silt to solidify around it, leaving an impression after the shell decomposes. Most of the steinkerns that have been found along the canal are early types of mollusks and snails, but there are also shark's teeth, tube casings of ancient worms, and burrow tubes of early crustaceans.

Besides fossils, the seaborne sediments in northern Delmarva contain glauconite, a complex mineral containing potassium, iron, and aluminum. Sediments containing glauconite, or "greensand" as it came to be known, were dug from marl pits and used for fertilizer in the nineteenth century. A layer up to forty feet deep that lies under the farmland between Odessa and Middletown,

Delaware, makes it among the most fertile on the peninsula. Today, greensand is used as an exchange medium to purify water and as a lining for landfills, where it filters out heavy metal ions.

Meanwhile, the dinosaurs and flying reptiles disappeared and starfish, sea urchins, and lobsters joined the inhabitants of the sea, along with fish such as cod, herring, and salmon. By the close of the Cretaceous period, the class of mammals known as marsupials were common. Our familiar opossum is a survivor.

As tens of millions of years passed, the sea continued to rise and fall and the rivers to wash sediments off the land. Layer covered layer on the lower peninsula and the next geologic era, the Cenozoic, began.

The first five epochs of the Cenozoic era (the Paleocene, the Eocene, the Oligocene, the Miocene, and the Pliocene) are often lumped together by geologists into the Tertiary period which lasted until the beginning of the Ice Age, about one million years ago.

The majority of our present-day mammals, insects, and flowering plants trace their roots to Tertiary times. At the start of the period, sometime around sixty-five million years ago, a honeybee got caught in the sticky resin of an ancestral sequoia tree on the coastal plain in what is now southern New Jersey. Over time, the resin turned to amber, preserving the bee, which is now in the collection of the American Museum of Natural History in New York City, conclusive evidence that honeybees had already been on earth long enough to develop remarkably modern features by the early Cenozoic era.

True birds, notably cormorants and snipe, had evolved by Eocene times, about sixty million years ago, as well as many flightless species that are now extinct. Crabs and squidlike creatures were added to the growing list of creatures in the sea. The dinosaurs were gone, but their descendants remained as crocodiles, lizards, and turtles.

As the Cenozoic climate turned cooler, the palm trees and tropical ferns disappeared from the peninsula. The conifers persisted, however, and were joined by temperate trees like hickories, oaks, and lindens. Mammals now grew to enormous sizes. Elephantlike mammoths and mastodons roamed the land, together with rhinoceros thirty feet long and fifteen-foot armadillos. There were giant hogs and sloths, tapirs, and saber-toothed tigers. Large whalelike mammals swam in the sea, along with sharks big enough to have teeth eight inches long. Fossilized specimens of these teeth are still brought up by oystermen from the bottom of the Chesapeake Bay.

About forty million years ago, at the beginning of the Oligocene epoch, something happened to cause a twenty-five-million-year gap in the geologic record of the peninsula. Delmarva's only undisputed Oligocene sediments are on the extreme southern tip. Did the sea wash them off the rest of the peninsula, or did the land remain exposed and undisturbed until the end of the Miocene epoch? Either way, fifteen million years ago, the sea again swept over the land, bringing more sediments and leaving more fossils. Oddly enough, this time there was no glauconite. It is a geologic mystery why glauconite, still present in modern seas, never appears in these later sediments.

The Ice Age on Delmarva

Although many perhaps may say, it is a physical absurdity to suppose there ever was water enough in the sea to cover the highest mountains: But let such remember, that he who from nothing created the universe, can meet with no difficulty in executing his designs.

—*A Citizen of Delaware, 1797*

After the fourth epoch of the Tertiary period (called the Miocene) another ten-million-year gap occurs in the geologic record of the peninsula, lasting until the beginning of the Ice Age. The Ice Age began in the Pleistocene epoch, also known as the first part of the Quaternary, one million years ago, and may, in fact, be still with us. Already, the glaciers have advanced and retreated across the North American continent four times. At present, the ice has receded to the Arctic, where it continues to melt, causing the sea to rise and flood the land at the rate of at least one-quarter foot per century, and in some places as much as one foot per century. This rate is now accelerating because of a buildup of certain gases in the atmosphere resulting from the burning of fossil fuels. This "greenhouse effect" is not an abstract threat for Delmarva: twenty more feet will flood most of the peninsula!

In the east, the ice penetrated as far south as central Pennsylvania and northern New Jersey. Although it never reached Delmarva, the peninsula was profoundly affected nevertheless. Each time the ice advanced, it incorporated so much water that the sea fell to as much as five hundred feet below its present level and meltwater running off the southern face of the glacier cut deep ravines in the landscape. The ancient Susquehanna and Delaware rivers flowed at the bottom of two of these ravines, some two hundred feet below the level of the plain.

The History

Each time the climate warmed, the amount of water released by the melting ice floe caused the sea to rise high enough to inundate the peninsula. During one early melting phase, called the Sangamon age, about eighty thousand to one hundred thousand years ago, the water rose thirty to forty feet *above* its present level, depositing a thick layer of sandy soil on southern Delmarva. Some think it also left behind the poorly drained depressions that are now known as Delmarva bays.

In the last advance, about twenty-five thousand years ago, the so-called Wisconsin Glacier stopped just north of Trenton. It was a veritable mountain of ice, several thousand feet thick. Part of a sheet that covered the entire top of the globe, it incorporated so much of the earth's available water that the sea dropped over three hundred feet, causing the continental shelf to emerge from the sea east of Delmarva. Pollen samples dating to 11,500 B.C., when the Wisconsin Glacier was at its height, show that extensive grasslands covered its exposed face, interspersed with patches of pine, spruce, and deciduous trees, while the ancestral Delaware and Susquehanna rivers flowed fast and cold down deeply incised channels to the sea.

Ice Age weather must have been stormy, as cold air from the ice sheet continually mixed with warm air from the south. This extensive frontal activity would have kept it cloudy, wet and cold, with little or no change from season to season. Scattered deposits of loess, a type of loamy soil carried by the wind, have been found in the center of the peninsula and along the Eastern Shore of Maryland. They are considered geological evidence that high winds sweeping across the grasslands were blocked at those sites by forests.

Ice Age wildlife on the peninsula included boreal species, such as lemmings and ground squirrels, that are found in very different habitats today. Huge Pleistocene musk oxen, mammoths, and mastodons grazed on Delmarva's plains and browsed at the edge of the woods. In the patches of spruce forest, peccaries mingled with white-tailed deer, caribou, and elk. Giant beaver and moose inhabited the peninsula's extensive swamps, and there were huge bats as well as wolves, skunks, otters, weasels, and fox.

Man Comes to Delmarva

Between the swamp and the sea shore, the woods must have been full of Indians, and doubtless the theatre of many bloody scenes; vestiges of many of their towns are still to be seen; and perhaps no part of the continent could have furnished them with the necessaries of life in equal abundance on so easy terms.
—A Citizen of Delaware, 1797

It is thought that humans first migrated to North America over a land bridge from Asia, arriving anywhere from twenty thousand to thirteen thousand years ago. The first groups in our area probably arrived between twelve to fifteen thousand years ago, when the Wisconsin Glacier was beginning to retreat. They were Paleo-Indians, nomadic hunters and gatherers who had followed the vast herds of lumbering mammoths and mastodons east across the Pleistocene grasslands. However, firm archaeological evidences of their presence here is scarce because so much of the peninsula as they knew it is now underwater.

Mammoths and mastodons were principally differentiated by the structure of their molars. They and other Ice Age animals provided meat and warm clothing for the Paleo-Indians, who killed them with spears (stone points lashed with rawhide into the split head of a wooden shaft). By chipping flakes from the edges of a piece of high-quality flint, they fashioned spearheads that were sharp on both sides. These could also be used as butchering knives and to clean animal bones and hides.

Obviously, a source of good stone was critical to the Paleo-Indians' survival. There are three kinds on northern Delmarva that can be flaked to hold an extremely sharp edge: jasper, chert, and chalcedony. All can be found in Cecil County, Maryland, and at Iron Hill near Glasgow, Delaware, and there is ample evidence that roving bands of hunters regularly visited these sites to replenish their supplies of tools and weapons.

There was no such thing as a stone quarry on the sandy coastal plain of lower Delmarva, but archaeologists theorize that glacier meltwater might have carried quantities of cobbles down the ancestral Delaware and Susquehanna rivers, depositing them on bars where currents converged at the mouths of major rivers. There is, in fact, archaeological evidence that Paleo-Indian hunting bands gathered on the headlands that overlooked the Choptank and the Nanticoke rivers.

The Paleo-Indians had no way to store meat, so they had to move continually with the herds. They apparently had a network of base camps on the peninsula from which parties of hunters made periodic forays. One of the choicest of these hunting sites, according to tools that have been found there, was along the "backbone" of the peninsula, the midpeninsular divide that separates the headwaters of rivers that drain west to the Chesapeake from those that drain east to the Delaware Bay. During the Ice Age, this area was full of freshwater lakes and swamps, which attracted the animals the people depended on for food and also provided precious drinking water.

13

The Ice Recedes

After covering the northern part of the continent for several thousand years, the Wisconsin Glacier began to retreat. Meltwater rushed to the sea, spreading a sheet of sediment over much of the coastal plain and filling the river valleys with eroded sand and gravel. The sea rose at a rate of about one and a half inches per decade and crept slowly westward across the continental shelf, flooding into the mouths of the ancient Susquehanna and Delaware rivers.

The melting was the result of a profound change in the weather which, according to pollen studies, did not occur gradually as might be supposed, but in periods of radical and abrupt shifts. Prevailing westerlies swept warmer and drier air over the peninsula and seasons gave shape to the year for the first time. As the climate warmed, plants and animals gradually were able to extend their ranges and a large variety of species from both glaciated and nonglaciated regions moved into that part of the coastal plain that is now the Delmarva Peninsula.

As the soil thawed and the growing season lengthened, trees spread into previously open land, an incursion that eventually would have a devastating effect on the Pleistocene megafauna. The mammoths, mastodons, and musk oxen of Ice Age Delmarva were adapted to grazing in grasslands or browsing at the forest edge. The boreal spruce forest that increasingly covered the peninsula forced them northward in the wake of the receding ice. While there is evidence that elk and moose continued to inhabit the swamps of the lower peninsula long after the great herds of grazing animals were gone, they, too, eventually disappeared. While elk and moose continue to thrive in parts of North America today, the other great animals of the Ice Age were less adaptable and ultimately perished.

After 8,500 B.C., a mixed woods began to replace the boreal forest of the postglacial period, and the people were able to gather a larger percentage of their food supply. Milling and grinding stones, as well as other plant processing tools, are found in the archeological record for the first time, hard evidence that the people consumed wild fruits, nuts, and grains. Because a wide variety of stone could be used to make such tools, they were no longer dependent on particular quarry sites and could establish settlements wherever they chose. In the north, people used rocky outcrops as shelters. Farther down the peninsula they gathered near wooded swamps in "macroband base camps," that contained as many as twenty to thirty families. While hunting parties continued to make periodic forays from these settlements, the men no longer had to travel great distances in pursuit of grazing animals. Deer, rabbits, bear, and wildfowl were plentiful everywhere and were killed by stone points lashed into a wooden shaft. The points of this Archaic period were lighter than those made by the Paleo-Indians, and their efficiency against the faster moving game of the forest was augmented by a new device called a spear thrower: a wooden stick about two feet long that served as a lever to increase the velocity of a hurled spear.

By 6,500 B.C., the warmer climate had completely changed the character of the forest. Boreal species such as spruce had migrated northward or moved off the peninsula into the higher elevations of the Appalachian Mountains. They were replaced by hemlocks, pines, and oaks. Pollen studies show that over the next two thousand years, the peninsula gradually became covered with a dense "mixed-mesic" forest. Mixed-mesic is a botanical term meaning a forest growing in rich, well-drained soil with no single dominant species. A remnant of that ancient forest still exists in the Great Smoky Mountains National Park in the southern Appalachians; it includes every deciduous tree association found along the eastern seaboard, including those on Delmarva.

Deer and turkey were plentiful in those rich mesic woods and were probably the major game animals for Archaic hunters. Birds included wintering juncos and nuthatches, red-winged blackbirds, bluejays, Carolina wrens, flickers, and others. Turkey vultures, bald eagles, blue herons, wood ducks, and osprey all fed and bred on the peninsula as, in greatly diminished numbers, they still do today.

Meanwhile the sea continued to rise at a rate of about one inch per decade, too fast to permit the stable concentrations of water that we know as estuaries. Drill cores dating to this period taken from the bottom of the Chesapeake and Delaware bays do not contain shellfish, but there is evidence that shad and herring were already coming up the rivers every spring to spawn.

By 3,000 B.C., at the start of the so-called Woodland period, the rising sea had begun to drown the ancient Delaware and Susquehanna river valleys, gradually transforming them into the Delaware and Chesapeake bays. By 1,200 B.C. the *rate* of rise had slowed enough for the development of estuarine shellfish communities, and stone cooking bowls and rudimentary ceramics appear in the archaeological record for the first time—two events that are undoubtedly connected. The advent of cooking hints of more permanent villages and a sedentary life-style that is only possible when there is a handy and reliable source of food.

A few hundred years later there occurred another radical shift in the climate. A pronounced drying trend, called a xerothermic, swept over the entire northern hemisphere. The prolonged drought killed off vast tracts of forest, allowed western prairie environments to penetrate far to the east, and severely restricted both the range and populations of many of Delmarva's woodland plants and animals.

15

The History

The lack of rainfall also lowered the water table and lessened the flow of fresh water into the rivers. By this time, the sea was about thirteen feet below its present level, and the rate of rise was still decreasing. Anthropologists have found evidence of settlements dating to this period along the banks of rivers, possibly indicating that the people were searching for new sources of food and water. Anadromous fish, such as shad and alewives that spawned in the rivers, would have had to penetrate farther upstream for fresh water, but the effect of the saltier water on shellfish communities is unclear.

Sometime after 800 B.C., a cooling trend brought increasing moisture to eastern North America and ended the long drought. Forests much like the ones we know today gradually refurbished the peninsula, and the Chesapeake and Delaware bays filled to their present boundaries and became havens to huge flocks of migrating ducks and geese.

Agriculture also began to be practiced on the peninsula. Some archaeologists argue that it was the pressure of feeding an increasing human population that forced the development of agriculture, while others say it was a serendipitous development that arose when discarded seeds sprouted and grew on refuse heaps. In any case, it is clear that human populations did increase on the peninsula as elsewhere. Plants from Central and South America, such as beans, Indian corn, *Zea mays*, and squash, *Curcurbita* spp., became the staple crops of tribes all over the continent, but there is little evidence that they were grown much on Delmarva. However, remains of amaranth, another South American plant that is now naturalized on the peninsula, have been found in early middens and storage pits on the lower peninsula. Examples of these pits can still be seen on both the Atlantic Coast of the peninsula and the shores of the Chesapeake Bay. They contain shells, the bones of deer and other animals, as well as other debris left after hundreds of years of Indian meals.

The Woodland people cleared garden plots on the floodplains of rivers by the method known as "slash and burn." They peeled off the bark of trees and burned stacks of dry wood at their base. Crops were then planted between the dead or dying trees. When the soil in one plot was exhausted, they simply moved to another. When all the land surrounding the village had been used, they moved the village. Because the Indian population was small and their villages widely scattered, this wasteful system of agriculture had little effect on the environment.

By 600 B.C., elaborate funerals were taking place on Delmarva, evidence that a more complex society had developed, particularly among the Indians of the middle peninsula. Graves containing the remains of over a hundred people have been excavated at Island Field in Kent County, Delaware. Many contained nonlocal artifacts such as pipes and beads indicating trade to the north.

16

However, the Indians did not trade for profit, but for power and influence. Gift giving was a subtle way to maintain good diplomatic relations with neighboring tribes; a valuable gift not only enhanced the giver's stature, it also made the recipient beholden to him and insured his support if needed. For reasons that are not entirely clear, this widespread trade slowed by 900 A.D., and many of the peninsula's Indian settlements fragmented into smaller and simpler communities.

During the long silent centuries that followed, the peninsula's rivers and estuaries teemed with fish, shellfish, otters, and beaver. Cougars, black bears, wolves, deer, and a host of smaller animals roamed a forest filled with flowers, ferns, rich mosses, and songbirds. There were also numbers of wild turkeys, hawks, and owls. Ospreys and eagles fished in the rivers, turtles and muskrats abounded in the marshes, rafts of waterfowl blackened the surface of the Chesapeake in fall and winter, and huge flocks of shorebirds migrated up the Delaware Bay every spring. Passenger pigeons were so numerous they clouded the sky and so tame, it was said, that they could be knocked out of the trees with long sticks.

The Woodland Indians described by the first Europeans lived in domed huts constructed of bark or grass mats laid over a framework of bent saplings. They were seminomadic, constructing their villages near a river or a wooded swamp in winter and moving to the coast in summer. Each tribe had sovereignty over a certain territory, but their boundaries tended to shift with tribal allegiances. The Indians saw the land as theirs to use, but not to own: a crucial difference from most of the Europeans who were to come.

It is thought that the Indians regularly burned the woods to increase the amount of sunlight in woodland clearings and encourage the cover and browse relished by deer. In December of 1632, the navigator of a Dutch ship standing off the coast of Cape May wrote in his diary that the land gave off a "sweet perfume . . . [that] comes from the indians setting fire . . . to the woods and thickets, in order to hunt." Such burning would also have increased the abundance of edible berries and seeds. Whether the Indians realized it or not, frequent burning also enhances the fertility of the soil and prevents the accumulation of litter that can cause major forest fires.

The life of a Woodland Indian was based on a seasonal cycle of want and plenty. Summer was the season for tending crops and gathering wild berries and edible plants. In the early fall, the hickory and walnuts were ripe, and the first migrating waterfowl came into the marshes and were caught in nets and snares. In late fall, when the animal pelts were at their best, the people moved inland to hunt deer, bear, beaver, and raccoon. Late winter and early spring was the dangerous time; the ground was frozen, the plants dormant and the animals lean. Many people starved to death before the shad, herring, and sturgeon began to come up the rivers to spawn and the cycle began again.

> *The Susquehannock Indians are for the most part great Warriours and . . . keep
> . . . the several nations of Indians round about them in a forceable obedience
> and subjection.*
>
> *—George Alsop, 1666*

Most of the Indians on the Delmarva Peninsula were members of the social and linguistic family known as the Algonquians. The Susquehannocks were Iroquois. Their principal territory extended up the Susquehanna River and its feeder streams, but after the Europeans came, the tribe regularly entered the headwaters of the Chesapeake and traveled up the rivers of the northern Eastern Shore to trade with them.

The Algonquians living in what is now Delaware called themselves the Lenni-Lenape, or the "original people." They occupied territory on the west bank of the Delaware River, from the headwaters south to what is now Bombay Hook. The people living south of the Choptank River on the Eastern Shore were Nanticokes; there were also a host of other tribes, such as Wicomicoes, Choptanks, and Assateagues among others. Most were ruled by a local chief, with the possible exception of the Accomacs and Accohannocs on the southern tip of the peninsula. They were said to be under the authority of Chief Powhatan whose principal village was on the western shore of Virginia. These various tribes apparently had little contact with one another (to be an Algonquian apparently meant only that they sprang from the same ancestral stock and belonged to the same linguistic group). The Nanticokes and the Lenni-Lenape became bitter enemies of the Susquehannocks as the borders between their respective territories were increasingly violated by the Susquehannock incursions.

Because the Indian tribes had no written language, our knowledge of their life and culture must be pieced together from archaeological evidence and the sometimes inaccurate, and often biased descriptions given by early European observers. We do know that, except for a limited amount of agriculture, Delmarva's Indians were essentially hunters and gatherers, dependent on the natural resources of their immediate surroundings. We also know that these natural resources were incredibly rich and abundant. Viewed from the present environmental crisis, the number and variety of North American plants, birds, fish, shellfish, and animals remarked on by the first Europeans are difficult to imagine. Within less than two hundred years, much of it had disappeared.

That the European settlement of this continent was an historic event of immense political and cultural importance is well known. Less well known were the environmental ramifications. Finding a way to balance the needs of a modern civilization with the needs of a healthy natural environment has become one of the crucial questions of the twentieth century: unfortunately, it was a question that occurred to almost no one in the early days of our nation.

Settlement

*I, Seketarius & Kalehickop Nochcotamen & Toonis & Leleghanan
& Wippais do hereby promise and Engage to give or Sell all our
Land lying between Christina & Upland Creek unto William Penn
Proprietary & Governr of ye Province of Pennsilvania after ye
same manner as Keklappan and others sell theirs in Spring next.
Of wch I have already received a very good Gun, some powder
and Lead, two pairs of Stockins, one Match Coat and Tenn bits
Spanish money. In witness whereof I have sett my hand and Seal*

　　　　　　　　　　　　　　　　　　his
　　　　　　　—Seketarius X Mark
　　　　　　　　Philadelphia. ye 19th 10th Mo. 1683

*This same Indian . . . told me . . . God then waited until the moon
was full and made a white man, who he said knew every thing but
Wynota or God　　And that Wynota was sorry he had made white
men, because they drove the Indians from the salt water, or sea.*
　　　　　　　　　　　　—A Citizen of Delaware, 1797

The first white man known to have set foot on the Delmarva Peninsula was
Giovanni da Verrazano in 1524, an Italian in the service of the French king. His
ship *Dauphine* entered Chincoteague Bay and, according to his own account, a
landing party penetrated inland about eight miles until stopped by swamps,
undoubtedly those of the upper Pocomoke River. Verrazano's party saw several
Indians, probably Assateagues, and attempted to capture two of their children,
a thoughtless act that was to have grave consequences for the next man to
explore the peninsula, nearly a century later.

The History

He was Bartholomew Gilbert, who sailed down the coast from New England in 1603 in search of survivors from Sir Walter Raleigh's lost colony at Roanoke. Gales blew his ship into the mouth of the Chesapeake Bay. It is thought that he went ashore somewhere between Pocomoke Sound and the Big Annemessex River where he was ambushed and killed by Indians.

In 1607, three ships under the command of Captain Christopher Newport were also blown into the mouth of the Chesapeake by a gale, but they apparently left as soon as the storm subsided, giving only a cursory look at the "great inland sea" that lay before them. However, the following year, 1608, the irrepressible Captain John Smith left the colony of Jamestown, Virginia, to sail northward up the Bay. He crossed to Cape Charles in an open barge with fourteen men, only three of whom, he tells us, knew how to sail. After many adventures and encounters with various Indian tribes, he explored and mapped the Chesapeake all the way to the mouth of the Susquehanna River.

The next year, 1609, Henry Hudson sailed his ship the *Half Moon* into the mouth of Delaware Bay while looking for a passage to the Orient. Encountering dangerous shoals, he soon abandoned the South River, as he called it, and sailed northward to explore the river that now bears his name. While none of these early voyages immediately resulted in settlements, they were portents of drastic change for the peninsula and its people.

The Fur Trade

Of beavers, Otters and martens, black foxes and furs of price may yearly be had six or seven thousand.
— *John Smith, 1614*

Wolves are pretty well destroy'd by the Indians, for the sake of the Reward given them by the Christians for that Service.
— *Gabriel Thomas, 1697*

A more terrible enemy . . . had invaded them—the small pox.
— *J. Thomas Scharf, 1879*

The fur trade is frequently cited as evidence of how easily the Indian was corrupted by the superior goods of the European and induced to forsake his traditional way of life. The Indians' fascination with guns, metal tools, iron pots, cloth, and liquor made them increasingly dependent on the white man and the allure of sudden wealth from the fur trade caused the Lenni-Lenape to eradicate the bear and beaver populations from their territory as early as 1644. However, some historians think that the quick destruction of both the Indian way of life and the ecology it depended on must be viewed against the ravages of disease. Tragically, up to 90 percent of the Indian population along the East Coast of North America had died by the close of the seventeenth century. Thus it could be argued that it was the introduction of Old World diseases that was actually responsible for the first big environmental change in the New World.

Along with the colonists and provisions, European ships brought measles, smallpox, and influenza to the coast of North America. While these and other diseases were common in the crowded living conditions of European cities, they were virtually absent among the Indians. Some think that the micro-organisms that caused them had been killed by the constant cold during the Ice Age migrations from Asia thousands of years before. Their absence left the Indian society remarkably healthy, but also pathetically vulnerable. Once exposed, whole villages succumbed, not only to lethal diseases like smallpox, plague, and tuberculosis, but also to the childhood diseases of chicken pox and measles. It does not take much imagination to understand what a devastating effect this would have had on an Indian's religion and cultural identity, not to mention his trust in his tribe's traditional healing practices. At the time, few of the Indians connected the spread of pestilence with the coming of the white man; they believed instead that some kind of punishment had been visited upon their people. (Unfortunately, some white men were very much aware of the devastating effect of European diseases on the Indians and evidence suggests that disease was often deliberately introduced by way of smallpox-infected blankets.)

The History

In addition to the scourge of disease, there were profound philosophical differences between the Indian and the white man that led to the destruction of the Woodland Indian's very existence. Whereas the Indian saw the natural world as the sacred provider of everything that was needed to sustain life for himself and his descendants, the European saw a seemingly inexhaustible supply of valuable commodities such as furs and timber that were scarce and expensive at home. This contrast between resource to be preserved and commodity to be sold is crucial to understand the destruction wrought by the fur trade, as well as by the settlers to come.

In 1631, a fur trading post was established by William Claiborne on Kent Island. Claiborne had been appointed Secretary of State for the colony of Virginia (which included Maryland at the time) by Charles I in 1625 and given license to trade with the Indians. Since his post was the principal market for furs brought in by the Susquehannocks, it had the obvious effect of increasing their power over, and enmity toward, the Nanticokes. The Susquehannocks also regularly traveled up the Elk River and into "Minquas Creek" (an early name for the Christina River) to trade with the Dutch and Swedes in what was then Lenni-Lenape territory. Claiborne, like many other European fur traders, became adept at pitting one tribe against another, exploiting their traditional enmities while creating appetites for European goods.

Claiborne's trading post was the first permanent settlement in Maryland, but it was not the first on the peninsula. One Thomas Savage had moved his family from Jamestown to the Eastern Shore of Virginia in 1619 where he was given a large tract of land by the Assateague Chief, Debedevon, also known as "the laughing king." Other settlers from Jamestown soon followed Savage. They are said to have thrived in the climate of the peninsula while many of their countrymen left behind in Virginia succumbed to sickness and starvation or fell prey to Indian massacres.

In 1631, the ill-fated colony of Swanendael, or "Valley of the Swans" was established for trade with the Indians by the Dutch near Lewes, Delaware. According to one version of the story, a Sickoneysinck Indian stole a piece of tin that had been painted with the Dutch coat of arms and nailed to a post. When the Dutch official in charge, Gillis Hossitt, angrily demanded retribution, some of the Sickoneysincks, thinking to please him, killed the thief and brought a "token of the dead" to the horrified Hossitt. On December 6, 1632, friends of the slain Indian, seeking revenge, entered the settlement and massacred all the inhabitants.

In 1638, a colony was established by the Swedes and Finns at present-day Wilmington. Finland, at that time, was a part of Sweden. This first Wilmington settlement was small, never more than a few hundred farmers, hunters, and

fishermen. In seventeenth-century Sweden, people still farmed in small plots cleared by the slash and burn method and hunted the intervening woods with crossbows and spears, a cultural similarity that kept their relations with the Lenni-Lenape relatively peaceful. Also, all the land in the colony was owned by its sponsor, the New Sweden Company. Individual Swedes and Finns did not own land in their own name until Johan Rising became Governor of New Sweden in 1654. When the Dutch claimed sovereignty over the territory in 1655, many Swedish farmers quickly changed their allegiance in order to keep their land, a move apparently welcomed by the Dutch.

The bands of Lenni-Lenape Indians in the area traditionally came together in early spring for the fish runs, stayed to grow corn at their summer stations, then dispersed in the fall to hunt waterfowl and deer. Still, anthropologists consider the Lenni-Lenape foragers, rather than true agriculturalists, because they made little attempt to store corn for the winter, but consumed most of the crop at their fall harvest festivities. Even so, by the 1640s they were growing corn specifically to sell to the Swedes, trading it for metal tools, cloth, and alcohol as part of a network that included the Susquehannocks to the west, the Dutch in New York, and the English in Virginia.

This trade network collapsed after 1684 when what is now the state of Delaware was claimed by William Penn as part of his charter. Again, the Swedish and Dutch farmers quickly changed their allegiance, this time swearing to uphold the English king in order to retain title to their land.

When the Swedes, and later William Penn, systematically bought the Indians' lands instead of merely appropriating them, Penn thought he was acting fairly, but the Indians did not understand the European concept of land ownership. We now know that when they "sold" land, the Indians thought they were contracting for the use of its resources, as they commonly did with other

The History

Indian tribes. They had no way of visualizing what would happen when thousands of English settlers arrived and set about clearing the forest and fencing the land. To make matters worse, these new English settlers had little interest in trading for the Indians' corn.

Meanwhile the Susquehannocks had become ravaged by disease and continuous wars against the Seneca and other tribes of the Five Nations to the north. When some of Maryland's colonists joined with the Seneca against them, the tribe was decimated. The Lenni-Lenape, having lost their land in Delaware and eastern Pennsylvania, moved into Susquehannock territory in the first step of their long westward migration.

Wherein is set forth how Englishmen may become Angels, the King's Dominions be extended and the adventurers attain Land and Gear; together with other advantages of that Sweet Land.
—A Declaration of the Lord Baltemore's Plantation in Mary-land, 1633

In 1632, Charles I granted a charter for land in the new world to George Calvert, the first Lord Baltimore. However, George Calvert died before his new land could be settled, and the charter was transferred to his son, Cecilius. In 1634 two ships, the *Ark* and the *Dove*, brought two hundred settlers under the leadership of Cecil Calvert's younger brother, Leonard, into the Chesapeake. They founded an English colony on the western shore in what is now St. Mary's County. Apparently dismissing the fact that he had already apportioned some of the same territory to the fur trader, William Claiborne, the king had included the peninsula "between the ocean and the Bay" in Calvert's claim, an oversight that was to cause much friction, first between the Calverts and Claiborne, and later with William Penn.

A charter was a conveyance of land from the king, who claimed it all, to the holder for a token yearly rent. The rent in Calvert's case was two Indian arrows and one fifth of all gold and silver ore "that may, from time to time, be discovered," but his charter was also unique because it gave Calvert absolute power in the administration and defense of his province. Writs could be issued in his name, rather than the king's, and it was he who fixed the rents and services on all the manors he created.

In the "headright system," the holder of a charter in the New World gave a certain amount of land to anyone who paid his own way, plus extra for each member of his family. In Pennsylvania (which included Delaware at the time) a man received one hundred acres for each person over sixteen years of age, including his wife and himself, and fifty acres for every child under that age.

26

According to Cecilius Calvert's "Conditions of Plantation," however, "Gentlemen" who paid one hundred pounds and brought "five able men" with them were entitled to a grant of two thousand acres "for them and their heyres for ever in that Country." These grants were subject to quitrents, to be paid annually to Lord Baltimore in the "commodity of the country." The quitrents seemed nominal (they were valued at about one shilling per one hundred acres), but it has been estimated that the Calverts took in over four thousand pounds sterling every year in quitrents in the mid-seventeenth century. Each gentleman was also given the right to make and administer laws on his manor, the right to free trade with Holland as well as England, and freedom from taxation by the crown. He became, in effect, the equivalent of an English Lord.

*In shirts & Drawers of Scotch-cloth blue, With neither Stockings, Hat, Nor Shoe
These sot-weed Planters Crowd the Shoar . . . In hue as tawny as a moor.*
                                                                    —Ebenezer Cooke, 1708

Lord Calvert's "Gentlemen" soon established large plantations along the rivers of the Chesapeake Bay. Little by little, Delmarva's ancient woods were cleared and all land not needed to grow food was given over to tobacco, or "sot-weed," a commodity in great demand in seventeenth-century Europe. As in England, an owner of thousands of acres parceled them out in tracts of a few hundred under the care of tenants, a system that worked especially well for tobacco, because that crop required a series of painstaking operations to bring it success-fully to market.

Because Lord Baltimore's "Conditions" gave each planter the right to conduct trade, the tobacco was shipped directly from his plantation to an agent in London or Bristol, often in the planter's own ships loaded at his own river-side wharf. Leading planters also acted as merchanting agents for the crops of their neighbors. In such a system, there was no need for towns, and none devel-oped on Maryland's Eastern Shore until well after 1680.

*Indentured Servants are preferable to all others, because they are not so
expensive. To buy a Negro or a black slave requires too much money at one
time; and men or maids who get yearly wages are likewise too costly.*
                                                                    —Peter Kalm, 1761

Maryland's first tobacco plantations were far from grand or elegant. Seven-teenth-century planters lived in what have been described as small, ramshackle farmhouses, surrounded by a cluster of similarly ill-kept farm buildings. Floors were dirt or crude planks and the furniture homemade from local wood. Even so, by the end of the century there were black slaves working in Delmarva's fields. The first had come into Virginia in 1619 as a direct result of the opening of west Africa to free traders from the New World. Eastern Shore tobacco planters, like those in tidewater Virginia, became slaveowners because they needed field laborers; indentured servants gradually worked off their contracts and tenant farmers soon owned land of their own. Gradually, the English population spread along the banks of the estuaries from Kent Island in the north and the Annemessex and Manokin rivers in the south. In Delaware, it moved southward along the shore of the Delaware River and Bay. Although in 1720, only a narrow ring composed of the Eastern Shore of Maryland and the coast of Delaware Bay from Wilmington to Cape Henlopen and the southern tip of the peninsula had been settled, forty years later, this ring of settlements had widened several miles inland and moved down the Atlantic coast south of Cape Henlopen. The bays and rivers provided the only convenient transport; the few existing roads were described as "impassable after the least rain."

The population of Delaware as recorded in the nation's first census of 1790 was about 60,000, equally divided among the state's three counties. The population density on the Eastern Shore of Maryland and Virginia was probably comparable. (Maryland as a whole is listed as having 319,728 people.) By that time, all of the land on the peninsula had been claimed although much of the interior was not populated until the coming of the railroads nearly a century later.

Changes to the Land

It was remarkable that any progress has been made, when we consider the small number of the first settlers . . . coming from an old cultivated country to thick woods . . . It may be said that in a sort, they began the world anew.

—Jared Elliot, 1748

[The oaks] will bear two foot and a halfe square of good timber for 20 yards long.

—John Smith, 1600s

The English settlers on Delmarva transplanted their economic life and culture to the peninsula with astonishing speed, yet from the start, there were profound differences between the Old World and the New. Ancient British social strictures appeared ridiculous in a land where everyone must fend for himself, so it is no wonder that the seeds of what would become the peculiarly American belief in the rights of every man—to make what he could of his own life and property—took root very early.

The first English on the peninsula, as in all British settlements, subscribed to the theory of mercantilism. That is, they thought it the purpose of a colony to provide needed commodities for the mother country. Many of those commodities were the natural resources of the land. The fact that England's own forests had disappeared long since did not inspire them to conserve wood in the New World. Also, a certain arrogant pride in their own superior culture kept them from assimilating any part of the Indian concept of resource preservation.

Not only were there no rules here to limit the cutting of trees but the supply of wood seemed virtually endless. The peninsula's great forests of white oak, *Quercus alba*, were the first to go, cut to supply the colonial shipbuilding

31

industry. The Murderkill, St. Jones, Mispillion, and Broadkill rivers all had thriving shipyards before 1700, and Delmarva oak was also considered the material of choice on the eastern seaboard. The peninsula's trees were taller and stouter than those found in New England and the wood firmer than that of more southern species. Many of the barrels used to import sugar, molasses, and rum from the West Indies were also made from Delmarva oak.

The bark of Spanish oak, *Q. falcata*, and black oak, *Q. velutina,* were used for tanning hides, and quercitron, the bright yellow inner bark of the black oak, was also used for dye. Because, to the colonists, conserving labor was far more important than protecting trees, they simply burned the ones without market value to make it easier to extract those that had value. By the late eighteenth century all the large trees close to settled areas on the peninsula were gone, and even firewood had become scarce.

The peninsula's baldcypress, *Taxodium distichum*, and Atlantic white cedar, *Chamaecyparis thyoides*, grow in wooded swamps and the wood is extremely resistant to rot. Huge numbers of these trees were cut for boat timbers as well as shingles. Unlike hardwoods, these wetland conifers do not resprout from stumps, so, except for a few isolated stands, they have disappeared from the peninsula. The swamps where they grew have been taken over by red maple and sweet gum or drained for farming.

Farming

The soil appears particularly fertile and strawberries, vines, sassafras, hickory nuts & walnuts we tread upon everywhere in the thickest woods.
— *Father Andrew White, 1634*

The farms are in general small and ill-cultivated; they receive little or no manure and are in every respect badly managed.
— *La Rochefoucauld, 1800*

Of course, the colonists were probably terrified of the forest. Not only did it shelter wild beasts and hostile Indians, but, because it made farming impossible, it threatened their very survival. So, right from the beginning, agriculture had a profound impact on the peninsula's natural areas and wildlife communities.

Like their Calvert counterparts on the Eastern Shore, a few upper-class Delaware families received thousands of acres in grants from William Penn. On both sides of the peninsula, the holders of these large warrants tended to claim the most fertile land in the district, contiguous or not, and to divide their holdings into farms of a few hundred acres. On the Eastern Shore of Maryland, it was not unusual for a planter to claim virtually all the land along the banks of a particular river or creek.

In the lower counties of Delaware, tobacco was also the major cash crop in the seventeenth and early eighteenth centuries. In fact, the cultivation of tobacco was so widespread in the Chesapeake region that it served as currency for the payment of debts, quitrents, and stipends. Delmarva's sandy soil proved ideal for its cultivation, and the peninsula's miles of navigable waterways made it comparatively easy to transport the harvested crop back to English markets. Tobacco, in fact, was the peninsula's first monoculture, and early tobacco planters faced the same problems of fluctuating prices and proliferating pests that afflict single crop farming today. When the market was strong, the planters cleared and planted as many fields as they could to take advantage of the price. But, when prices dropped, they found they had to continue to clear and plant more land in order to maintain their former level of income.

To raise the best quality leaf, the preferred procedure was to burn a plot of woods in early spring and plant the tiny tobacco seeds in the layer of ash that covered the so-called "virgin mould." After about two months, the young seedlings were transplanted into an older, previously cleared field. This system, coupled with the fact that tobacco exhausts soil very quickly, meant that "fresh" land had to be cleared almost continually. Tobacco farming spawned a demand for virgin land that not only destroyed hundreds of acres of forest, but also led to widespread land speculation since the buying and selling of land became the most reliable way for an ambitious man to make his fortune.

The first woods to be cleared were along the peninsula's major waterways, which resulted in clogging the waterways with silt and floating trees. Formerly deep and navigable rivers became impassable, a problem that was compounded by ships dumping excess ballast at anchor. It was not long before buildings originally built along the banks of navigable creeks became isolated. There are many examples of these stranded early buildings on the peninsula today, even though the Virginia House of Burgesses passed an act forbidding the dumping of ballast as early as 1680. At the Third Haven Meeting House in Easton, Maryland, for instance, a swale on the lawn is all that remains of the creek that once carried local Friends to meeting.

In 1730, the tobacco market suffered a serious setback, and much "old" land on the peninsula was abandoned to "pine sedge and sorrell." Some Maryland planters, anticipating the collapse, had already shifted to grain, a move that proved so profitable that they soon replaced their early farmhouses, described as "weatherproof but cheaply built," with the elegant Georgian manor houses that still grace the waterways of the Eastern Shore.

The aim of the farmers in this country, if they can be called farmers, is not to make the most they can from the land, which is . . . cheap, but the most of the labor, which is dear. The consequence . . . [is] much ground . . . scratched over and none cultivated or improved as it ought to have been.
— George Washington, 1791

The majority of Delmarva's early farmers knew nothing of farming before they came here, and even if they had, would have found the English farming traditions of the time largely irrelevant. The American climate was both hotter in summer and colder in winter than the English; droughts were more frequent and farm workers scarce. Yet land was there for the taking, a "wasteland" of "empty" woods and marshes that required only labor to clear or drain them. Unfortunately, it took far less labor to burn woods than to husband soil; according to a disturbing number of early accounts, American farmers neither rotated their crops nor manured their fields even though this was a common practice in Europe.

The principal environmental effect of burning and cutting was an increase in the shrubby plants that thrived in clearings and at the borders of woodlands and a corresponding increase in the populations of birds that fed and nested in them, such as jays, mockingbirds, and cowbirds. Animals like rabbits, foxes, skunks, possums, and woodchucks, which frequent hedgerows and fields, pro-

34

liferated, while those of the forest interior began to decline. On Delmarva, these included wild turkey, cougars, otters, beavers, and bears, many of which had already suffered serious declines due to the pressures of hunting and the European fur trade.

By the first decades of the eighteenth century, the intensive plantings of tobacco had seriously depleted much of the peninsula's soil. Even though some of the old land could still support crops, much of it was abandoned to invading broomsedge and used for grazing. By 1750, corn had replaced tobacco as the principal cash crop on the peninsula. Wheat was also grown on northern Delmarva and, like tobacco before it, served in place of currency to pay rents and other expenses. During the Revolution, wheat was even used to pay government officials.

Delmarva's tobacco had always been handled through British agents, but her grain was a wholly American enterprise. Merchant mills grew up along piedmont rivers like the Brandywine and Red Clay. Unlike earlier mills that ground a local farmer's grain for a fee, the miller now bought the grain himself, sold it as flour, and transported it in his own ships throughout the colonies and as far away as the West Indies and southern Europe. The economic importance of these mills is underscored by the fact that the British razed every one they could find en route from the Elk River to Philadelphia in 1777.

The cultivation of one crop is, by definition, a monoculture and monocultures are always an affront to the balance of nature. Unfortunately for us, that balance dictates that a population explosion in any one species always results in a corresponding increase in the organisms that feed on it. Thus, the prevalence of wheat fields on eighteenth-century Delmarva invited widespread attack by the Hessian fly, a European pest thought to have arrived in the bedding of horses brought to the colonies by the Hessians (German mercenaries who fought with the British in the Revolution). The Hessian fly, like so many imported pests that were to follow it, had no natural controls in this country. It proliferated and spread throughout the colonies, attacking the stalks of wheat and ruining both the harvest and the peninsula's thriving grain business.

Hogs are the most numerous of the domestic animals; . . . these animals never leave the woods, where they always find sufficient food, especially in autumn and winter. They grow extremely wild and generally go in herds . . . Every inhabitant recognizes his own by the particular manner in which the ears are cut.
— *Francois Andre Michaux, 1804*

Groups of cattle and horses dot the marsh . . . feeding on salt grass.
— *Robert Wilson, 1876*

The History

Delmarva farmers did not raise hay until the nineteenth century when it was needed to supply city horses with winter fodder. Before that, they grazed their sheep and cattle on floodplains, salt marshes, and barrier islands and allowed their hogs to roam free in the woods, a practice from which the herbaceous layer in many Delmarva woods has not recovered. Everywhere, domestic livestock stripped the bark from trees, grazed on wild plants, compacted the soil with their hooves, and polluted streams with their manure. Because wolves, foxes, hawks, and eagles found the young of these wandering cattle and sheep to be easy prey, they were inevitably denounced as "varmints" and bounties were offered for their destruction.

The first cattle on the peninsula were massacred with the Dutch at Swanendael in 1632. These Dutch cattle, although well thought of in Europe at the time, proved to be poorly suited to casual grazing on Delmarva's marshes and colonial farmers soon replaced them with a scrawny but hardy mix of Danish and English cattle that could subsist on a winter forage of dry grass and bushes. Large numbers of these animals were later slaughtered by the British army during the Revolution. Others persisted for generations as feral populations on the peninsula's barrier islands. The last remnants of these colonial cattle and sheep were removed from Hog Island, now part of the Nature Conservancy's Virginia Coast Reserve, in 1987. The famous ponies of Assateague, said to be the descendants of horses that escaped from a sinking Spanish galleon, probably interbred with early farm horses.

When the saltmeadow cordgrass, *Spartina patens*, of the marshes could no longer support the growing numbers of herds, farmers tried seeding drained marshes with English grass, now known as Kentucky bluegrass, *Poa pratensis*, a move that is thought to have substantially increased the peninsula's populations of mourning doves. The first English grass probably arrived in shipboard litter and manure, and is still found naturalized throughout the peninsula where the humid climate suits it well.

Cattle were not stabled until the nineteenth century, when peninsula farmers, finally recognizing the value of manuring their fields, sought to make it easier to collect. Stabling, in turn, led to an interest in improving the stock and dairy farms became a prominent feature on the peninsula. In the 1890s, however, there was an outbreak of the cattle disease, anthrax, which was thought to have come into Delaware Bay on a shipment of infected leather hides. When shipboard wastes infected with the bacteria were dumped into the Delaware River, the infection spread into the marshes and eventually to the peninsula's dairy herds. The problem was made worse when farmers, ignorant of the nature of the disease, disposed of their dead cattle in the streams. In the 1930s the Depression dealt another serious blow to the milk business, and the peninsula's herds and pastures began to be replaced by today's field crops of corn and soybeans.

Sheep were raised too. During the Civil War, the peninsula's woolen mills provided material for military uniforms. Few are raised today; Delmarva's sheep could not compete with the vast flocks of Australia and the American West.

Only the chickens survive. They were known as dunghill fowl until the 1930s, because they survived on a few handfuls of grain and what they could forage in the barnyard. The first broiler hatcheries, built in the 1920s, were one of the few agricultural enterprises to weather the Depression on the peninsula. In the 1950s, agribusiness began to take over the poultry business and the birds were raised in a carefully controlled environment by local farmers under contract to huge processing companies.

> The soil . . . is well worn and requires careful culture.
> —Robert Wilson, 1876

Soil fertility over much of the peninsula continued to decline. Much of it had not had time to recover from the early cycle of tobacco when the intensive plantings of wheat and corn, after the Revolution, again left it leached and exhausted. To make matters worse, many of Delmarva's rivers became so clogged with silt that they were no longer navigable and the once prosperous shipbuilding towns found themselves stranded.

It could be said that the future of farming on the peninsula was saved by the Chesapeake and Delaware Canal. The digging of the canal, finished in 1829, unearthed quantities of the same glauconite or greensand that had been laid down by the ocean millions of years ago. When this "marl" was spread on fields, it was found to vastly improve the soil. In fact, it is the thick layer of glauconite that underlies the land between Odessa and Middletown, Delaware, locally known as the "levels," that is responsible for that region's particular richness and fertility.

When James C. Booth, a professor at the Franklin Institute in Philadelphia, did the first geologic survey of the peninsula in 1841, he recommended the liberal use of marl, manure, and other organic matter to improve Delmarva's farmland. Lime was also used, made from burned oyster shells or quarried limestone from the Pike Creek Valley area near Newark, Delaware. Horseshoe crabs, high in both lime and organic matter, were caught by the thousands when they came ashore to lay their eggs in the spring. Guano (bird droppings) was even hauled in steamships from South America. After 1886, when a Dutch scientist found nitrogen-fixing bacteria in the root nodules of legumes, red clover was routinely planted on Delmarva's fields, and came to be known as the "mortgage lifter."

> *Without any question, this peninsula is capable of supplying the world, even if the world should very largely increase in capacity for eating canned peaches and drinking peach brandy . . . . The culture of the peach . . . gives a peculiar charm to the face of the country.*
>
> *—Robert Wilson, 1876*

> *Here's your peaches! Your nice Delaware peaches! Your sweet Delaware Peaches!*
>
> *—Nineteenth-century fruit peddlers*

The canal also provided easy transportation between major East Coast cities for the product the peninsula would become famous for: peaches. Delmarva's first commercial peach orchards were planted in 1830 in Delaware City, Delaware. Like all the crops that preceded it, the first peach trees were planted along the rivers and creeks for easy transport, but by the middle of the century, railroad lines allowed the orchards to spread inland over much of the peninsula. Robert Wilson wrote in 1876 that " . . . the banks of the Upper Chester form a continuation of orchards" and that "it required seven steamers and more than twice that number of sailing craft to carry [the] peaches to market, notwithstanding two lines of railroad." This was written at the peak of the industry, a time when many orchards had up to forty thousand trees. The imposing square brick houses that dot the countryside around Middletown, Delaware, were built by peach growers during the heyday of the orchards and are still known locally as "peach houses."

The first peaches were brought to the New World by Spaniards in the 1500s and were carried northward along the East Coast by the Indians. William Penn mentioned in 1638 that there is "not an Indian plantation without peaches," and Peter Kalm reported that they were so plentiful that they were fed to swine. Peaches had been grown on the peninsula for home consumption since the early 1700s, especially on the Eastern Shore, where they were made into peach brandy.

The early trees were grown from seed and varied greatly in quality. It wasn't until 1832, when the technique of budding was developed, that the commercial peach industry was born. However, because the budded trees, like all vegetatively propagated plants, shared the same genetic makeup, they also shared the same resistance or susceptibility to disease.

The appearance of the blight that came to be known as the "peach yellows" first appeared in Delaware City in 1842. We now know it was a virus, but viruses were not identified until the 1900s. At the time, theories about its spread ranged from bad soil and fertilizers, to bad winds and even sunlight. In fact, it was spread by leaf hoppers from diseased rootstock. By 1855 the yellows had destroyed all the orchards in Delaware City, and had spread to Middletown by 1862. As farmers in uninfected areas continued to plant orchards, the center of the industry gradually moved down the peninsula. Even so, by the 1890s the yellows had completely destroyed Delmarva's vast peach industry. They have not been grown here on such a scale since.

Other fruits had problems as well. Apples and strawberries were widely grown in the 1920s until they, too, were wiped out by a disease called red stele fungus. Pears got pear blight. All these cultivated fruits are members of the rose family, a family that seems to be especially attractive to pests and disease when selectively bred.

The coming of the railroad fostered steam-powered lumber mills which cut the remaining tracts of forest in the peninsula's interior. The wood was used to fuel the railroad engines and the lime and oyster-shell kilns used to make farm fertilizer. When farmers began to pen their livestock, the need for rail fences also took large numbers of trees. A farm directive of 1837 recommended that one-fifth to one-third of each farm must be kept in woods to meet this need. Many farmers were unwilling to do this and planted lines of osage orange, a native of Texas, instead. Remnants of these "hedge apple" fencerows are still common on the northern peninsula today.

In the end, however, it was the need for charcoal that destroyed the most trees. Charcoal was used to fuel the blast furnaces of the iron industry: the processing of bog iron on the lower peninsula and iron ore in New Castle County, Delaware, were important early enterprises. A kiln for making charcoal used two tiers of four-foot lengths of wood, piled end on end like a tepee. The outside was coated with mud and pine needles and the pile ignited and sealed so it would burn slowly over a long period of time.

Charcoal was also an important ingredient of gunpowder. Dogwood, willow, and alder were considered to make the best quality, resulting in the cutting of thousands of these trees to supply the duPont powder mills in the 1800s.

By the time the Great Depression arrived in the 1930s, the peninsula's fields had once again fallen into exhaustion. The thirties was also the time when the peninsula's largest holly trees were destroyed to supply a thriving Christmas trade. Holly wood was also good for toys, tool handles, and musical instruments. Unfortunately, the same pattern of exploitation without resource management prevailed until no hollies of marketable size were left on the peninsula.

The History

Meanwhile, the chestnut blight, an imported fungus disease, invaded the peninsula's piedmont forests. The American chestnut, *Castanea dentata*, once an important component of all Eastern forests, was completely gone from Delmarva by the 1920s, little more than a decade after the blight was first discovered. Chestnut blight was followed by Dutch elm disease in the 1940s and today the peninsula's loblolly pines are being attacked by southern pine beetle and the oaks by the gypsy moth. The damage inflicted by all these diseases and pests is thought to be compounded when trees are under stress from acid rain.

In order to help hard-hit Delmarva farmers, and others like them across the country, the Soil Conservation Service was formed during the depths of the Depression. The service taught sound conservation methods such as strip cropping to maintain fertility and combat erosion, as well as the value of fencerows and farm ponds, practices which also benefitted the peninsula's remaining wildlife.

After World War II, when agribusiness and the broiler industry took over Delmarva farming, most of these lessons were forgotten. Farming on Delmarva today is homogenous and mechanized, dominated by endless fields of corn and soybeans, grown principally to supply the poultry business. The use of enormous tractors, corn pickers, and combines has caused farmers to remove every hedgerow that might be an obstacle to these machines. Even the islands of old trees that once sheltered farm animals are gone. Everywhere, farm fields grow larger and larger, while woodlands continue to shrink.

In spite of improved breeding, this lack of crop diversity can still result in a proliferation of pests. Now the response is a heavy use of pesticides and a growing worry about the effects of residues in our food and groundwater. Also, the use of herbicides to kill weeds on cropland threatens our surviving wild plants, while silt from farm fields and algae blooms caused by livestock manure and agricultural fertilizers are major pollution problems for the estuaries.

Huge flocks of blackbirds, cowbirds, and starlings, attracted by endless fields of ripening corn, are now common on the peninsula, but the red-cockaded woodpecker is gone and the Delmarva fox squirrel threatened, both victims of the relentless clearing of mature woods for cropland and housing developments. The quantities of grain left behind by mechanical corn pickers has not only increased the population of Canada geese, but actually changed their migration patterns. They are now so numerous that they are crowding out other waterfowl and may be one of the factors contributing to the decline of the redhead and the American black duck. In agriculture as in so much else, the first lesson of a healthy environment is the preservation of diversity.

Of course, agriculture is certainly not Delmarva's only environmental culprit. Cities like Wilmington, Baltimore, and Philadelphia dumped their municipal and industrial waste into the peninsula's waterways with impunity until the early 1970s. While laws are now on the books forbidding such practices, enforcing them requires vigilance as well as political skill. The problems of polluted runoff from city streets, acid rain, or the safe disposal of urban trash and toxic wastes have yet to be solved. Burgeoning development along parts of the coasts continues to interfere with natural processes and poses serious threats to the well-being of inland bays.

Today, two and a half centuries after settlement, the oysters are dying, the fish are declining, and the marshes have been widely invaded by common reed, *Phragmites australis.* Virtually nothing remains of the peninsula's original forest.

Farms, industry, and houses are at the base of modern civilization. At the same time, it is increasingly clear that, in the long run, the preservation of a healthy economy depends on a quality environment. On the peninsula, as around the world, a burgeoning human population continues to exploit the riches of the earth in an effort to improve its own condition. Only recently has there been a growing awareness that in despoiling the land and water and ruining the rich natural resources, the human race has endangered its survival.

It will take serious commitment and painful sacrifices to reverse the trend, but there are many hopeful signs. At last people are beginning to

appreciate and protect the peninsula's remaining natural areas and allow the natural ecosystems to survive and prosper. In Delaware a strong Coastal Zone Act protects the marshes and shores of Delaware Bay from being despoiled by heavy industry, and there is a serious effort underway to restore water quality in the Chesapeake. Farming without chemicals, once a fringe movement dismissed as impractical and idealistic, is now, according to the U. S. Department of Agriculture, moving closer to the mainstream of American agriculture as farmers discover that, if done correctly, it can lower their costs and increase their profits. The wild turkey has been reintroduced to Delmarva and seems to be doing well, the bald eagle is slowly increasing, thanks to the banning of DDT, and the beaver, missing since the early eighteenth century, has returned.

The Land

Woods

Generally the Country is covered with great Woods. Oakes and
Walnut, both black and white, are the most common Trees . . .
Likewise Elme, Ash, and Chestnuts, which equall the best in
Spaine, France, Italy or Germany.
                          —Lord Baltemore's Declaration, 1633

Despite the reckless use of the axe during more than two
centuries, there may yet be found in portions of Talbot and
Dorchester . . . groups of virgin pine of the finest quality, while
the white oak and tulip poplar attain an immense size . . . there
was a stump . . . in Kent into the hollow of which a horseman
might ride and turn his animal.
                                   —Robert Wilson, 1876

There are no accurate descriptions of the original forest on the peninsula. Most early writers were so preoccupied with the necessities of survival that they paid little attention to their natural surroundings, while the few that did often indulged in exaggerated hyperbole in hopes of attracting new colonists. A few accounts survive from New England, however, that describe immense, widely spaced trees in a parklike setting kept open by Indian fires, a description that was probably valid for this area as well.

What is known is that every patch of woods on the peninsula that exists today has been cleared and logged repeatedly. Most have also been invaded by exotic species of plants such as Japanese honeysuckle, *Lonicera japonica*. There are few old pines anywhere, and most of the oldest hardwood forests are in the piedmont section of the northern peninsula. It is hoped that with the new enthusiasm for preserving natural areas, more will be allowed to develop in the years to come, especially since it has become increasingly evident that large areas of old-growth woods are needed to provide safe breeding habitat for many woodland species of birds and animals.

Because of pervasive disturbance, it is not clear to botanists how many of the differences between the peninsula's coastal plain and piedmont forests are a reflection of age and how many are due to differing soil conditions and climate. It seems clear that, if left alone, much of Delmarva's pine woods would eventually be replaced by deciduous hardwoods. Indeed, this is already happening in some areas. Nevertheless, we know, both from early descriptions and from our own knowledge of forest ecology, that the woods that once covered the peninsula were not all alike, but a patchwork of tree associations that varied according to the site. For instance, in the piedmont section of the peninsula, the woods were originally dominated by oaks, chestnuts, and hickories. In areas with well-drained soil on the lower peninsula, these same trees mixed with loblolly pines in a forest type known as the coastal plain hardwoods. On lower and less-well-drained land, white oak mixed with sweet gum, sour gum, willow oak, and pin oak. Scrub oaks and pines grew in sandy soils near the coast and the extensive wooded swamps of the interior peninsula were dominated by bald-cypress and Atlantic white cedar.

The ecology (the word comes from the Greek *oikos* or a place to live) of any forest community is complex. It is also in a constant state of flux, like a dance in slow motion. Each new season brings a change in temperatures as well as a shift in the balance between daylight and darkness, causing different plants to take a turn in the spotlight and display their flowers, fruits, fall color, or evergreen foliage. Over time, there are dry decades and wet decades, as well as cool ones, hot ones, storms, insect infestations, diseases, and fire, all of which profoundly influence the number and distribution of forest species.

In summer, the sunlight slants through forest trees making dappled patterns of light and shade. The warm air hums with insects. A hawk may be glimpsed circling high above the trees or a songbird heard scratching among dry leaves on the forest floor. With the coming of dusk, the temperature falls and the humidity rises. Reversing their daytime cycle, the plants now take in oxygen and give off carbon dioxide. Hawks and songbirds find roosts for the night. Deer begin to stir from their daytime cover, and owls and other night predators emerge to hunt in the gathering darkness.

As winter approaches, the pace of activity slows. Most herbaceous plants die to the ground. Deciduous trees and shrubs drop their leaves to prevent loss of moisture while the ground is frozen and water unavailable. Some birds leave the peninsula to fly south for the winter while others arrive from their northern breeding grounds. Chipmunks, mice, and snakes crawl into underground dens;

squirrels also den up in the coldest weather, yet they and foxes continue to hunt actively all winter. Many insects freeze, but others hide under rocks or tree bark along with the eggs and pupae of a new generation. In November, the deer enter their rutting period, and, sometime after the start of the new year, the great horned owls begin to nest.

He hath found the said Country full of trees, to wit: Oaks, hickory and pines; which trees were in some places covered with vines.
—Cornelius Hendrickson, 1616

While trees are the backbone of any forest community, the particular species of trees found in a given woods is influenced by the texture of the soil. The peninsula receives about forty inches of rain a year, yet some of Delmarva's upland forests are dry and others moist, because the size of the soil particles, which are largest in sand and smallest in clay, determines how fast the water drains away.

Sandy soils leach easily, keeping them both dry and sterile. If the soil is also extremely acid, as in many of the peninsula's coastal pine forests, soil organisms such as earthworms, weevils, grubs and some soil bacteria cannot survive and little humus accumulates. In the moist well-drained soils preferred by hardwoods, however, these organisms continually enrich the soil by converting the nutrients found in organic debris into soluble compounds that can be used by plants. This process also tends to increase a soil's capacity to hold water, and may, over time, even change its character enough to allow different species to move into the woods.

Light is also an important selector of woodland species. The trees in a forest canopy are always bathed in sunlight, yet in summer, only a very small fraction of that light penetrates to the forest floor. For this reason the plants at the lowest level, or the herbaceous layer, are the first to green up in spring, followed in succession by the shrub layer, the understory trees and finally the trees in the canopy. Many of the woodland flowers of the northern peninsula's piedmont forests are so well adapted to take advantage of this sequence that they bloom, set seed, and relapse into dormancy in the brief period of light and warmth available to them before the canopy trees leaf out. Botanists call them "spring ephemerals."

As an open stand of pine or young hardwoods grows, the light reaching the interior diminishes, inevitably weakening some species. Some will fall victim to disease while others will be unable to reproduce. The loblolly pine, *Pinus taeda*, for instance, is a tree that needs almost full sun for maximum growth. Old loblollies often persist in the canopy of a mature forest, but their seedlings cannot survive the shade and therefore will not replace them.

The Land

Even in a so-called climax forest, there are always changes. Individual trees die and are replaced by islands of sun-loving plants within the forest, a few of which may survive to a great age. However, large numbers of early successional, sun-loving trees in the canopy of a mature forest are usually a signal that the woods have been cut repeatedly in the past.

Piedmont Woods

Full of groves of oak, hickory, ash and chestnut trees.
—*David Pietersen deVries, 1633*

The oldest forests in the piedmont section of the peninsula have not been lumbered for seventy-five years or more. They are full of old beech trees, *Fagus grandifolia*, perhaps because early loggers left them behind. There are beech at all layers of these woods: seedlings scattered across the forest floor, half-grown saplings in the understory, and the great gray elephant feet of trees reaching high into the canopy.

In winter, beech leaves of tan parchment rustling in the wind are a distinctive feature of these woods. Beech, oaks, and the vanished chestnuts of the original eastern forest are all members of the same botanical family, Fagaceae, and it is a peculiar characteristic of young trees in this family to retain their dried leaves in winter, a trait that often persists on the lower branches as the trees grow older.

In moist soils at the bottom of valleys and along woodland streams the beech mix with black gums, *Nyssa sylvatica*, red maples, *Acer rubrum,* and tulip trees, *Liriodendron tulipifera*. Red maples and tulip trees are adaptable trees that are also found on more upland sites among several species of oak, including white and black oak, *Quercus alba* and *Q. velutina*, red oak, *Q. rubra,* and chestnut oak, *Q. prinus*.

Because tulip trees are also among the first trees to appear in a developing piedmont forest, their widespread presence in these older forests is a sign of early logging. Deep-rooted and long-lived, the tulip trees found on Delmarva and in other eastern woods are one of only two species in the genus *Liriodendron* in the world. The other grows in China and Vietnam, evidence that the species is a survivor from some ancient worldwide forest.

Mingled with these trees in the moist forest bottomland are shrubs such as spicebush, *Lindera benzoin*, and pinxterbloom, *Rhododendron periclymenoides* (formerly *nudiflorum*). The flowers of spicebush, named for its aromatic twigs and foliage, paint the early spring woods with a delicate wash of yellow.

Pinxterbloom, one of the peninsula's lovely wild azaleas, is named for the Dutch word for Whitsunday. It has delicate pink flowers in spring.

At slightly higher elevations, flowering dogwood, *Cornus florida*, becomes the most conspicuous tree of the understory. Black haw, *Viburnum prunifolium,* and maple leaf viburnum, *V. acerifolium*, are common shrubs. Ferns are everywhere. On north-facing slopes, the forest floor may be virtually carpeted with the evergreen Christmas fern, *Polystichum acrostichoides.*

While a single spreading oak in a young forest is usually a survivor from a time when the land was farmed, the presence of oak and hickory trees in the canopy of a piedmont forest is a sign that the woods has begun to enter the climax stage of its development: a period of relative equilibrium characterized by deep soils and a rich woodland fauna and flora.

April and May is the season of wildflowers in Delmarva's old-growth piedmont woods. Spring ephemerals such as spring beauty, *Claytonia virginica*, bloodroot, *Sanguinaria canadensis*, toothwort, *Dentaria laciniata,* and Dutchman's breeches, *Dicentra cucullaria*, are interspersed with jack-in-the-pulpit, *Arisaema triphyllum*, wild ginger, *Asarum canadense*, and violets. Along stream banks are dense patches of troutlily, *Erythronium americanum*, another spring ephemeral, and the kelly green leaves of skunk cabbage, *Symplocarpus foetidus*. Skunk cabbage is one of the first flowers to bloom in the spring. Its maroon hoods may appear overnight in a warm February.

The Land

Dryer hillsides support bloodroot, partridgeberry, *Mitchella repens*, and isolated plants of rattlesnake plantain, *Goodyera pubescens*. There may be patches of trailing arbutus, *Epigaea repens*, a plant that was common here before it was dug out of the woods by collectors in the early years of this century. Showy orchis, *Galearis spectabilis*, and cranefly orchis, *Tipularia discolor*, can be found in some old-growth woods. Virtually all have carpets of mayapple, *Podophyllum peltatum*, wild ginger, and ferns.

Skunk cabbage, red trillium, and jack-in-the-pulpit all have a faintly fetid smell that attracts pollinating flies. Other early woodland flowers depend on the bumblebee, *Bombus* spp., an insect whose rapid wingbeats and dense "furry" coat allow it to maintain its body temperature on cold days in the early spring.

Spring wildflowers are also pollinated by solitary bees of the family Andrenidae or Halicitidae. The male bee visits many different species of flowers to collect nectar, but the female confines her foraging to a single species, collecting pollen on her hind legs. She then lays her eggs in an underground burrow, providing each one with a tiny pollen ball for nourishment. The larval bee hatches, eats the pollen, pupates, and emerges as an adult the following spring.

The seeds of some spring ephemerals also have nodules of lipids that are a favorite food of ants. The ants drag the lipids off to their tunnels to eat, and neatly plant the seeds in the process.

Coastal Plain Forest

Saxaphrasse, Pine, Firre, Bay and the like . . . sweet Gummes and Balsamum.
—*Lord Baltemore's Declaration, 1633*

The forest on the coastal plain section of the peninsula has a southern warmth not found in the piedmont, especially in winter when the dormant hardwoods are enlivened by the presence of evergreen pines and hollies, sweet bay and wax myrtle. These are young woods, for the most part, having been logged repeatedly for oak, loblolly pine, and other commercially valuable species. The Pleistocene soils on which they grow are geologically young as well, essentially a mix of silt and sand with a thin layer of acid humus.

Because of the warming influence of the Gulf Stream, Delmarva's coastal plain forests have a unique mix of species. Trees such as sycamore, *Platanus occidentalis*, black willow, red maple, and black gum, *Nyssa sylvatica*, that are found on moist bottomlands in the piedmont, mingle here with southern trees growing at or near the northern limit of their range, such as sweet gum, *Liquidambar styraciflua*, loblolly pine, water oak, *Quercus nigra*, and willow oak.

The southern red oak, *Q. falcata,* also called Spanish oak, is a particularly handsome tree common in these woods. Its glossy olive-green leaves are covered with a dense reddish-brown felt on the underside, which is distinctive from a distance when the leaves are turned over by the wind.

Live oak, *Q. virginiana*, a large spreading tree of southern plantations, reaches its northern limit on the eastern shore of Virginia. So does a rare and beautiful small tree known as the silky camellia, *Stewartia malacodendron.* A southern species of holly called yaupon, *Ilex vomitoria,* also grows on the southern peninsula, its specific name a reference to the caffeine contained in its leaves, once used by the Indians as an emetic.

Sweet bay magnolia, *Magnolia virginiana*, and Hercules'-club, *Aralia spinosa*, are southern plants that grow in wet, poorly drained soil along Delmarva's streams and ditches. Both are special in their way: sweet bay for its waxy sweet-smelling flowers and Hercules'-club for its huge creamy-white clusters of flowers in August.

Without the deep humusy soils found under old-growth hardwoods, coastal plain forests have comparatively few woodland wildflowers, although partridge berry and wintergreen, *Gaultheria procumbens*, are common, and ground pine, *Lycopodium flabelliforme*, ground cedar, *L. obscurum*, and running club moss, *L. clavatum*, often carpet the forest floor. Trailing arbutus can still be found in some woods and pink lady's-slippers, *Cypripedium acaule*, occasionally grow in poorly drained areas. Spring blooms in these woods are chiefly provided by dogwood, blueberries, and deerberry, *Vaccinium* spp., and the delicate complicated flowers of laurel. Mountain laurel, *Kalmia latifolia*, and the smaller sheep laurel, *K. angustifolia,* are both abundant.

The American holly, *Ilex opaca,* is common among the pines of the southern peninsula, particularly near the coast. So is wax myrtle, *Myrica cerifera,* a southern evergreen bayberry. The lovely and fragrant coast azalea, *Rhododendron atlanticum,* forms stoloniferous colonies about two feet high in sandy coastal plain woods. Pawpaw, *Asimina triloba,* a northern representative of the tropical custard-apple family, is also found here. Its edible fruits are eaten by opossums, squirrels, raccoons, and foxes. Box huckleberry, *Gaylussacia brachycera,* is a particularly beautiful shrub that is found only on two or three sites on the peninsula. Because its branches root where they touch the ground, a single ancient plant eventually may cover an acre of open woods.

While not many woods on Delmarva's coastal plain have burned in recent decades, fire is thought to be a major selector of the sort of pine forests found over much of the lower peninsula, although the picture has been clouded by the widespread use of herbicides to create pure stands of loblolly pine. However, both loblolly and Virginia pine, *P. virginiana*, also sprout quickly after fire leading some botanists to think that their broad distribution, in combination with dry land oaks such as post oak, *Quercus stellata*, and black jack oak, *Q. marilandica*, is indicative of early Indian fires.

Unlike logging and downed trees, fire favors species that need special conditions to survive. The cones of some pines, such as pitch pine, *Pinus rigida*, a northern species found on the peninsula, must, in fact, be burned before they will open and release the seeds. Fire also increases the incidence of blueberries, huckleberries, and junipers, all common plants on Delmarva.

The pines of the peninsula's coastal plain are known to botanists as "hard" pines. They are stiff, upright, and bristly, often growing in open groves. Most have two to three needles in a cluster and thick platy bark that effectively insulates them from the searing heat of fire. Pines have deep penetrating root systems, well adapted to sandy soil. With the single exception of pond pine, *P. serotina*, they do not grow well in wet, poorly drained areas.

In addition to influencing the selection of tree species, forest soils are natural communities in their own right, full of borers, beetles, and millipedes that feed on dead wood, rotting leaves and fruit. Predaceous centipedes and beetles hide in leaf litter on the forest floor. Springtails (order Collemboa), pill

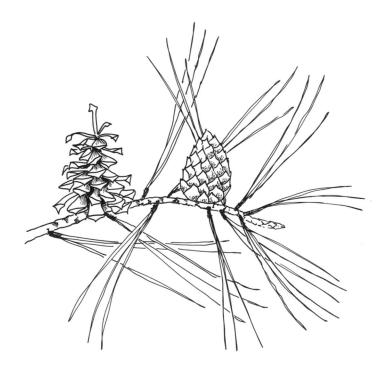

bugs (family Armadillidiidae), and sowbugs (family Oniscidae) feed on fungi and bacteria while spindly daddy longlegs (family Phalangidae) scurry over fallen leaves scavenging for dead insects.

Far above them, katydids and leaf hoppers feed on the leaves of canopy trees. Delmarva's piedmont and coastal plain woods also serve as a nursery ground for the larvae of many butterflies and moths that forage as adults in adjacent fields and meadows. Many of them are host specific, feeding only on particular species of plants. The larvae of the spicebush swallowtail, *Pterourus troilus,* for instance, only feeds on spicebush and sassafras, the larvae of the hackberry butterfly feeds on hackberries, and the zebra swallowtail larvae, *Eurytides marcellus,* feeds exclusively on pawpaw.

Many woodland moths are so well adapted to look like tree bark that they are invisible to all but the sharpest eye, yet both the promethea, *Callosamia promethea*, and the polyphemus moth, *Antheraea polyphemus,* have conspicuous and fearsome eye spots to frighten predators. The translucent green luna moth, *Actias luna*, on the other hand, hangs at the end of twigs exactly like a leaf. The larvae of all these species feed in the peninsula's woods, although many have suffered from the widespread use of pesticides to combat gypsy moths, an alien pest that was accidentally released in Massachusetts late in the nineteenth century. Voracious gypsy moths have defoliated wide swaths of oaks and pines on the peninsula as elsewhere and could eventually alter the composition of the forests in the future.

Solitary wasps are also common in the woods. Unlike social wasps, such as yellow jackets and paper wasps, solitary wasps are not aggressive. They sting only to capture their prey, which they then place in a nesting cell with an egg. When the egg hatches, the wasp larva eats the prey and pupates. Some species of wasp lay their eggs on caterpillars, which are then consumed by the developing larvae, while others are responsible for the galls found on oaks and other plants.

Spiders are everywhere. Wolf spiders (family Lycosidae) dash after beetles in the leaf litter. Jumping spiders (family Salticidae) are a favorite food of birds. Orb weavers (garden spiders) such as *Araneus diadematus* wait for their prey in a rolled leaf in the upper corner of the web. White and spined micrathena spiders spread sticky filaments from tree to tree and wrap and store their prey in vertical webs that look like bird droppings.

The larvae of many of the most bothersome insects of the woods also live in the forest. These include flies and gnats (order Diptera), chiggers, *Trombicula* spp., and wood ticks, *Dermacentor variabilis.* Recently, there have been several cases of Lyme disease on the peninsula. This disease is caused by a bacteria found in the intestines of the tiny deer tick, *Ixodes dammini.* Adult female ticks lay their eggs in early spring after feeding on deer throughout the winter. After hatching, the tick larvae attach themselves to mice, other small mammals, and birds—the true carriers of Lyme disease bacteria. After molting, tick larvae overwinter as nymphs without feeding, but a nymph that has been infected in the larval stage can spread the disease the following spring when it begins to feed. Nymphal ticks are most active between May and July, the period when humans and domestic animals are most vulnerable to infection.

Birds

There are . . . owsels and black-birds with red shoulders, Thrushes, and divers sorts of smaller Birds, some redde, some blew, scarce so bigge as Wrens.
—*Lord Baltemore's Declaration, 1633*

Birds, of course, range over huge areas. While no species could be considered endemic to the peninsula, its strategic geographic position invites a wide variety of northern and southern birds to nest here. Many others that breed in the north also winter on Delmarva or pass through during seasonal migrations.

Birds of the deep woods are usually adapted to a particular level of the forest. For instance, ovenbirds, woodcocks, and whippoorwills are birds of the forest floor. Chickadees, vireos, and titmice flit among the trees and shrubs of the understory and tanagers hide in the highest treetops.

Woodland birds that nest on the ground are invariably colored a mottled brown, like the dry leaves that surround them. Indeed, they blend into their environment so effectively that only their calls normally reveal their presence. Many also have large, protruding eyes, to help them see well in the dim light of the forest.

The loud cry of "teacher, teacher, TEACHER!" that reverberates through the woods in spring is that of the ovenbird, *Seiurus aurocapillus*. Although technically a warbler, the ovenbird looks like a small brown thrush with pink legs and an orange stripe on his crown. He typically wags his rump as he walks over the woods floor, flicking over the leaves with his feet in search of hidden worms, slugs, and insects. The ovenbird's nest is built directly on the ground, but so skillfully, that it is virtually invisible from above. It is a domed structure of leaves and twigs with the entrance at the side, like an old-fashioned oven.

Recent studies have shown that the ovenbird, like many deep woods birds, needs large areas of old woods to protect it from the depredations of the brown-headed cowbird, *Molothrus ater*. Cowbirds are prolific birds of open fields and woods' edges that build no nests of their own, but lay their eggs in those of others, sometimes destroying the eggs of the host bird. The usual practice of leaving small islands of fragmented woods surrounded by fields of corn or other crops has not only resulted in a population explosion of cowbirds but also made it far easier for them to penetrate to the interior of the woods and prey on the nests of woodland birds. Birds of open lands and forest edges seem to know the difference between a cowbird's egg and their own. Robins and catbirds will puncture and destroy the invader while yellow warblers and phoebes will repeatedly bury them under new layers of nesting material. Woodland birds have no such defenses. Perhaps, because they have been preyed on for a relatively short time, they are apt to incubate and rear the young cowbirds as their own. The trouble is, cowbird eggs hatch sooner and the nestlings grow more rapidly than the young of the host bird. While it is true that, on average, a single parasitized nest may mean the death of but a single host nestling, the number of nests that are preyed upon has now multiplied to the point that whole populations are being adversely affected.

The woodcock, *Philohela minor*, is nocturnal. It is another species of the forest floor that probes the woodland soil for succulent worms and insect larvae. A member of the sandpiper family, Scolopacidae, the woodcock does indeed resemble a misplaced shore bird with its long bill and large brown protruding eyes. In spring, the male puts on a unique breeding display. With his round chunky body and absurdly long bill, he looks as comical as a child's toy as he spirals upward on whistling wings into the soft evening air. At the top of his flight, he bursts into a clear warbling song before plummeting earthward.

A single male woodcock mates with several females, each of whom lays her eggs directly on the leaves near the site of the male's nuptial flight. She builds the scantiest of nests, but sits tightly on her clutch so that her protective coloration protects the eggs from marauding snakes, foxes, or weasels.

One of the loveliest sounds in Delmarva's spring woods is the lilting song of the wood thrush, *Hylocichla mustelina*, floating through the trees at dusk like the clear sweet flute of a woodland Pan. The wood thrush is a brown bird, slightly smaller than a robin, with a spotted breast and pinkish legs. It characteristically hops along, flipping through the fallen leaves in a methodical search for food. Its nest and blue-green eggs resemble those of its cousin, the robin, *Turdus migratorius* (also a thrush), although the nest is made of leaves instead of grass. It is usually placed about six feet off the ground, often in the forked limb of a dogwood.

The wood thrush is also vulnerable to cowbird predation, particularly where the woods are small and fragmented. Also, like many of our woodland birds, it spends its winters in Central America, and has been adversely affected there also by rampant development and loss of habitat.

The Land

On hot summer nights the northern whippoorwill, *Caprimulgus vociferus,* and its southern cousin, chuck-will's-widow, *C. carolinensis,* both repeat their names over and over in a sort of mechanical litany. The ranges of these two birds overlap on the peninsula, but the whippoorwill prefers deciduous woods and the chuck-will's-widow the pines of southern Delmarva. Neither species builds a nest; the female simply lays her eggs on top of the leaf litter, relying on her own effective camouflage to hide them. Both birds sleep by day and catch moths, beetles, ants, and termites by night. When perched, their small weak feet make them appear to be resting directly on their body. If flushed, they fly noiselessly, like large brown moths. For reasons that are unclear to ornithologists, the whippoorwill is declining, while the chuck-will's-widow is slowly extending its range to the north.

Woodland birds that dart after flying insects include the vireos, gnatcatchers, and warblers. Vireos are small olive-green birds with lighter undersides that dart quickly from tree to tree. Both white-eyed vireos, *Vireo griseus,* and red-eyed vireos, *V. olivaceus,* are so common in Delmarva's deciduous woods that there may be as many as one nesting pair per acre. The white-eyed vireo has a splash of yellow on its side and the red-eyed vireo a black and a white stripe over the eye, somewhat like an eyebrow and eye shadow. Vireos tie their cuplike nests into the fork of a branch with strands of grapevine bark. The nests are small fairy structures that are glued together with spider webs and, in the case of the red-eyed vireo, decorated on the outside with cocoon silk and lichens.

The warbling vireo, *V. gilvus*, and the yellow-throated vireo, *V. flavifrons*, are less common, but can also be found in Delmarva's piedmont woods. The warbling vireo looks like a small red-eyed vireo without the eyebrow and eye shadow, but the yellow-throated looks rather like a warbler with its bright yellow breast and yellow spectacles.

The tiny blue-gray gnatcatcher, *Polioptila caerulea*, resembles a tiny mockingbird but it cocks its tail like a wren. Gnatcatchers nest in both deciduous and pine woods, building intricate cuplike nests of plant down, oak catkins, spider webs, and lichen. It is said that if the bird is discovered in the midst of building the nest, it will immediately tear it apart and build another with the same materials.

Nesting warblers in the peninsula's woods include the hooded, the cerulean, the Kentucky, the black-and-white, the northern parula, and the pine warbler. The hooded warbler, *Wilsonia citrina*, and the cerulean, *Dendroica cerulea*, both nest in deciduous woods although the hooded warbler is also partial to the peninsula's deep wooded swamps. The male has a conspicuous black hood surrounding his yellow face. In the female, this "hood" is a mere black line that outlines her face.

The cerulean warbler chooses the tallest trees of the peninsula's oldest deciduous woods for its nest. The male has a cerulean-blue back, white underparts, and a black line across his chest. He also has white wing bars and black stripes on his wings and sides. The female is entirely different. She is blue-green above and white below, with black wings and white wing bars.

Delmarva pine woods are the home of the pine warbler, *Dendroica pinus*, and the northern parula warbler, *Parula americana*. True to its name, the pine warbler nests only in pine trees. The bird creeps over tree limbs and around the trunk, where its gray-olive coloring blends almost perfectly with the bark. The northern parula warbler builds a unique hanging nest of lichens almost like that of an oriole.

Black-and-white and Kentucky warblers both build their nests on or near ground level. The black-and-white warbler, *Mniotilta varia*, is distinctive, both for its color, and its habit of crawling up and down tree trunks. It hides its nest at the base of a tree or under a fallen log. The Kentucky warbler, *Oporornis formosus*, on the other hand, builds its nest on a small pile of fallen leaves. It is a small bird with yellow spectacles. Both these species are severely preyed upon by cowbirds.

The Land

The eastern wood peewee, *Contopus virens,* is another resident of the forest canopy. The peewee is a small, upright, rather inconspicuous bird that darts into the air after flying insects. Its loud "pee WEE" is unmistakable as it echoes through the trees in spring. A peewee's nest is built near the top of a woodland tree. From below, it resembles a small lump of lichen.

Both the brilliant red and black scarlet tanager, *Piranga olivacea*, and the all red summer tanager, *P. rubra,* nest in Delmarva's woods. Both species also winter in Central and South America, making them doubly vulnerable to the worldwide destruction of forests. The brilliant coloring of the males does make them look like misplaced residents of the Amazon rain forest. In fact, some ornithologists consider both tanagers and warblers to be South American birds that happen to nest in North America. Like so many other species, the northern range of the scarlet tanager overlaps on the peninsula with the southern range of the summer tanager. Both species haunt the tops of Delmarva's oak trees where they feed on the larvae of the oakworm moth, *Anisota* spp., the oakleaf caterpillar, *Heterocampa mantea,* and the buckmoth, *Hemileuca maia.*

Most of the chickadees found in Delmarva's woods are Carolina chickadees, *Parus carolinensis*, although the northern black-capped chickadee, *P. atricapillus,* may also be present in the piedmont section of the peninsula. Some ornithologists think that the two species hybridize where their ranges overlap. Although very similar, the Carolina is a slightly smaller bird and has less white on its wings than the black-capped. Their voices are slightly different as well.

Chickadees eat both seeds and insects, and they are easily attracted to feeders. During fall and winter they travel in flocks, moving around a closely defined feeding territory. These flocks often attract other birds, such as tufted titmice, *Parus bicolor*, nuthatches, and red-bellied and downy woodpeckers, that apparently capitalize on the chickadees' talent for finding food and spotting predators. Both chickadees and titmice nest in natural tree cavities and old woodpecker holes. Woodland birds that could be called tree climbers include brown creepers, nuthatches, and woodpeckers. Unlike the black-and-white warbler who spirals around a tree in both directions, most of these typically climb in only one direction, either up the tree or down.

The brown creeper is a small brown bird that spirals *up* a tree from the base. Nuthatches go down the tree. They are small blue-gray birds that descend head first in a straight line, carefully extracting grubs from the tree bark. The white-breasted nuthatch, *Sitta carolinensis,* is the one most commonly seen here, but the brown-headed nuthatch, *S. pusilla*, is a southern species that breeds in the pine woods of the lower peninsula. The red-breasted nuthatch and the brown creeper, *Certhia familiaris*, nest to the north of here and are only present on the peninsula in winter.

Woodpeckers, on the other hand, hitch their way up a tree trunk in jerks, like a wooden toy, while balancing on their stiff tails. Woodpeckers' feet have two toes forward and two toes behind. Their bills are as strong as chisels and they probe holes in the tree bark for insects with long barbed tongues. Species commonly found on the peninsula include the flicker, the downy, the hairy, and the red-bellied. Less common are the red-headed and the pileated.

While flickers, *Colaptes auratus*, are here all year, they may be more numerous in winter when the resident population is joined by northern migrants. A flicker's bill is relatively weak compared to other woodpeckers, so the birds choose soft dead wood in which to excavate holes for their nests. In woods where dead snags are scarce, they may return repeatedly to the same tree, making a new hole each year. Such "flicker trees" are a good place to find nesting birds in the spring. Flickers also indulge in complicated head-bobbing displays and a mated pair will often drum on the nesting tree to communicate with each other.

Downy woodpeckers, *Picoides pubescens*, are a familiar sight around suburban suet feeders and are far less shy of human contact than their larger cousin, the hairy woodpecker, *P. villosus*. Both extract insects and beetles from crevices in the bark with their barbed tongues and usually choose a dead or dying branch on a live tree for their nesting holes. They also drum on resonant tree limbs in late winter to advertise their territories.

The red-bellied woodpecker, *Melanerpes carolinus,* seems poorly named: the small spot of red on its belly is far less evident than its zebra striped body, white rump, and red crown. The red-bellied is another southern bird that seems to be extending its range northward despite the fact that it often competes with starlings for nesting sites.

The red-headed woodpecker, *Melanerpes erythrocephalus,* our only species of woodpecker with a completely red head, on the other hand, has been crowded out of nesting sites in much of the east by the aggressive competition of starlings. Happily, there is some evidence that they are now returning to the peninsula, but to fully recover, the species will need abundant dead snags in the woodland. The birds will not use birdhouses, and some have been poisoned by creosote when attempting to nest in telephone poles.

The pileated woodpecker, *Dryocopus pileatus*, is the most spectacular of the woodpeckers. The largest one found on Delmarva, it is about the size of a crow, with a brilliant red crest and conspicuous black and white neck stripes. In flight, one can also see blotches of white on the underwings. The nest hole of the pileated woodpecker is oval or rectangular, not round like other woodpeckers. It is also large, about eight inches long, and is usually found on the south side of a living tree. Abandoned holes are often used by gray squirrels. The pileated is a secretive, deep woods bird that only inhabits large tracts of mature woodlands. Where such tracts are scarce, so is the pileated.

The red-cockaded woodpecker, *Picoides borealis,* has been extirpated on the peninsula, but some efforts are being made to reestablish it here and in other parts of its former range. The red-cockaded drills its nesting cavities only in living pines that are at least sixty years old and infected with a fungus called "red heart" that softens the core of the tree. It is easy to understand why the widespread harvesting of mature loblollies and other pines on Delmarva, as elsewhere, has seriously threatened its survival. The last Delmarva sighting was in Dorchester County in 1976.

Raptors of the Woods

Hawks there are of sundry sorts; which all prey commonly upon fish:
Sparrow-hawkes, Lanerets, Gosse-hawkes, Falcons, and Osperaies.
—*Lord Baltemore's Declaration, 1633*

Delmarva's two most spectacular woodland raptors, or birds of prey, are the red-tailed hawk and the great horned owl. The two species complement each other: they hunt the same territory and feed on the same prey animals, one by day and the other by night. They even compete for nesting sites.

The red-tailed, *Buteo jamaicensis*, often sits on a dead snag at the edge of the road. The birds also soar on the wind or circle buoyantly on hot summer thermals. When seen from below they appear almost white, but one can glimpse their distinctive red-brown tail as they wheel in the sunlight. Red-taileds are buteos, a type of hawk that has wide rounded wings made for soaring. They have a poor sense of smell, but their hearing is acute, and, like other hawks, they have both monocular and binocular vision. Hawks' eyes are also tubular; that is to say, the distance between the cornea and retina is greater than the width of the eye, which enables the birds to see well at great distances.

The high descending "keeeer-r" of the red-tailed is most often heard over open country, but the bird builds its nest in a forest tree, usually at the edge of the woods where it has a wide view of the surrounding countryside. On flat Delmarva, they frequently choose the highest crotch of the tallest tree. The peninsula's mature forests may have as many as one red-tailed nest per square mile—large, bulky, collections of sticks and twigs about thirty inches across and lined with strips of cedar bark, grapevines, grasses, or even corn shucks.

Red-taileds may be seen on their courtship flights soon after the New Year. High in the sky they cross and re-cross each other's path. At times, the smaller male dives at the female, even touching her back with his talons. This ritual is repeated each year even though the pairs mate for life and generally return to the same nest.

The eggs are laid in late winter and take about a month to incubate. The female stays on the nest until the nestlings are a few weeks old, relying on the male to bring her food. Young red-taileds require almost constant feeding for six to seven weeks and, even when out of the nest, stay close to the home tree until they have learned to hunt effectively.

These are adaptable birds. They feed on a wide variety of animals found in the woods and nearby open country, and can readily alter their diet if the need arises. Meadow mice, shrews, and voles are most commonly eaten although they also take young rabbits, squirrels, or chipmunks. Even though they were once commonly shot by farmers as "chicken hawks," they fly far too slowly to catch birds.

A mature pair of red-taileds may occupy a particular area for many years, but their young must leave to establish new territories. In early fall, these immature hawks, singly or in groups, can sometimes be seen moving southward on the forward edge of an incoming cold front.

Another buteo found in the peninsula's upland forests is the crow-sized broad-winged hawk, *Buteo platypterus*. Far less obvious than the soaring red-tailed, the broad-winged spends most of its time deep in the woods, where it feeds on toads, frogs, insects, and small rodents. The nest is hidden in the thick foliage of the forest canopy, and is usually home to two or three downy young. Like red-taileds, broad-wingeds mate for life. Unlike red-taileds, however, broad-wingeds regularly change their nesting sites and hunting grounds. The broad-winged is a secretive bird that only betrays his presence by his call, a sudden shrill scream that sounds like "kwee-ee." When hunting he gazes down at the forest floor from an overhanging tree limb before dropping down on an unsuspecting vole or snake. In early fall, Delmarva's broad-wingeds join the huge flocks of eastern hawks that migrate down the coast or along the ridges of the Appalachians to wintering grounds in South America.

Accipiters are woodland hawks that dart through the trees after small birds. When flying, they characteristically spread their flight feathers like splayed "fingers" at the outer edges of their wings. The two species that nest on the peninsula seem to be declining, apparently victims of pesticides.

The sharp-shinned hawk, *Accipiter striatus*, twists and banks like a fighter plane, spreading his tail and quickly sinking his talons into an unsuspecting victim on the forest floor. Flocks of chickadees, sensing a sharp-shinned hawk in the area, will immediately stop their busy feeding and calling and freeze, effectively vanishing from sight. This hawk prefers coniferous trees, but will also nest in oaks, building a broad platform of sticks and twigs where a large limb meets the trunk of a tree.

The cooper's hawk, *Accipiter cooperii,* looks and acts much like a sharp-shinned. The cooper's hawk has a rounded tail, the sharp-shinned, a square one. The cooper's hawk is also larger, but since the females of both species are generally larger than their mates, a female sharp-shinned may be about the same size as a male cooper's. Cooper's hawks will attack chickens, and are responsible for the bad reputation all hawks have with poultry farmers. They have now disappeared from much of their former breeding range and are officially listed as a threatened species.

> *The owls here are the largest I ever saw; my son shot one some time ago that measured four feet nine inches from the tip of one wing to the tip of the other; his head was as big as that of a large calf, and looked more like one than the head of a bird. His legs were feathered quite down to the claws, which were two inches long; these formidable talons he well knew how to use, and frequently exercised them on my pigs, turkeys and geese.*
> —*A Citizen of Delaware, 1797*

The owl in this description was undoubtedly the great horned owl, one of four species of owls present in Delmarva's upland woods. The others are the long-eared owl, the tiny screech owl, and the barn owl.

While hawks have some degree of binocular vision, the owl has the widest field of binocular sight of any bird. It is the only bird whose eyes face forward. An owl's retina has many light-gathering receptor cells and its pupils can dilate almost to the edge of the iris; both adaptations help it to see in the dark. Owls can also turn their heads 180 degrees to face backwards. Contrary to popular belief, an owl is not blind in the daytime, although in bright light its pupils may contract into a tiny speck in the center of the eye. Owls blink with their top lid, making them appear thoughtful and "wise." They also raise their lower lid when sleeping and, like all birds, have a nictitating membrane to clean and moisten their eyes. Owls also have soft downy tips on their flight feathers, enabling them to fly as silently as a shadow and swoop down on their prey without warning.

The great horned owl, *Bubo virginianus,* is the largest "eared" owl on the peninsula, although the ears are actually tufts of feathers on the side of the head and have nothing to do with hearing. Great horned owls are efficient predators whose soft mournful notes of "who, who, who are you" float on the night air. These "hoot owls" as they are often called, are huge birds, eighteen to twenty-five inches long with a wingspread of more than four feet. During the day they hide in dense vine-draped trees, often returning to the same one for weeks at a time.

The owls emerge from their roosting tree at dusk to hunt through the night. Rabbits, skunks, mice and other small rodents are their preferred prey, but they will also eat snakes, lizards, and frogs, as well as young geese, ducks, crows, hawks, and other birds. The prey is swallowed whole but later the bones, mixed with feathers or fur, are regurgitated as the "owl pellets" that litter the ground under an owl's roosting tree.

The permanent home range of a great horned owl covers one to three square miles. This includes a woodland nesting site and roosting cover as well as open hunting territory. Studies have shown that pairs of owls systematically hunt the territory over several years, moving from one part to another until they have circled back to the start.

Courting owls sing hooting love songs to each other, snapping their bills and sometimes rubbing them together as if they were kissing. They mate for life, although if one member of the pair dies prematurely, the survivor will often invite a new mate into the home territory.

A great horned owl does not build a nest, preferring instead to move into one belonging to a red-tailed hawk and, if food is scarce, may not nest at all. Because the eggs are laid very early in the year, they, as well as the young owlets, must be brooded almost continually by the female to prevent them from becoming chilled. The male brings the food. Great horned owlets often leave the nest before they can fly, at five or six weeks, and roost near the home tree where they are fed by their parents. By spring, when they can fly short distances, the songbirds are migrating and small mammals have young, providing the owlets with easy prey.

The long eared owl, *Asio otus,* is a smaller, thinner, more upright version of the great horned owl, about the size of a crow, with vertical stripes on the breast and long "ears" set fairly close together on the top of its head. It is a northern species whose breeding range includes only the northern third of the peninsula. They may also be found on southern Delmarva in the wintertime where, on rare occasions, one may be spotted huddled against the trunk of a tree. They are among the most secretive and nocturnal of owls and nest in abandoned crows' nests (sometimes actively evicting their owners), old hawks' nests, and tree cavities. Their call is a soft moaning "hooooo."

Screech owls, *Otus asio,* are best known for their ghostly tremulous wail drifting through the night woods. They are tiny eared owls, less than ten inches long, either brown or gray, whose daytime roost may be revealed by flocks of scolding mockingbirds. The little owl rarely moves, even in the midst of the onslaught, and can be closely observed. Screech owls usually nest in abandoned woodpecker holes, but they can also be enticed into suburban nesting boxes.

The monkey-faced barn owl, *Tyto alba*, is a year-round resident of the peninsula, as well as most temperate zones of the world. The barn owl, while originally a cavity-nesting woodland owl in this area, has adapted so well to human development that it now also builds its nests in barns and other buildings as well as church steeples, silos, and nesting boxes. These owls return to the same site year after year and if the supply of prey is plentiful, may produce more than one brood a year, unusual in raptors.

> *Of fowl of the land, there is the Turkey (Forty and Fifty Pound weight) which is very great.*
> —*William Penn, 1683*

> *Large game, as the deer and the turkey, has entirely disappeared, owing to the restricted range which has been left to it.*
> —*Robert Wilson, 1876*

Wild turkeys, *Meleagris gallopavo*, once the principal game bird of the Indians, had disappeared from the peninsula by 1880, victims of widespread forest clearing as well as market gunners who slaughtered them by the thousands for sale in the cities. Later, remnant populations in the remote mountains of Pennsylvania, Virginia, and West Virginia suffered further damage when the chestnut blight eliminated their principal food.

In the 1970s, attempts were made to re-introduce the species to Delmarva. The first turkeys released were pen-raised birds that proved unable to adapt to the wild, but game managers now report that turkeys seem to be increasing, despite the general scarcity of forest habitat.

Turkeys are huge birds; the male is nearly four feet tall, and the female is not much smaller. They roost in the upper branches of trees, changing their perch nightly. The birds do not migrate, but a foraging flock may wander over many miles, feeding on forest mast and tubers, berries, wild grapes, grass, and seeds. They also eat insects such as grasshoppers and beetles and, like grouse, wallow in the dust to rid themselves of vermin.

In spring the toms put on a spectacular breeding display, gobbling furiously to attract the attention of the hens, while dragging their wings over the ground, puffing out their chests, and fanning their tails. The hens choose their mates and two or three may select the same tom.

The hen then scrapes out a hollow in the leaves on the forest floor, and lays eight to twelve eggs, covering them carefully whenever she leaves the nest

to feed. Hen turkeys fiercely defend their broods against predators like hawks, foxes, raccoons, skunks, crows, and owls. Turkey poults, as the young are called, are very susceptible to cold and hide beneath their mother's wings until they are about a month old. Thereafter, they roost in the trees on their own.

Reptiles and Amphibians

Rattlesnakes, a kind of large, horrible and abominable snakes; they have jaws like a dog; they cut and bite off a person's leg as if it had been cut with an ax . . . on its tail it has horny joints which rattle like the children's rattle do.
— *Peter Martenson Lindestrom, mid-seventeenth century*

Snakes are not everyone's favorite wildlife! This quotation is from a rather fanciful, not to say absurd, description of the animals found in New Sweden in the 1600s. There are no rattlesnakes on Delmarva today. The peninsula's only poisonous snake is the copperhead, *Agkistrodon contortrix*. Present, although extremely rare, it can be found in rocky outcrops and old stone walls in the piedmont woods of the northern peninsula. It is also found around the cypress swamps and adjacent agricultural land of southern Delmarva. While the copperhead is secretive and rarely encountered, it is well to be able to recognize one quickly. It is a light tan snake with red-brown markings in the shape of an hourglass. The narrowest part of the hourglass is on the top of the snake's back with the wider part spilling over the side. The young have yellow tails.

The copperhead, like the rattlesnake, is a pit viper, so named for the heat sensing pit that lies between the eye and nostril on either side of the snake's head and helps the animal locate the small warm-blooded mammals and birds that are its prey. The eyes of the copperhead (should you get that close) have vertical pupils instead of round. Its bite, while rarely fatal, is extremely painful and requires prompt medical attention.

While few snakes are poisonous, all snakes are predators. They feed on mice, toads, birds, and insects, depending on the species. At the same time, raptors and predatory mammals regularly dine on them. Snakes do not hear well, due to an absence of external ear openings, but they have an acute sense of smell and relatively good eyesight. The purpose of their flicking forked tongues is to detect and identify scents.

The snakes most likely to be encountered in Delmarva's woods are the northern black racer, *Coluber c. constrictor*, the eastern hognosed snake, *Heterodon platyrhinos*, and the black rat snake, *Elaphe o. obsoleta*.

The black racer is a smooth satiny black, with some white on its chin and throat. Racers are extremely quick and agile and usually hunt with their heads held high. The snake that tears across a country road in front of your car is usually a racer. For the most part they are not good climbers, but if sufficiently alarmed may flee into the lower branches of a shrub.

The eastern hognosed snake is mostly found in Delmarva's sandy coastal plain woods, although it may also inhabit old fields on the northern peninsula, and dunes. Named for their upturned snout, which looks rather like a pig's, these snakes are highly variable in their color and markings. They are usually spotted, but the background color may be yellow, brown, gray, or even black. A hognosed will hiss loudly and inflate its neck when alarmed. This is a bluff; the snake is quite harmless. If the initial tactic does not work, the snake may turn itself upside down, open its mouth and loll out its tongue as if it were dead, calmly turning over and continuing on its way when the danger is past.

The black rat snake is the largest of Delmarva's snakes, sometimes reaching a length of six feet or more. Black snakes are a vivid shiny black with a white or cream colored chin. They are found in both deciduous and pine woods on the peninsula, as well as in old fields and farm buildings, where they may be tolerated for their superior mousing abilities. A black snake is also a good climber and can sometimes be seen sunning himself high on a tree limb at the edge of a field.

The eastern garter snake, *Thamnophis s. sirtalis*, is a woodland species that has become so tolerant of man that it is now more often encountered around his fields, gardens, and abandoned barns than in the woods. This is a small snake with longitudinal yellow stripes, although like many snakes, there are numerous variations in its color and markings.

The corn snake, *Elaphe guttata*, is another woodland species that has moved into barns and abandoned houses. Corn snakes are relatively rare on the peninsula, and only occur on the coastal plain. They are good climbers and, although primarily nocturnal, may be seen in the early evening as they emerge for a night of hunting mice, rats, birds, or bats. During the daytime, corn snakes hide underground, resting in old rodent burrows. Although somewhat variable, corn snakes are usually a pale yellow ocher with black edged, red-brown markings, a combination that was once thought to resemble the multicolored kernels on an ear of Indian corn.

Eastern milk snakes, *Lampropeltis d. triangulum*, are fairly common in the rocky woodlands of the piedmont section of the peninsula. They hunt only at night, usually hiding beneath fallen trees during the day. Milk snakes are white, with vivid red-brown blotches edged with black. There is also a subspecies that is more yellow known as the coastal plain milk snake, *L. doliata temporalis*, that is also found on the peninsula. While milk snakes are completely harmless, many have been killed by mistake for their superficial resemblance to copperheads. They were once thought to milk cows, hence their common name.

The eastern kingsnake, *Lampropeltis g. getulus*, while not common here, is another example of a southern species that finds its northern limit on Delmarva and southern New Jersey. It is a shiny black snake with white markings that feeds on other snakes as well as lizards, birds, and mice. Basically terrestrial, kingsnakes are also good swimmers and sometimes haunt the banks of streams in search of young water snakes and turtle eggs, two of their favorite foods.

The peninsula also has a few snakes so small, scarce, and secretive that they are rarely found even by researchers. They include the eastern worm snake, *Carphophis a. armoenus*, the most common of the group, the northern redbelly snake, *Storeria o. occipitomaculata*, and the eastern earth snake, *Virginia v. valeriae*. All have adult lengths of up to only twelve inches.

Some species of snakes lay eggs while others bear live young. Both eggs and young are usually hidden beneath rocks and old logs or in decaying vegetations. Breeding usually takes place in spring and the young snakes hatch or are born in late summer or early fall.

Dragons . . . [and] land tortoises.

—Peter Martenson Lindestrom

Lindestrom's "dragons" were probably skinks—smooth, shiny, usually terrestrial lizards that hunt by day and hide under rocks and logs at night. Skinks bite, and if caught by the tail, will simply drop it off in your hand. Three kinds are found in Delmarva's woods as well as throughout the east. They are the five-lined skink, *Eumeces fasciatus*, the ground skink, *Lygosoma laterale*, and the broadheaded skink, *E. laticeps*. Of these, the five-lined skink is the most often encountered. It is a small lizard, between five and eight inches long, black or brown, with five broad light stripes down its back. These stripes are most conspicuous on young lizards and tend to fade with age. The tail is blue or gray and breeding males have a bright red-orange head. Five-lined skinks normally hide among the leaves on the forest floor where they feed on insects and their larvae, as well as spiders, earthworms, and occasionally small mice. While they do not climb trees, they may occasionally be seen basking on stumps or on the base of a tree trunk.

Ground skinks are another example of a southern species that reaches the northern limit of its range on Delmarva. Ground skinks hide in the leaf litter on the floor of the forest and search for insects. They are small, only about three inches long, the color of an earthworm but with a black stripe down either side. One peculiar characteristic of the ground skink is a transparent lower eyelid which allows the animal to see while protecting its eyes from dirt.

The broadheaded skink is truly a miniature dragon! Eight to twelve inches long, it is a brown lizard with five broad light stripes down its back and a wide flat head which in the males is colored bright orange. Juveniles are a brilliant black with a bright blue tail. This is another southern species that is found only as far north as Delmarva. Broadheaded skinks are arboreal: they live in holes in dead and dying trees and hunt insects high in the forest canopy.

Also found on Delmarva are northern fence lizards, *Sceloporus u. hyacinthinus*, so named for their habit of clinging to rail fences as well as rotting logs and stumps. Fence lizards are spiny lizards, a large genus with keeled and pointed dorsal scales. Male fence lizards have a blue throat patch that is surrounded by black. These lizards dash up a tree trunk when surprised, usually hanging motionless on the opposite side of the trunk. If approached again they dodge around the tree and cling at a slightly higher level, repeating this maneuver until they are out of reach.

Lizards have scales on their bodies and claws on their toes. Salamanders are smooth skinned and clawless. Most salamanders live in or near water, but the redbacked salamander, *Plethedon c. cinereus*, is a terrestrial species that is commonly found in Delmarva's woods, where it hides under rocks and logs. This salamander comes in two color phases, red-backed and lead-backed, both of which are found here. The species is unusual in that its eggs hatch into miniature adults with no intervening larval stage.

The common land tortoise of Delmarva's woods is the gentle box turtle, *Terrapene carolina*. Box turtles are easily recognized by their hinged lower shell, or plastron, which closes tightly against the upper shell, or carapace. The males have red eyes and the females brown. In June, a female box turtle is sometimes seen in the act of burying her eggs in the sandy dirt of a sunny bank or trail. The eggs, which are about the size of a hen's with thin flexible white shells, hatch, in about three months, into miniature turtles about an inch in diameter.

A box turtle may live to a great age, yet spend its entire life in an area the size of a football field. These turtles are often discovered leisurely dining on earthworms or wild strawberries, early in the day or after a summer rain. Because they eat mushrooms that are poisonous to man, box turtles should never be eaten. The shell was a sacred symbol for the Lenni-Lenape Indians. Their creation myth centered around a turtle that rose from the sea. The Indians used the shell to make ceremonial rattles and often buried them with their dead.

Wood turtles, *Clemmys insculpta*, are a pond species that often wander far from water into Delmarva's piedmont woods and fields. The southern boundary of the wood turtle's range crosses the northern peninsula. This turtle has red markings on its neck and legs and a rough, sculptured shell without the hinge found on the plastron of the box turtle.

Woodland Mammals

Large lions but smooth, bears, coal black, large and grim, wolves, lynxes, polecats, elks . . . raccoons, minks, beavers, otters, red deer, hinds in abundance, foxes, grey, spangled and black, . . . hares . . . and squirrels.
    —*Peter Martenson Lindestrom, mid-seventeenth century*

Of living creatures . . . and Beasts of the Woods, here are divers sorts . . . for food as well as Profit, the Elk as big as a small Ox, Deer, bigger than ours, Beaver, Raccoon, Rabbits, Squirrels . . . some eat young Bear and commend it.
    —*William Penn, 1683*

Several animals mentioned on these early lists were extirpated from the peninsula, as well as throughout much of the east, soon after settlement. They fell victim to the early fur trade and to the loss of their woodland habitat, and those that survived were later destroyed by bounty hunters and farmers who saw them as a threat to domestic livestock.

Large herds of eastern elk, *Cervus elaphus*, once roamed the entire Chesapeake Bay region. The last one was killed in Clarke County, Virginia, in 1855, an event that effectively ended their existence. The peninsula also had black bears, *Ursus americanus americanus*, gray wolves, *Canis lupis lycacon*, and eastern cougars, *Felis concolor couguar*, at the time of settlement. The bears have now retreated into the Appalachian mountains (the last bear sighting on Delmarva was in the Great Cypress Swamp about 1900), while the gray wolf, with the exception of a remnant population on Michigan's northern peninsula, has been extirpated from the entire eastern United States. The eastern cougar is a nocturnal predator that requires a large and remote hunting territory. It was gone from Delmarva by 1899 and was thought to be extinct until recent reports of sightings in the Appalachians.

It seems ironic today that an important reason for the decline of both cougars and wolves was the widespread decimation of their principal prey animal: the white-tailed deer. There were no deer on the peninsula by the turn of the century. That they have now returned in force is due partly to the proliferation of the kind of second growth, shrubby woodlands they thrive on, and partly to the lack of these natural predators. Deer, like many prey animals, are strong reproducers, and without predators to keep them in check, tend to proliferate beyond the capacity of their habitat to support them.

The most common mammal inhabiting our woods both now and in the past is arguably the white-footed mouse, *Peromyscus leucopus*. A species of deer mouse, white-footed mice are found in every kind of woods on the peninsula as well as in hedgerows and brushy areas. They are appealing little rodents, either gray or brown with white underparts and a relatively short hairy tail. By day, these mice hide in the shelter of hollow stumps or trees, emerging at dusk to scrounge for nuts, berries, and seeds. Their large bulging black eyes, long whiskers, and big ears all help them to navigate in the dark. Like many animals of the eastern forest, white-footed mice thrive on acorns, beech and hickory nuts, and the seeds of pines and other conifers, but they are particularly fond of the fruits of the wild black cherry, *Prunus serotina,* and the first evidence of their presence is often a small cache of cherry pits. Blackberries, raspberries, shadberries, the fruit of various species of viburnum, and the seeds of jewelweed, *Impatiens* spp., are all favorites as well. The mice also eat groundbeetles, caterpillars, centipedes, and snails.

The white-footed mouse is active all winter. It often moves into an old bird's nest, capping it carefully with a blanket of leaves or thistledown to keep snug in the cold weather. These mice are extremely prolific. The females begin to breed at the early age of two months, and produce several litters a season for most of their lives. Our woods would be overrun with mice if they were not preyed upon by many snakes and every hawk, owl, weasel, or fox in the neighborhood. In fact, it is the number of mice in a woodland that determines how many of these higher predators it can support.

Another tiny inhabitant of the woods on the northern half of the peninsula is the short-tailed shrew, *Blarina brevicauda*. Slightly smaller than mice, shrews have pointed snouts, small ears, and short tails. Unlike mice, they are carnivorous. They use their hard, sharp noses and powerful little paws to plow through the leaf litter and forest humus in search of invertebrates. Shrews have a high rate of metabolism and voracious appetites, consuming huge quantities of food for their size. There is some evidence that they are also able to paralyze earthworms and snails with a toxic secretion in their salivary glands in order to store them for later use.

The short-tailed shrew hides its nest of leaves and grass beneath a fallen log, where the female may produce three to four litters of five to seven young a summer. Great numbers of shrews are killed by hawks, owls, weasels, skunks and snakes, although not all are eaten because of an offensive odor emitted by a pair of glands on the animal's flanks.

The masked shrew, *Sorex cinereus*, is also found in Delmarva's woods. Masked shrews are tiny, only about a third of the length of the short-tailed shrew, but they are found in a wide variety of habitats.

> *Here also is that Remarkable Creature the Flying-Squirrel, having a kind of Skinny Wings, almost like those of the Batt, though it hath the like Hair and Colour of the Common Squirrel, but is much less in bodily substance. I have (myself) seen it fly from one tree to another in the Woods, but how long it can maintain its flight is not known.*
>
> *— Gabriel Thomas, 1697*

The southern flying squirrel, *Glaucomys volans*, is one of five members of the squirrel family in Delmarva's woods. There also gray squirrels, *Sciurus carolinensis*, Delmarva fox squirrels, *Sciurus niger cinereus*, red squirrels, *Tamiasciurus hudsonicus*, and eastern chipmunks, *Tamias striatus*.

The range of the southern flying squirrel includes all of the eastern United States, from central Vermont and New Hampshire into Florida. They may actually outnumber the gray squirrel in Delmarva's woods, but flying squirrels emerge only at nightfall, and so are seldom seen. They are just as fond of birdseed as gray squirrels, and regularly rob suburban feeders.

Flying squirrels do not actually fly. They glide from tree to tree buoyed by a loose fold of skin that stretches between the fore and hind leg on either side of the body. They fling themselves into space from the top of one tree, land on another, then run up the trunk to launch themselves again.

The Land

They are attractive little animals with a rich glossy coat of blended gray and cinnamon, a flat silky tail, and white underparts. They eat insects and birds' eggs as well as the usual berries, nuts, and seeds and are preyed on in turn by hawks, owls, and foxes, as well as by the neighborhood cat.

Flying squirrels do not hibernate but hunt actively all winter, even though several may huddle together in one nest to keep warm. By flattening its body, a squirrel can squeeze through a very small hole, and can invade attics or other spaces under the eaves of a house.

> *The squirrel frolics among the hickory-groves and gum-swamps.*
> — *Robert Wilson, 1876*

The excited chattering of the gray squirrel is one of the first woodland sounds that children learn to recognize. These quick nervous rodents are a familiar presence. Suburban yards and city parks are as much to their liking as the deep woods. While they are certainly plentiful today, early accounts tell stories of mass migrations of these squirrels; thousands of them apparently moved periodically from one area of the eastern woods to another. The populations were said to be so dense that that a hunter could kill more than a hundred in just a few hours, yet by 1900, so much of their forest habitat had been cut that it was feared that the gray squirrel might actually become extinct.

Despite its evident skill in adapting to human civilization, the gray squirrel is still an arboreal species, and is only found where mature deciduous trees or pines produce plentiful crops of nuts and seeds. For the most part, they only come down from the trees in order to collect and bury nuts for later consumption. Because many of their caches are never recovered and eventually sprout, they are also responsible for much forest regeneration.

Each squirrel has a home range of several wooded acres, although the territories of several individuals may overlap, causing the resident squirrels to form loose social hierarchies. Gray squirrels forage most actively in the early morning and late afternoon, a habit well known to great horned owls and foxes, who stalk them in the low light. They mate in late winter and the young are born in bulky nests hidden in tree hollows, or in one of the large globular leafy nests that are so obvious in the trees of a deciduous forest. Gestation is about forty days. A pair usually has more than one litter of two or three young a season.

The red squirrel is primarily a northern species; the peninsula is near the southern edge of its range. Red squirrels also like acorns, beech, and hickory nuts, as well as tulip tree and sycamore seeds. They bury the green cones of pine trees before they have opened so they do not lose the seeds and also eat berries, fungi, and birds' eggs.

Red squirrels are a rich red-brown and about half the size of the gray squirrel. In winter they usually develop ear tufts, the only squirrel indigenous to the peninsula to have them. They are busy, quick little animals and dig industriously for buried acorns and maple seeds, spending far more time on the ground than the gray squirrel. They build nests of shredded grape bark, usually in a deserted woodpecker hole or natural tree cavity, but sometimes in an excavated burrow at its base. They occupy these nests all through the year. In late winter, during red squirrel breeding time, the males can often be seen chasing the females through the trees. A litter of from three to seven young is born after a gestation period of about thirty-eight days, and, if conditions are good, a second litter is produced in late summer.

Some forest mammals, such as the red fox and the eastern raccoon, have actually benefitted from the drastic changes that have occurred in the landscape. The Delmarva fox squirrel has not. It is a subspecies of the eastern fox squirrel, *Sciurus niger*, indigenous to the Delmarva Peninsula and probably evolved because of the peninsula's comparative isolation from the rest of North America.

Any interbreeding population of a plant or animal collectively contains a diversified gene pool: a sort of genetic reservoir of potential adaptation to change. In the absence of environmental pressures, this level of genetic diversity tends to remain steady, and, except for slight individual variations, no evolution occurs. However, if a small group of breeding individuals becomes isolated for one reason or another, their recessive genes may begin to combine in such a way as to allow recessive characteristics to become dominant. The isolation may be geographical, as on a peninsula largely surrounded by water, or the species may find itself trapped in a surviving fragment of an earlier ecosystem that has been superseded. In either case, when the resulting genetic shifts are important enough to prevent the isolated population from interbreeding with their original parent population, a new subspecies is said to exist. Such a situation gave rise to the Delmarva fox squirrel.

Although the gray coat and white underparts of Delmarva fox squirrels superficially resemble those of gray squirrels, fox squirrels are considerably larger and have a brown head and a much bushier tail. Far less arboreal than gray squirrels, they are typically seen running along the ground.

The historic range of the Delmarva fox squirrel once included the entire peninsula where they thrived in the forests of mature loblolly pines and hardwoods. However, the widespread clearing of the woods in the nineteenth century, combined with the continual harvesting of marketable trees in the twentieth century, eventually reduced their numbers to a tiny remnant on the Eastern Shore of Maryland. Luckily, there is a new interest in preserving some of Delmarva's older forests, and successful efforts are being made to reintroduce Delmarva fox squirrels into much of their former range.

Chipmunks, too, are more often seen on the ground than in trees. In fact, the eastern chipmunk is more closely related to the ground squirrels of the West than to our eastern tree squirrels. Chipmunks are appealing, gregarious little beasts, a rich red-brown color with black and white stripes down their back and over their eyes. If alarmed, they typically utter a sharp "chuck" and scurry off with tails held high in the air.

Chipmunks sleep away all but the mildest days of winter. They are solitary animals, for the most part, each living in its own burrow, an intricate system of tunnels that wander far underground beneath entrance and exit holes that may be only a few feet apart. At various locations along the length of these tunnels are nest chambers and storehouses for the chipmunk's impressive collection of nuts and seeds. Chipmunks have two breeding periods a year, one lasting from February to April and the other in June and July. After mating, they separate and the female bears and raises the young on her own.

And that strange Creature the Possam, she having a false Belly to swallow her Young ones, by which means she preserveth them from danger when anything comes to disturb them.
— Gabriel Thomas, 1697

The opossum, *Didelphis virginiana,* is North America's only marsupial, an order of mammals principally characterized by their manner of bearing young. After a brief gestation period of twelve to thirteen days, the tiny naked embryos are born. Scarcely the size of a honeybee, each must crawl into its mother's pouch, which it apparently locates by smell, and latch onto a teat. The teat then expands in the newborn's mouth, effectively binding it to the mother opossum for about two months.

Young opossums grow fast. After two months they are about the size of a full grown mouse and leave the pouch for short periods to cling to their mother's back. By three and one-half months, they are ready to go off on their own. Two broods a year are normal, and occasionally three, so that there may be young in the mother's pouch most of the year from February through October. The mother opossum builds her nest in a fallen log, hollow tree, or abandoned woodchuck hole. She picks up nesting material in her mouth, then transfers it to her tail for transportation.

Opossums are omnivorous. They eat all sorts of fruits and berries as well as insects, frogs, snakes, and birds. In turn they are preyed on by owls and foxes. They are shy, secretive, and nocturnal, so that while plentiful in our woods, they are seldom seen alive. Unfortunately their habit of eating road-killed carrion makes them particularly vulnerable to speeding cars.

The fox, both red and gray, the raccoon and the opossum, are found in scarcely diminished numbers.

—Robert Wilson, 1879

The gray fox, *Urocyon cinereoargenteus*, is more a creature of the woods than his larger cousin the red fox. Gray foxes were originally a southern species but they have gradually extended their range far to the north and are now common in New England. They are adept at climbing trees, using their stout nails like a cat. Gray foxes den in a hollow log or tree, often on the border of swamps or bottomlands, and produce a litter of three to five young foxes in early spring. They are solicitous parents, tending their young well into summer. Their principal prey animal is the cottontail rabbit, although, like red foxes, they will eat all kinds of fruits, birds, and small mammals as well as insects, snakes, and turtles.

Raccoons, *Procyon lotor*, are also common in Delmarva's woods. Raccoons are related to bears, and they are found in every woodland that provides suitable den sites. Young raccoons are born in early April and are well cared for by their parents who often keep them with them until late fall.

Their sharp claws and long dexterous "fingers" make raccoons accomplished climbers; they can scurry up any size tree with alacrity. Raccoon tracks can be found on the sandy banks of almost every woodland stream; their favorite foods are crayfish, frogs, and fish, but they also feed on a variety of fruits, berries, nuts, and insects. They are particularly fond of stripping ears of corn, a habit that does not endear them to farmers. While the raccoon sleeps away the coldest days of winter, he does not actually hibernate, and is readily up and active during mild spells.

Raccoons are nocturnal, crafty, and secretive. In fact, any individual that does not exhibit such behavior should be treated with extreme caution, because raccoons are highly vulnerable to rabies.

Bats, these resemble a small hawk.

—Joseph Scott, 1807

Bats are also feared as carriers of rabies, yet it has been estimated that only one bat in a thousand actually becomes infected with the disease and it usually dies very quickly. Still it is always prudent to leave any wild animal you suspect of being sick strictly alone.

Six species of bats are known to occur in Delmarva's woods. Most common in deciduous woods are the red bat, *Lasiurus borealis*, and the big brown bat, *Eptesicus fuscus*. Less often encountered are the hoary bat, *L. cinereus*, which prefers pines and other evergreens, the silver-haired, *Lasionycteris noctivagans*, the eastern pipistrelle, *Pipistrellus subflavus*, and the little brown bat, *Myotis lucifugus*.

Red bats are solitary tree bats. The females give birth alone high in the trees, in late May or early June, and the litters of two to four young then cling to their mother until they can fly on their own, usually when they are between two and six weeks old. Big brown bats, on the other hand, collect in large colonies of nursing females with young, either in hollow trees or man-made structures.

Solitary bats, such as the hoary, silver-haired, and red, tend to migrate south in winter. Others, such as the big brown, little brown, and eastern pipistrelle, collect in hollow trees, buildings, or tunnels to hibernate.

Bats are the only true flying mammals. Their wings are actually membranes that stretch between the bat's front and hind legs and are attached to the side of the body. The finger bones support this membrane during flight like the ribs of an umbrella. When at rest, bats hang upside down, clinging to their roost with their hind feet and folding their wings like a fan. In order to find their way rapidly in the dark, bats emit a series of supersonic sounds that bounce off objects and are picked up by their large and sensitive ears, a process called echolocation.

Bats are the subject of many ghostly tales, but they are valuable animals to have around, eating thousands of flying insects. It has been estimated that a single little brown bat eats more than five hundred mosquitoes per hour.

Open Lands

I should be able to turn the poorest ground, which would hardly afford food for a cow, into the richest and most fertile meadow where great flocks of cattle would find superabundant food and grow fat.

—Peter Kalm, 1761

Coarse grass, rushes, horse-mints, and other noxious weeds, are the general production of lands overcharged with moisture.

—John Spurrier, 1793

While virtually all the open land on the lower peninsula is still actively farmed, working farms are increasingly scarce in Delmarva's piedmont, making abandoned pastures, old fields, and thickets common features of the landscape north of the fall line.

Piedmont farms have been abandoned in both good times and bad. In the nineteenth century many farmers deserted the piedmont's hilly terrain for the flat Midwestern prairies. Many more went out of business during the Depression when they could not meet their mortgage payments. Yet, in the long run, the largest number of piedmont farms appear to have gone out of production in times of economic prosperity. Rising land prices and steep inheritance taxes contributed to reasons owners sold for housing and commercial development. Today, open space in the northern peninsula is disappearing at an alarming rate.

For the most part, farms in the piedmont never entered the age of agricultural specialization. Most had a mix of field crops, pastures, hayfields, and hedgerows. Some of this cleared land is still kept open by periodic mowing, but many old cow pastures, hayfields, and former cropland have been invaded by

77

broomsedge, red cedar, and dense thickets of blackberries, sumac, honey-suckle, and multiflora rose.

The changes going on in these neglected fields occur in a roughly predictable sequence that is known as plant succession. Not surprisingly, the first plants to appear in an abandoned field are always fast-growing and sun-loving. Because Delmarva, like the rest of the eastern United States, was originally covered with woods, these early successional plants are predominantly alien weeds that thrive on disturbed soil, or prairie species that spread eastward when the land was cleared. However, because their seeds cannot germinate in the shade, their numbers dwindle as soon as the first seedling trees and shrubs appear in the field.

As the woody plants take over, their falling leaves add humus to the soil, gradually creating the environmental conditions needed for native shade-loving woodland species to return. Between fifty and a hundred years after a field has been abandoned, the original components of the peninsula's indigenous woodland will once again be in place, yet even with no further disturbance, it will take another hundred years for the young woods to truly resemble Delmarva's pre-colonial forest.

In practical terms, this means that a field that has been plowed but not planted will be quickly covered with crabgrass, *Digitaria sanguinalis*, and horseweed, *Erigeron canadensis*, usually mixed with rosettes of winter annuals, such as daisy fleabane, *Erigeron annuus*, and members of the mustard family, genus *Brassica*. Biennials such as common mullein, *Verbascum thapsus*, and Queen Anne's lace, *Daucus carota*, will come next, followed by perennials like yarrow, *Achillea millefolium*, and chicory, *Cichorium intybus*. Swathes of white oxeye daisies, *Chrysanthemum leucanthemum*, and yellow black-eyed Susans, *Rudbeckia hirta,* may spread into the field by the second or third year.

The seeds of most of these plants were already in the soil when the field was abandoned. Most are natives of Europe and Asia that arrived accidentally in packing materials or mixed in with hay brought for livestock, although both dandelion, *Taraxacum officinale*, and Queen Anne's lace were grown as vegetables before 1700, and the root of chicory was used as a coffee substitute. Buttercups, *Ranunculus acris,* and field daisies were grown as garden flowers.

A hayfield or pasture that is already covered with grass when abandoned, is often invaded by broomsedge, *Andropogon virginicus*, a native tufted grass with densely fibrous roots. For years, a few red cedar, dogwood, hawthorne, *Crataegus* spp., and isolated clumps of goldenrod, *Solidago* spp., may be the only other plants in a field of *andropogon*. It was thought that the soil in such areas was too poor to support other vegetation, but recent research has shown *andropogon* is allelopathic: its roots exude a chemical which inhibits other plant growth. Because these broomsedge clearings contain predominantly native species, it appears that they may have existed in the original forest as well.

Where mats of allelopathic broomsedge are not a factor, the early grasses and field flowers are soon crowded out by thick stands of goldenrod and asters. There are seventy-five species of goldenrod native to the eastern United States. Three that are common on Delmarva's piedmont are tall goldenrod, *Solidago altissima*, rough-stemmed goldenrod, *S. rugosa*, and Canada goldenrod, *S. canadensis*. The most common asters in upland fields are usually the white frostweeds, *Aster ericoides*, *A. pilosus*, and *A. simplex*.

In a few years, these herbaceous plants will give way to early pioneer hardwoods such as sassafras, *Sassafras albidum*, and wild cherry, while islands of blackberries, *Rubus* spp., and sumac, *Rhus* spp., as well as invasive aliens like multiflora rose, *Rosa multiflora*, Asiatic bittersweet, *Celastrus orbiculatus*, and Japanese honeysuckle will appear in the field.

The Land

Bittersweet and honeysuckle are rampant vines that were originally brought here as garden ornamentals. They twine over other vegetation, choking out woody plants and smothering herbaceous ones, often to the point of slowing the natural sequence of succession. Multiflora rose is another Japanese species that is used as a rootstock for grafting hybrid tea roses. When an enterprising nurseryman began marketing it as a "living fence" about twenty years ago, it proved to be so attractive to mockingbirds and cardinals that it substantially expanded their ranges. While undoubtedly a good wildlife plant, multiflora rose is so prolific that it is now crowding out our native pasture roses, and, to some extent, our blackberries and sumacs.

The first potential canopy trees to appear in a field in the piedmont section of the peninsula are usually tulip trees, *Liriodendron tulipifera*, white ashes, *Fraxinus americana*, and red maples. Along roadsides and in abandoned upland on the coastal plain, sweet gums, *Liquidambar styraciflua*, are early pioneers, while Virginia pines and post oaks, *Quercus stellata*, are the first invaders in sandier soils.

Farm Fields

The Corne is very plentifull in each of three Harvests in the same yeare. This Corne maketh good bread and beere.
—Lord Baltemore's Declaration, 1633

Corn and soybean fields, hayfields that are regularly mowed, and pastures still grazed by cattle or horses are all prevented from entering this cycle of succession and remain as open land. Of course, in the case of cropland, the numbers and relationships of plants, pollinators, pests, and scavengers have been artificially altered by the lack of diversity and the use of pesticides. Cornfields are not natural ecosystems, yet both deer and foxes hide in them and their tracks may be seen in the soft soil. Various sparrows flit among the corn stalks and, to the dismay of farmers, raccoons strip and eat the ears. Newly plowed corn or soybean fields also turn up organisms that lure gulls in the spring and the gleanings left by mechanical corn pickers attract huge flocks of Canada geese and whistling swan in the fall and winter. Smaller birds like the horned lark may be seen walking over Delmarva's farm fields in winter and both turkey vultures and black vultures often circle high in the air above them.

Killdeers are also birds of open farm country and cultivated fields. The killdeer, *Charadrius vociferus*, is a plover that, unlike others of his clan, inhabits inland fields. The birds can often be heard early on a spring morning, calling "kill-dee, kill-dee" as they fly overhead or run about a newly plowed field picking up exposed earthworms, beetles, and ants. Killdeer nest in a scrape in the ground, typically choosing a pile of rubble or oyster shells at the edge of a country lane or field that has an open view of the surrounding countryside. If an intruder approaches her nest, the female killdeer will scream and flutter away, dragging one wing as if it were broken in a desperate effort to distract attention from her brood.

Pastures

Lamb's quarter, snake weed, which is esteemed a safe remedy for the bite of a snake, nettles, dog fennel, toad flax, wild vines, blazing-star, cinque foil, ground cherries, purslane and yams, which grow without cultivation, in fields, and open ground.

—Joseph Scott, 1807

Pastures, too, have their own ecology. For the most part they are covered with spreading fescue grasses, *Festuca* spp., and Kentucky blue grass. Both are species that can withstand the continual trampling and cropping of cattle or horses. These low-growing pasture plants offer little protection for wildlife, however, so large butterflies are rare and perching birds present only if there is a protective hedgerow. Ants can be important aerators of a pasture's packed soil, but the only grasshoppers are likely to be crickets and short-horned grasshoppers of the family Acrididae, so called because their antennae are less that half their body length.

However, some species of plants survive in pastures because they are prickly, like thistles, *Cirsium* spp., and *Carduus* spp., foul tasting, like buttercups, or poisonous to eat like pokeweed, *Phytolacca americana*. Some plants are all three, like horse nettle, *Solanum carolinense*, a deadly member of the tomato family.

Horse nettle may be scattered throughout an upland pasture but pokeweed is a disturbed soil species that typically appears in the bare soil at the edge of cowpaths. It is a tall distinctive plant, with small bell-like pink flowers and rich purple fruit that was used by the Indians for dye. Pokeberries are loved by many animals and birds; flocks of robins can become drunk on fermented pokeberries after a frost, causing them to fly erratically and bump into trees and buildings.

Pokeweed is one of the few plants of disturbed soil that is native to North America. Experiments have shown that the seed must, in fact, travel through the digestive system of a bird or animal before it will germinate. The seeds may lie dormant for years, sprouting only if the land is disturbed. Young shoots of pokeweed are edible with careful cooking, but the roots and fruit contain a substance called phytolaccin which is poisonous to humans.

Most of the invasive prickly thistles of pastures are aliens. The Canada thistle, *Cirsium arvense*, which is actually European, is the most aggressive. It is a perennial that spreads by underground stolons as well as by floating thistledown, and can quickly dominate a pasture. Bull thistles, *C. vulgare*, and nodding thistle, *Carduus nutans*, also flourish in pastures but they are biennials and will not spread if the plant is cut before going to seed. Native thistles found in pastures include pasture thistle, *Cirsium pumilum,* which has the largest flowers, field thistle, *C. discolor*, a plant easily recognized by the thick white wool on the undersides of its leaves, and tall thistle, *C. altissimum.*

A thistle, actually, is a rewarding hunting ground for the naturalist. Larvae of butterflies and moths as well as snails, click beetles, and grasshoppers hide among a thistle's thorns while aphids and tree hoppers suck the plant's sap and are "farmed" by ants for their sugary fluids. The flowers attract pollinating flies, mosquitoes, bees, and wasps as well as ruby-throated hummingbirds, *Archilocus colubris*. Crab spiders, family Thomisidae, and ambush bugs, family Phymatidae, hunt near the base of the corolla. Salticid spiders wait to pounce on pollinating skippers and, in turn, are captured by orb-weaving spiders, or five-lined skinks.

Nettles, both the alien stinging nettle, *Urtica dioica*, and the native slender nettle, *U. gracilis*, are common at the edge of pastures and along Delmarva's roadsides. While a nettle's minute stinging hairs make them repellent to humans, they are important host plants for the larvae of butterflies, particularly red admirals, *Vanessa atalanta rubria*, and question marks, *Polygonia interrogationis.*

Aggressive social wasps, such as yellow jackets and hornets of the family Vespidae, dig tunnels in the bare dirt of pastures. So do many species of harmless solitary wasps. One, called a cicada killer, *Sphecius speciosus*, builds a network of branching tunnels used as nesting chambers by the females. After being stung by a cicada killer, an egg is laid on the paralyzed cicada which is then sealed into a cell to serve as food for the larvae.

Song sparrows, *Melospiza melodia,* are common in pastures, especially in spring when they sing their melodious territorial song, interpreted by some as "maid, maid, maid, put the kettle on!" Vesper sparrows, *Pooecetes gramineus*, too, can occasionally be observed in summer taking a dust bath in dry pasture soil. Vesper sparrows hunt insects in short grass, but they need a conspicuous singing perch for territory selection, and will not nest if the pasture lacks a nearby hedgerow or fence. While vesper sparrows may sing throughout the day, their song is most noticeable in the early evening: two long low notes, two higher ones and then a short rippling trill. With the possible exception of the plain field sparrow, *Spizella pusilla*, virtually all sparrows are brown, striped birds that dart quickly into cover, making them extremely difficult to tell apart. The song sparrow has a conspicuous black dot in the center of its chest and the vesper sparrow is the only one with white outer tail feathers. The boundary between the vesper sparrow's summer and winter ranges neatly crosses the peninsula. The birds only nest on northern Delmarva yet they may be present on the southern peninsula in winter. All three of these sparrows nest on the ground in tussocks or at the base of a shrub, although the song sparrow may also nest in the shrub itself.

Hayfields

As lovely a farming country as the eye can wander over. Should it chance to be early summer, the rolling surface presents its slopes on every side clothed in varied shades of green.

—*Robert Wilson, 1876*

Hayfields that are harvested for cattle or horse feed are traditionally mowed two or three times a summer, although many piedmont fields are now mowed only once a year and the hay sold as compost to mushroom growers. Livestock hay is made up of European forage grasses like timothy, *Phleum pratense*, or orchard grass, *Dactylis glomerata*, that green up quickly in the spring and flower in early summer, mixed with legumes such as red clover, *Trifolium pratense*, and alfalfa, *Medicago sativa*.

Legumes, members of the pea family, Leguminosae, are the only plants able to capture nitrogen from the air and convert it to a chemical form. This feat is actually performed by bacteria of the genus *Rhizobium* that are contained in tumorlike nodules on legume roots. Therefore, quite apart from their value as forage plants, clover and alfalfa act as natural fertilizers in hayfields in the same way that another legume, the soybean, restores nitrogen to exhausted cornfields.

Delmarva's hayfields are also full of field flowers like bedstraw, *Galium* spp., purple vetch, *Vicia americana*, Queen Anne's lace, chicory, and asters as well as stray native grasses. Delmarva's native grasses are warm season grasses. They do not begin to grow until the soil has warmed in late spring and generally flower in late summer and fall. A conspicuous one in Delmarva hayfields is a waxy-panicled species called purple top, *Triodia flava*. The ear turns a deep purple in September. A field of purple top rimmed with red-berried dogwoods whose foliage is just beginning to turn is one of the peninsula's loveliest sights.

Grass is wind-pollinated. Nevertheless, hayfield grasses are hosts to countless insects of the order Orthoptera, such as grasshoppers, crickets, mantids, and walkingsticks. Grasshoppers feed on the shoots of forage grass. The males "sing" by scraping parts of their wings together to establish territory and attract females. After mating, the females cut slits in plant stems with their ovipositor to deposit their eggs. The newly hatched nymphs resemble small wingless adults. Grasshoppers are, in fact, the basis of the hayfield's intricate food web. Not only are they relished by birds, reptiles, and mammals, but orb weaving spiders also catch and wrap them in their webs for later consumption.

Crickets, family Gryllidae, hide in the grass of meadows and hayfields where they glean detritus on the ground and at the base of plant stems. The soil is also full of ants and ground beetles of the family Carabidae that feed on other insects and moth larvae. Crab spiders, *Misumena* spp., hide in goldenrod flowers; hunting spiders (Lycosidae and Salticidae) lurk in the grassy forest; and small, round shamrock spiders, *Araneus trifolium*, wait beside webs spun between grass stems for the tug of a captured prey on their signal strand. Spiders, grasshoppers, and bees do not metamorphose like many insects but molt their external shells like crabs as they grow. Grasshoppers and hatching spiders look like tiny replicas of their parents and step out of their split skins up to twenty times before they reach adult size.

The keel-and-standard flowers of hayfield legumes are pollinated by flies (Diptera), bees (Hymenoptera), and butterflies (Lepidoptera). Most hayfield flowers veritably hum with bees, including bumblebees, honeybees, and small green metallic bees of the family Halictidae. Bees are selective. They visit only one species of flower at a time, carrying pollen from blossom to blossom until the blooming time for that particular species is over. A bumblebee visiting red clover will ignore a blooming alfalfa plant immediately adjacent.

Butterflies are everywhere. The most common is the alien cabbage white, *Artogeia rapae*, the larva of which feeds on cruciferous plants of the mustard family, Brassicaceae. The female falcate orangetip, *Anthocharis midea*, a species that visits field chickweed, *Cerastium arvense*, in early spring looks like the cabbage white except for the scalloped edges of her wings. Only the male has orange wingtips.

The larvae of sulphur butterflies, family Pieridae, feed on hayfield legumes like clover and alfalfa and pollinate the flowers as adults. Small gold coppers and blue hairstreaks, family Lycaenidae, can be seen resting with folded wings, while orange and black pearly crescentspots, *Phycoides tharos*, seem to blow from flower to flower on the breeze. Pearly crescentspots lay their eggs on the leaves of aster plants, and the adults take nectar from composite flowers like fleabanes and thistles. They, too, fold their wings when at rest.

Because the larvae of the monarch butterfly feeds on toxic milkweed plants, neither the caterpillar nor the adult monarch are palatable to birds. The viceroy, *Basilarchia archippus*, on the other hand, is quite palatable, but avoids being eaten by mimicking the toxic monarch. The viceroy feeds on the nectar of asters, goldenrods, and other late summer composites.

Monarch butterflies, *Danaus plexippus*, are famous for their long and essentially mysterious migrations. Huge flocks may be seen all along the East Coast of the United States in the fall on their way to the mountains of central Mexico where they spend the winter in a semi-dormant state, hanging onto trees like orange and black leaves. In spring those same butterflies begin the flight north, but since they lay their eggs and die en route, it is the new adults from this itinerate brood that arrive back on Delmarva. More broods follow over the summer; those that pupate in July and August spend their entire lives on the peninsula, but the butterflies that hatch from their eggs again set off for Mexico in September.

Some large butterflies feed on the nectar of Delmarva's field flowers. Milkweed, red clover, thistles, and dogbane are favored by tiger swallowtails, *Pterourus glaucus*, mourning cloaks, and red admirals. The spicebush swallowtail, the zebra swallowtail, *Eurytides marcellus*, and the regal fritillary, *Speyeria idalia*, also visit milkweed. The buckeye, *Junonia coenia*, prefers late season goldenrod, asters, and other composites.

Birds of Open Lands

The cheery pipe of [the Quail] is heard from every stubble field . . . the numbers have greatly decreased, however, since the introduction of reapers and mowing machines, which destroy many nests and mother-birds . . . [whereas] little damage was done by the sweep of the scythe and cradle, which cut high and left a tall irregular stubble.

—Robert Wilson, 1876

Birds that nest in Delmarva's meadows and hayfields include the eastern meadowlark, *Sturnella magna*, the bobwhite, *Colinus virginianus*, and three sparrows, the grasshopper, *Ammodramus savannarum*, the Savannah, *Passerculus sandwichensis*, and the Henslow, *Ammodramus henslowii*. Although declining in recent years, ring-necked pheasants, *Phasianus colchicus*, also nest on the ground in weedy fields and at the edge of woods in Delmarva's piedmont. Pheasants are a Eurasian species that have been widely introduced in this country. For some reason, they are quite scarce south of the Chesapeake and Delaware Canal.

The meadowlark is present in Delmarva's grassy fields all year. When flushed, meadowlarks alternately glide and fly with short rapid wingbeats, showing conspicuous white patches on either side of the tail. The yellow breast crossed with a black V that is so conspicuous in the field guides is only visible when the bird is perched. The meadowlark builds a nest at ground level, cleverly weaving a cover of loose grass into the surrounding vegetation to disguise it. As a further precaution, the brooding female avoids flying directly to the nest, but walks into it from some distance away, a diversionary tactic that is

shared by many meadow-nesting birds. When establishing their territory in early spring, male meadowlarks whistle from exposed perches and flutter upwards with their wings held high and their feet dangling, a behavior called a jump-flight. After a pair has been established, the female will answer the male's whistle with a so-called chatter call and the two will chase each other and indulge in more jump-flights. Meadowlarks are polygamous, however, so a single male may have several brooding females in his territory.

Bobwhites are usually thought of as birds of the hedgerows, but they actually nest in tussocks, hiding their clutch under an arch of woven weeds. Bobwhites' nests are almost never found, but after hatching, the chicks can often be seen running after the mother at the edge of a field. The young of bobwhites, like pheasants, turkeys, and many shorebirds, are precocial, which means they can run about immediately after breaking out of the egg. Newly hatched precocial chicks can also feed themselves and are already covered with down. Perching songbirds, on the other hand, are altricial. When hatched, the young are naked, blind, and helpless and must be fed entirely by the parents for several weeks before they are able to fend for themselves.

Nesting sparrows found in meadows and hayfields are shy, small birds that hide their nests in depressions at ground level and camouflage them with surrounding vegetation. The most common is the grasshopper sparrow, a bird so perfectly attuned to its hayfield habitat that its territorial song imitates and blends with the buzz of meadow grasshoppers. Savannah sparrows may occasionally be found on Delmarva as well, although the peninsula is at the extreme southern edge of their breeding range. The Henslow's sparrow is a shy secretive bird with an unbirdlike song, a weak flyer that runs through the grass when flushed. While Henslow's sparrows are not easily seen in the best of conditions, they are now seriously declining, victims of a pesticide that is spread on soybean fields.

Red-winged blackbirds, *Agelaius phoeniceus,* weave nests among the grass stems of meadows and hayfields as well as in marshgrass and cattails on the peninsula's wetlands. The liquid "konk-la-reee" of the returning red-winged is an evocative sound of early spring.

The American goldfinch, *Carduelis tristis,* builds its nest in nearby trees, but its breeding cycle is entirely dependent on the maturing thistles found in old fields and meadows. Goldfinches indulge in breeding displays in spring at about the time that the males change to their brilliant yellow plumage, singing from prominent perches and chasing after the females. Yet the pairs do not actually nest until mid-summer when the first thistle flowers go to seed. Goldfinches depend on soft thistledown to line their nests and feed thistle seed to their nestlings. At this time, the males indulge in long looping undulating flights, quite different from their usual short singing bounces.They sing as they go up and sometimes warble from a mid-air stall.

Many birds that nest in nearby hedgerows and thickets also hunt in the open fields, including our familiar robin, *Turdus migratorius,* who hunts insects in short grass. Flocks of robins often collect in sunny meadows in fall and winter. Pine warblers and chipping sparrows, *Spizella passerina,* forage for both seeds and insects in open fields and the soft notes of the gentle eastern bluebird, *Sialia sialis,* may be heard caroling from a tree at the edge of the field. Bluebirds typically drop to the ground to snare a grasshopper or cricket and immediately fly back to their perch to eat it. In recent years stiff competition with aggressive starlings for the knotholes, old posts, and broken tree stubs that serve as bluebird nesting sites caused their populations to decline. Fortunately, a widespread effort to provide them with nesting boxes seems to have reversed the slide.

One of the most conspicuous birds of Delmarva's open fields is surely the crow, *Corvus brachyrhynchos*. In fall and winter, crows collect in raucous bands that roam over open land in loose undisciplined flocks. In spring this large flock separates into smaller bands, believed to be made up of a breeding pair and their non-breeding young from the previous year. The birds become uncharacteristically quiet and secretive until the nest is built and the nestlings hatched. The nests are substantial basket-like structures of twigs and bark built high off the ground in nearby woods.

In summer these birds may often be seen "crow hopping" through the high grass in search of grasshoppers and meadow rodents, but probably their most distinctive behavior is their habit of mobbing birds of prey, particularly great horned owls. The sight of an owl at any time of the year will immediately cause a flock of crows to collect and harass him.

> *Under the influence of judicious legislation, the various species of hawk and falcon have been greatly thinned out.*
> —*Robert Wilson, 1876*

Owls, northern harriers, and red-tailed hawks all hunt small mammals in Delmarva's open land, but the typical raptor of upland fields is the kestrel or sparrow hawk, *Falco sparverius*. Kestrels are small hawks, about the size of a blue jay. They nest in nearby tree cavities or buildings and hunt rodents, insects and small birds in grassy meadows. On the peninsula, they can often be seen sitting on exposed telephone wires or fenceposts. When hunting they hover, facing into the wind on rapidly beating wings. Male kestrels have distinctive metallic-blue wings, but the females are brown. All kestrels have the quick darting flight and slim pointed wings typical of falcons.

> *Several kinds of hawks, owls, thrushes, turkey buzzards.*
> —*Joseph Scott, 1807*

> *T, U, Urkey, Iky Turkey. B, U, Uzzard, Izzard, Buzzard. Turkey Buzzard.*
> —*Nineteenth-century children's spelling rhyme*

True buzzards are African birds not found in North America, so popular custom aside, no ornithologist would call a turkey vulture a turkey buzzard. They call them TVs instead.

Turkey vultures, *Cathartes aura*, have four times the lift of a hawk. Typically, they soar for long periods on the rising columns of air called thermals, circling and rocking with their wings in a characteristic V. An adult vulture has a naked red head, but the immature birds have dusky black heads until they are about three years old.

Black vultures, *Coragyps atratus*, are a southern species. With the exception of a small resident flock around the Winterthur Museum near Wilmington, they are found on Delmarva only as far north as Smyrna, Delaware, and Chestertown, Maryland. They are smaller and chunkier than the more common turkey vulture and alternately flap and glide on level wings that are marked on the underside with white bull's-eyes at the outer edges. Both species like to roost on radio towers, a location that gives them a good view of the surrounding countryside. Vultures do not build nests, but lay their eggs directly in a hollow log or stump or on the ground in dense shrubbery.

Reptiles and Amphibians

The body of a snake is capable of prodigious extension—one of moderate length will take in a full grown rabit [sic] or squirrel.
—*A Citizen of Delaware, 1797*

Snakes are versatile creatures that adapt to a variety of habitats. Corn snakes, hognosed snakes, black rat snakes, black racers, and eastern garter snakes are all found in the tall grass of meadows and fields, as well as in the woods. A black racer will track field mice along meadow runways, looping itself around the little rodent's body while suffocating it in his mouth. Garter snakes hide in low meadows to hunt insects and amphibians. Copperheads, too, occasionally hunt mice in the grass, but usually prefer to hide beneath logs or stones. The fact that all these snakes are food for the red-tailed hawk and the horned owl keeps them secretive and wary.

Toads are also common in fields and meadows, where they eat insects, snails and slugs. Although toads must have water for their eggs and tadpoles, adult toads range far afield and may be found in a variety of habitats. The two species on Delmarva are the American toad, *Bufo americanus*, of the northern peninsula, and Fowler's toad, *B. woodhousii fowleri*, of the sandy coastal plain. The two species are extremely difficult to tell apart, and in areas such as Delmarva where their ranges and habitats overlap, they may even hybridize.

Toads spend the winter burrowed in loose dirt and the high trill of their mating song is heard from every farm pond and stream in early spring. Toad tadpoles are small and black and develop quickly, emerging onto dry land in a matter of weeks. Although handling toads will not cause warts, the fact that their skin glands secrete a substance that is extremely irritating to mucous membranes helps protect them from marauding foxes and other predators.

Mammals of the Open Fields

The fox . . . is found in scarcely diminished numbers . . . [while] the rabbit harbors in every brier patch.

—*Robert Wilson, 1876*

Generally speaking, the length of grass in a field or meadow determines what mammals will be found there. Moles, for example, particularly like the short grass and loose soil of pastures. We have two species of moles on the peninsula, the eastern mole, *Scalopus aquaticus*, of the East Coast, South, and Midwest, and the more northern star-nosed mole, *Condylura cristata*. The eastern mole is the one usually found in Delmarva's upland fields. The star-nosed prefers damper locations like mucky pastures, moist meadows, and the borders of ponds. Moles have short, nearly naked tails and heavy broad forefeet that are used for digging. The star-nosed mole's unique, fleshy pink projections surrounding its nose are apparently used for detecting the presence of food.

The ridges of soil that are pushed up in lawns, pastures, and cultivated fields after a rain are made by the eastern mole as it hunts worms, insect larvae, and other soil organisms in the softened topsoil. His regular burrow is actually ten or more inches below the surface. Moles do not hibernate but they do retreat underground in winter when the ground is frozen and during long periods of dry weather in summer. Each mole nest has several approaching tunnels, one of which may come up from below. Unlike most rodents, moles have only one litter a year, an indication that their underground habits efficiently protect them from predators.

The most numerous mammal of Delmarva's open country is doubtless the meadow vole, *Microtus pennsylvanicus,* a small rodent that looks very like a short-tailed mouse. Voles, or field mice as they are often called, hide under the protective cover of dead grass and herbs in open fields and marshes. While an individual vole has a range about the size of a tennis court, the ranges of different individuals crisscross a grassy meadow with interlacing runways. The runways are kept clear by the voles' habit of continually nibbling off the young grass.

Voles are particularly active in the early morning and late afternoon, but they seem to alternately feed and rest in short periods pretty much around the clock. In winter, they feed on the bleached shoots of grasses, seeds, and rootstocks as well as on the bark of young trees.

Meadow voles are champion breeders. From March to November, litters of young follow one another in rapid succession, and in mild winters breeding may continue all year. The nests are compact balls of dried grasses and roots, sometimes lined with moss, on or near the surface of the ground. The gestation period is three weeks. The litter of three to twelve young are weaned at about two weeks of age and the new young females may begin to breed before they are a month old. In one study, a captive female produced seventeen litters in a single year, and one of her daughters produced thirteen families of her own before she was a year old. Abundant population of these little mice are important, however. Their numbers are the most important single factor that determines whether a particular area can support healthy populations of predators such as foxes, weasels, hawks, owls, and even crows.

The eastern cottontail rabbit, *Sylvilagus floridanus*, also feeds on meadow grasses and broad-leaved plants. They, too, begin breeding in March and have several litters over the summer, nesting in skillfully camouflaged depressions lined with finely shredded leaves, grass, and fur pulled from the mother rabbit's own underside. Newborn bunnies are naked, blind, and helpless, and weigh less than an ounce, but they grow quickly and are ready to leave the nest in a little more than two weeks.

Rabbits are most active in the early morning or late afternoon but they also feed through the night, nibbling on grasses and herbaceous plants in summer and the buds, twigs, and bark of bushes in winter. They are particularly plentiful in fields bordered by hedgerows. Like other lagomorphs, rabbits practice coprophagy. Rapidly swallowed food is later defecated as soft green pellets and reingested. Cottontails are gentle creatures with no defense except their

speed to escape the foxes, skunks, crows, snakes, hawks, and owls that continually stalk them.

The fact that groundhogs, *Marmota monax*, were originally a woodland species seems evident from their habit of retreating to a winter den in the woods to hibernate. They are also skillful climbers, easily scurrying up young trees if pursued by dogs. Yet, for the most part, these animals prefer meadows and open fields, and their numbers seem to have increased on the peninsula when the land was cleared.

Groundhog burrows are elaborate constructions of tunnels and underground chambers about five feet below the surface of the ground. The main entrance with its conspicuous domed mound of excavated earth is ringed with concealed escape holes up to thirty feet away, which can be a real threat to horses and cattle. While individual groundhogs are solitary animals, several may build their burrows in a single field. Abandoned groundhog holes also provide serendipitous shelter for rabbits, opossums, raccoons, skunks, and foxes.

The groundhog is our only true hibernator. In summer, the animals eat almost continually, stuffing themselves with grass and other herbaceous plants, fruit and, if they get the chance, corn and young vegetables. By the first frost they have grown exceedingly plump and are ready to crawl into their dens for the long winter sleeps. Throughout the long months of hibernation, their body temperature drops and their breathing and metabolism slow. At this time, the groundhog neither eats, drinks, nor excretes, but is nourished solely by its layer of accumulated fat.

On Groundhog Day, February 2, legend says that groundhogs emerge from their den to look for a mate. If the sun is out, they will be frightened by their shadow and retreat underground, signalling six more weeks of winter. In fact, groundhogs mate in February or early March. A litter of four or five naked and blind young is born about a month later. They leave the parent den when they are about six to eight weeks old to establish their own shallow burrows.

Not counting humans, the principal natural enemy of groundhogs is the red fox, *Vulpes vulpes*, another animal that benefitted substantially when the land was cleared. The fox's preferred habitat is open farmland mixed with woods, marshes, and streams: a good description of Delmarva. Yet, while red foxes are abundant here, they are not found on the coastal plain south of the peninsula, preferring the higher and perhaps cooler land of the southern piedmont.

Foxes are every bit as crafty as legend says they are. Often fox prints in the snow are the first indication that one is in the vicinity. The track of a trotting fox looks like that of a small dog, but, unlike a dog, it runs in a nearly straight line.

Foxes are active all the year. They usually begin their hoarse nocturnal barking in late winter at the start of the mating season, although they can also be heard at other times of the year. The young foxes are born in March or early April, but do not emerge from the den until they are about five weeks old. A pregnant vixen moving into an old groundhog hole will first disperse the conspicuous mound of excavated dirt. She is always cautious and secretive; if her den is discovered, she will promptly move the kits. Foxes begin to mate when they are less than a year old. They are devoted parents, watching out for their brood until the young foxes are old enough to establish their own hunting territories, usually in late summer.

Skunks, *Mephitis mephitis*, like the same habitat as the red fox and are most abundant in open country where they feed on field mice, blackberries, wild cherries, crickets, and grasshoppers, not to mention field crops and garbage. Like the groundhog, a skunk will eat until it can barely waddle, in an effort to build up a sufficient layer of fat to sustain itself over the winter. They do not hibernate, however. They sleep away the coldest days, but a warm spell will lure them from their nest. By February, the mating urge is upon them. The young are born fifty-one days later. They nurse for about six weeks, then they are ready to learn to hunt on their own.

During the day, skunks hide in burrows or under buildings, emerging at nightfall to run nimbly about in the moonlight in search of crickets and sleeping beetles. They are basically gentle creatures, relying on their powerful smell to keep them safe from prowling foxes.

Thickets

Thickets and hedgerows are ecotones, or zones where different plant communities meet and overlap. Because of the innate shelter they provide, and their proximity to both woods and fields, thickets often have large and diverse populations of wildlife. Not only are hedgerow trees and shrubs usually dense fruiting species like sassafras, wild cherries, and dogwoods, but the many vines and creepers that inevitably drape themselves over branch and fence also provide birds and animals with abundant food and cover.

Broadly speaking, however, there are fewer insects and spiders in hedgerows, thickets, and early successional woods than in open fields. It could be said that, for the insect world, the invasion of woody plants into an abandoned field signals a shift from a foraging ground for adults to a nursery for their larvae. The abundance of larvae, of course, attracts its own populations of predators such as parasitic wasps of the family Braconidae, which lay their eggs on the bodies of caterpillars.

Tiny micrathena spiders spin their snares in young trees and more troublesome arachnids like ticks and chiggers are also abundant in woody thickets. Adult chiggers are small orange-colored mites, covered with hairs, that feed on plant and animal detritus. Their eggs are laid in the soil. A chigger egg is surprisingly complex. The outer egg breaks open to reveal a second egg and from this emerges the minute larvae that burrow into the skin of lizards, birds, or mammals, including humans. The larval chigger does not bite, but injects a digestive enzyme that actually dissolves the patch of skin to be ingested. After three days, it drops off to begin a two-stage metamorphosis into adulthood.

Caterpillar larvae of sphinx moths, family Sphingidae, hide among the vines at the edge of woods, feeding on Virginia creeper and wild grapes, while the adult moths eat fermenting tree sap and decaying fruit. Paper wasps, *Polistes* spp., also feed on crushed and rotting fruit. Females build the familiar large gray paper nests, constructed of wood pulp and saliva. Only the young mated queens overwinter in the soil and they start the new generation in the spring. All the workers, old queens, and undeveloped larvae die with the coming of frost.

Birds of the Thicket

That Strange and Remarkable Fowl, call'd (in these parts) the Mocking-bird, that imitates all sorts of birds in their various notes.
— *Gabriel Thomas, 1697*

Roben [sic] Red Breasts and many other kinds of birds take up their winter quarters here, and the variety of berries afford them plenty of food.
— *A Citizen of Delaware, 1797*

Thickets and hedgerows are full of nesting birds, including many of Delmarva's most familiar species like robins, mockingbirds, gray catbirds, and cardinals. The American robin builds its nest in the forked branches of dense early successional trees, as well as on the roof ledges of buildings. Robins are among the earliest songbirds to nest in spring, breaking up their winter flocks and setting up territories around the end of March. They raise successive broods until early August and if parasitized by the brown-headed cowbird, a robin will push the intrusive egg out of the nest.

Mockingbirds, *Mimus polyglottos*, also nest in thickets beginning in early spring. Mockingbirds are extremely territorial. From April until late summer, the males can be heard singing their loud imitative song almost continuously from exposed perches. They even sing at night, especially when the moon is full. Mockingbirds will defend their nesting sites aggressively against any intruder, including dogs, cats, snakes, and humans.

Unlike most birds, the mockingbird also has a fall territory. From September until February both male and female mockingbirds will actively protect a food source, usually berried shrubs in a thicket or hedgerow, by uttering loud "chick-chick" calls as they chase away other fruit-eating birds, including other mockingbirds.

Gray catbirds, *Dumetella carolinensis,* and brown thrashers, *Toxostoma rufum,* are closely related to the mockingbird and also build their nests in the dense thickets, briers, and vines of hedgerows and woodland borders. They, too, are known for their skill in imitating other birds' songs but while the mockingbird usually repeats a phrase three or more times, the brown thrasher repeats it twice and the catbird only once. The distinctive catlike "me-ow" of the catbird is a warning signal of alarm.

Cardinals, *Cardinalis cardinalis*, also seek out the tangles of grapevines, honeysuckle, and multiflora rose, as well as the dense pines of the lower peninsula. In spring, male and female cardinals sing to each other, repeating and matching each other's phrases. A courting male will also feed his intended mate, a behavior that can sometimes be observed at backyard bird feeders. The cardinal's distinctive undulating flight and the brilliant red color of the males make it an easy bird to identify.

Mourning doves, eastern kingbirds, blue grosbeaks, and indigo buntings also like the cover of brambles and shrubs. Mourning doves, *Zenaida macroura*, are now among the peninsula's most numerous birds. The flocks gather in hedgerows to feed on corn left in farm fields in winter. Mourning doves nest in young evergreens or tangled shrubs and vines, often using old robin or catbird nests as foundations for their frail platforms of sticks.

Eastern kingbirds, *Tyrannus tyrannus,* also build their relatively bulky nests in the thick cover of thickets and hedgerows. The kingbird is a tidy, dark, upright bird with a conspicuous white band across the tip of its tail. It perches on snags and power lines and darts into the air after flying insects. Kingbirds also chase crows with reckless abandon, diving on them from above like diminutive fighter planes.

The peninsula, southeastern Pennsylvania, and southern New Jersey represent the extreme northern limit of the range of the blue grosbeak, *Guiraca caerulea*, a thicket-nesting blue bird with brown wing bars. Blue grosbeaks have the thick bill typical of grosbeaks. They are common on lower Delmarva, but may easily be mistaken for cowbirds in poor light when the males' dull blue color appears black. The females are a warm yellowish brown. The rapid warbling song of the blue grosbeak is typically heard in groves of red cedars. In the fall, flocks of these birds collect to feed in Delmarva's grain fields before heading to Costa Rica and Panama for the winter.

Blue grosbeaks build their nests in open brushy fields, hedgerows, and roadside thickets, often using a cast-off snakeskin in the construction. They particularly like the sweet gum as a nesting site. Their eggs are pale blue or white, without markings.

The indigo bunting, *Passerina cyanea*, is a smaller, brighter version of the blue grosbeak that also hides its nest deep in the shelter of dense shrubs or blackberry canes. The males sing their high paired notes from exposed perches nearby, incessantly defending the nesting territory. Indigo buntings are insect eaters, and consume quantities of webworms, weevils, beetles, and grasshoppers in the process of rearing their young.

Goldfinches, too, build their neat cups of thistledown in hawthornes and other densely branched trees. Loggerheaded shrikes, *Lanius ludovicianus*, like the osage orange hedgerows of the northern peninsula. Field sparrows and chipping sparrows are also thicket nesters, principally differentiated from one another by the pink bill of the field sparrow and the rapid buzzing song of the chipping sparrow. The chipping sparrow also nests in young conifers on the southern peninsula.

Song sparrows, *Melospiza melodia,* nest on the ground, building a cup of grasses, weed stems, and leaves in the shelter of dense bushes or brush piles. Rufous-sided towhees, *Pipilo erythrophthalmus*, also build their nests on or near the ground in the thick cover of hedgerows and forest edges. Both species are frequent victims of the parasitic cowbird.

Hedgerows and young woods with larger trees may attract blue jays, redstarts, *Setophaga ruticilla*, and orioles, *Icterus* spp. Both the northern oriole and the more southern orchard oriole nest on the peninsula and winter in South America. Flocks of cedar waxwings, *Bombycilla cedrorum,* are present here throughout the year; sometimes several pairs will nest in the same brushy area within twenty-five feet of one another. Waxwings are particularly fond of the fruits of bittersweet and red cedar as well as other fruiting shrubs and vines.

The great crested flycatcher, *Myiarchus crinitus*, is a cavity nester that prefers woods' edges and clearings. It resembles a kingbird with a yellow breast but minus the white tail band. The yellow-throated vireo, *Vireo flavifrons*, and the yellow-breasted chat, *Icteria virens,* also nest in brushy thickets. The chat commonly chooses blackberry thickets or low dense trees like crabapples and hawthornes. Like the mockingbird, the yellow-breasted chat, scolds, whistles, mimics, and chatters. It also sings while flying and at night.

Although larger than most warblers, the yellow-breasted chat is classified as a warbler, family Parulidae. Other warblers found in Delmarva's thickets include the prairie, *Dendroica discolor*, which also likes pine barrens and burned over areas, and the yellow warbler, *D. petechia.* Warblers eat loopers, the larvae of geometrid moths, and other hairless soft-bodied caterpillars. Under particularly favorable conditions, yellow warblers may build their soft white nests of thistledown and milkweed fibers in loose colonies, with each pair defending a territory of less than half an acre. When parasitized by cowbirds, they commonly bury the intrusive egg, and build a second story for their own clutch.

Slim, long-tailed, yellow-billed cuckoos, *Coccyzus americanus*, nest in vine-covered thickets on the peninsula and winter in Argentina. Cuckoos' nests are so frail that the eggs can sometimes be seen through the base. They also lay their eggs in other birds' nests. Cuckoo eggs have been found in the nests of robins, catbirds, and cardinals among others. The black-billed cuckoo, *C. erythropthalmus,* is a more northern species that may nest as far south as Delaware and Maryland's Eastern Shore, but usually prefers more wooded areas. Cuckoos, jays, and orioles are among the few birds that feed on both the gypsy moth caterpillar and the prickly tent caterpillars that infest wild cherry and other fruit trees found in hedgerows and forest edges.

The peninsula's young pine woods attract pine warblers, *Dendroica pinus,* while brown-headed nuthatches, *Sitta pusilla,* breed and winter in the pine woods of the Eastern Shore of Virginia. Both species will leave, however, if deciduous hardwood trees begin to dominate the woods. Brown creepers, *Certhia familiaris,* and golden-crowned kinglets, *Regulus satrapa,* also like the peninsula's young pines.

As soon as young sweet gums and tulip trees flower and set seed, they attract wintering flocks of purple finches, *Carpodacus purpureus,* house finches, *C. mexicanus* (an introduced species), and pine siskins, *Carduelis pinus.* Hard winters sometimes drive flocks of evening grosbeaks, *Hesperiphona vespertina,* as far south as the peninsula where they, too, dine on the seeds of tulip trees.

Reptiles and Amphibians

All the snakes that have been previously described can also be found in developing thickets and young woods, but there is one species that particularly likes the viney thickets at the edge of fields, especially when close to water: the rough green snake, *Opheodrys aestivus,* also called the vine snake. It dines on grasshoppers, crickets, and the larvae of moths and butterflies. The rough green snake is a dainty, slender serpent, green above and white or yellow below, and it blends so perfectly into greenbrier, *Smilax* spp., that it is nearly invisible. It is a southern snake, and the peninsula and adjacent southern New Jersey are the northern limits of its range.

The northern brown snake, *Storeria d. dekayi,* like the garter snake, was once a woodland species. It has become so used to living with man that it is now commonly found in city parks, cemeteries, and empty lots. It is small, about a foot long, and has two parallel rows of dark spots down its brown back.

Mammals

The animals indigenous to the state (Maryland) are the deer, wolf, bear, panther, raccoon, marten, otter, fox, oppossum, buffaloe, wild cat, skunk or pole cat, ground hog, rabbit, squirrel, mink, mole and musk rat.
—*Joseph Scott, 1807*

Most mammalian species like a variety of habitats so it is not surprising that thickets and hedgerows also provide food and shelter for foxes, rabbits, raccoons, skunks, and opossums. Bats also search for the moth larvae that are so plentiful in young woods.

There are numerous mice and shrews in thickets as well. Like the meadow vole of open fields, the pine vole, *Pitymys pinetorum,* is a ubiquitous resident of such places, threading its way beneath the thick carpet of leaves in burrows a few inches below the surface. In spite of its name, the pine vole generally prefers deciduous woods to pines, although it is found in many different habitats. The little rodents eat roots, tubers, green leaves, and stems and often girdle young trees. Also, like the meadow vole, they are prodigious breeders. Their subterranean habits protect them, somewhat, from predatory hawks and owls.

One species of mammal that particularly seeks out woody thickets, as well as swamps and marsh edges, is the long-tailed weasel, *Mustela frenata.* North of Pennsylvania, this weasel turns white in winter, like its relative, the ermine. It does not do so on the peninsula where the winters have little snow.

Long-tailed weasels build shallow earth burrows, usually under fallen tree stumps. The nest is at the end of a twisting tunnel and often contains the remains of the field mice, rabbits, and chipmunks, as well as shrews, birds, and snakes that the animals feed on. Long-tailed weasels mate in July, but the development of the embryo is delayed and the young are not born until the following April.

I have Venison of the Indians very cheap . . . I have four Dear [sic] for two yards of trading cloth which costs five shillings, and most times I purchased it cheaper.
—Thomas Paschall, 1682

It is hard to believe that the white-tailed deer, *Odocoileus virginianus,* now so numerous on farms, thickets, and woods' edges on the peninsula, was once all but extirpated from Delmarva. Deer are considered browsing animals that also graze. In winter, they eat the twigs of maple and viburnum, red cedar, and pine, and graze on grass, leaves, and herbs in summer. However, studies have shown that their most important food source, in terms of building an adequate fat layer to sustain them over the winter, may be the acorns and beechnuts that ripen in Delmarva's woodlands in early fall.

In summer, white-tailed deer are a bright reddish tan, but when cold weather comes, they change to a winter coat of dense gray that blends almost perfectly with the leafless trees and shrubs of the deciduous woods. Each hollow hair is filled with air, a feature that not only provides good winter insulation but also keeps them afloat while swimming. Deer are, in fact, excellent swimmers and frequently travel from one coastal island to another.

Deer are creatures of habit. They stick to certain paths within a relatively small territory and retreat to well-known thickets if danger threatens. A deer's home territory is quite small, about a mile in radius, but it knows every part of that territory so well that it is an easy shot only when caught outside its boundaries. A deer can hide in a surprisingly small thicket. It is said that a buck will press his head to the ground so that his antlers look like the surrounding brush. While deer may be active at any time, they generally bed down during the daylight hours and emerge at dusk to feed throughout the night. When alarmed they flash their white tails in warning and bound off. They do not travel far, but simply melt into the trees a short distance away.

A buck's antlers are deciduous. Fresh racks are grown every year beginning at about two years of age, making antlers the most rapidly growing osseous (bony) structures found in mammals. In summer, the newly developing antlers are covered with a skin, known as velvet, that contains quantities of blood vessels to nourish the growing tissue. As this covering dries and begins to peel off, it is common to find fresh deer rubs on young trees, places stripped of bark where a buck has scraped off the velvet and polished his rack. A buck only carries his antlers through the fall rutting season, shedding them in December or January. It used to be thought that a buck grew more tines each year; however, except for the first year, the size of a buck's antlers is not an indication of his age but the quality of nutrition available to him.

During the fall rutting season, the bucks, their necks swollen and their racks newly polished, search the woods for a doe, sometimes engaging in pitched battles for her favor. Deer mate in November and the young are born the following spring after a seven-month gestation period. The scentless newborn fawns are hidden in dense thickets where their spotted coats blend perfectly with the fallen leaves. In settled areas where they are not commonly hunted, deer can become quite tame. They are particularly fond of apples, and often feed on green ones in early summer.

It is thought that approximately half of young does mate in their first year, producing one fawn apiece. Mature does usually produce twins. The fawns stay with their mother through the following winter, sometimes joining with other does and fawns in herds of twenty or more.

Because all the original predators of the deer have been eliminated from the peninsula, the herds have a tendency to multiply beyond the capacity of their habitat to sustain them. When this happens, they not only degrade their surroundings and rob other animals of their share of the nutritious woodland mast, but may starve in winter. Also, diseases may spread readily and genetic defects become more common in conditions of overpopulation. The fact is that, with the exception of the occasional fox or feral dog that may kill a young fawn, deer have no enemies except man.

Wetlands

The Value of Wetlands

*The branches of the Indian River are navigable within a few miles
of the swamp, and afford numerous springs of the Spaw or iron
mineral waters. Here then is to be had in the vicinity of each
other, the sea water, the Spaw water, and the swamp water,
specifically different, and each possessing great medical virtues.*
                        —Citizen of Delaware, 1797

Wetlands, to most people on Delmarva, mean waterfowl and marshes; lazy
creeks, mud, and mosquitos in summer; biting winds and the whir of wings
in winter. The thousands of acres of marshland that rim the peninsula offer
a convenient stopover for the many thousands of ducks and geese that fun-
nel down the Atlantic flyway every fall. Yet waterfowl are not the only
flocks that depend on the peninsula's wetlands. Red-winged blackbirds,
bobolinks, a few northern hawks, and owls also rest in our marshes during
migration.

   Nor are marshes our only important wetlands. Far more common in terms
of total acreage are the shallow wooded swamps that occur on inland depressions and along the floodplains of rivers. We also have deep and ancient cypress swamps, wet meadows, and the peculiar round ponds known as Delmarva
bays.

*The exhalations from the swamps and freshwater marshes, which at that time
extended through the greater part of the state; producing among the people in
their vicinity agues and intermittent fevers in the autumn and plursies in the
spring of the year.*
            —Delaware Register and Farmers' Magazine, 1838-39

Wetlands

Marshes and swamps were a vital source of food for the early people on Delmarva—marshes for their abundant populations of migrating waterfowl and shellfish, and swamps for the game animals they attracted. The peninsula's vast inland swamps, and the freshwater rivers they fed, were also the only sources of drinking water.

The Europeans, on the other hand, thought all wetlands were unhealthy sinks of insects and disease and diked and drained them as a matter of public health. The dikes also allowed them to grow crops and pasture livestock, for in the beginning, the peninsula's wide grassy marshes were the only areas without trees. Israel Acrelius in his *A History of New Sweden*, first published in 1759, tells us how it was done:

> The mode of procedure is to enclose a certain amount of swamp with a bank thrown up quite high, so as to keep out the water (the ebb and the flood), or tides. This bank commonly rises as high as five feet; sometimes ten feet. Also to make a ditch to carry off the water which comes on it from the land, and at the same time to place drains in the bank to let the water out; and then, again; by a gate upon the drains, to prevent it from running in.

This was arduous work, so perhaps it is not surprising that these early dikes began to deteriorate as soon as the Civil War put an end to slave labor. The pattern of manipulation, however, continued. In the nineteenth century, so-called tax ditches were built upstream on many of the peninsula's rivers to drain the surrounding land for agriculture. These ditches tended to eliminate the natural floodplain and increase the amount of silt that washed into mill-ponds and river channels downstream.

> *The people [at Cape Henlopen] are afflicted with a evil, not much unlike, and almost as severe as, some of the plagues of Egypt. I mean the inconceivable swarms of muscatoes and sand flies which infest every place, and equally interrupt the tranquility of the night and the happiness of the day. Their attacks are intolerable upon man as well as beast. The poor cows and horses in order to escape from these tormentors stand whole days in ponds of water with only their heads exposed.*
>
> *—Anonymous, 1788*

Mosquitoes we have had with us always! It is said that workers who harvested salt hay from the marshes in the nineteenth century warded off the clouds of mosquitoes and gallinippers (biting flies) with whiskey and burning heaps of green vegetation called smothers. Later, a mixture of kerosene, arsenic trioxide, and copper acetate, called Paris Green, was spread over the surface of marsh pools to kill the larvae.

In the 1930s, marshes along Delaware Bay were ditched by the Civilian Conservation Corps in a further effort to control mosquitoes as well as to provide jobs for the unemployed during the Depression. The theory was that if marsh pools were drained of standing water, the insects could not breed. Several million more linear feet were added in the 1960s, until mosquito ditches crisscrossed many Delmarva marshes like a giant grid.

Grid ditching altered both the water level and the rate of drainage in the marsh, and studies dating from those years show that it had a profound effect on the distribution of marsh vegetation. The elimination of marsh pools also reduced the populations of waterfowl, shorebirds, and waders that depended on them for food and resting sites.

After DDT was developed during World War II, crop dusting planes regularly broadcasted the pesticide over Delmarva's marshes to kill mosquitos and biting flies. At the time, the long-term persistence of DDT and its associated compounds was extolled as a breakthrough, although from the beginning there were ominous signs of damage to other organisms in the marsh. Soon it became evident that the pesticides were accumulating in the flesh of fish and interfering with the reproductive cycle of fish-eating birds like eagles, herons, and ospreys. Not only was the spraying expensive (it had to be repeated every time a new brood hatched), but the insects soon developed a resistance. DDT was finally banned in 1972.

Next, areas of Delmarva's marshes were diked to create freshwater impoundments on the theory that this would eliminate mosquito breeding sites while providing resting areas for migrating waterfowl. Such impoundments are still a feature of most of the peninsula's wildlife refuges. They do attract waterfowl, but they also alter the natural flow of water through the marsh.

The first "champagne" pools were dug in Delmarva's marshes in the early 1970s. These were pools of varying sizes that were connected to tidal creeks, or in some cases to existing ditches, so that the tide could move freely through the marsh bringing with it the killifish and minnows that prey on mosquito larvae. Unlike grid ditching, the pools did not alter the water table in the marsh, yet were deep enough to allow the mosquito-eating fish to remain in the pools throughout the tidal cycle. This system, which came to be known as Open Marsh Water Management, or OMWM, was far more biologically intelligent and environmentally sensitive than previous methods. It is now the officially recommended procedure for mosquito control.

Of course, the early efforts to kill mosquitoes were not the only forces adversely affecting Delmarva's wetlands. Sewage and industrial wastes were freely dumped into our rivers and bays throughout the nineteenth and early twentieth centuries. Coastal creeks were regularly dredged and the spoil dumped on the marsh for fill. Farther inland, many thousands of acres in the Great Cypress Swamp, as well as in scattered smaller wetlands, were drained for farming and housing and thousands more were channelized to facilitate the harvesting of timber.

In estuarine marshes where the natural action of the tide had been inhibited or water levels artificially altered by ditching or the dumping of dredge spoil, spreading stands of common reed, *Phragmites australis,* appeared. *Phragmites* is virtually useless to wildlife, yet it has now invaded some 40,000 acres of brackish marsh along Delaware Bay. Unlike most invasive weeds, *Phragmites* is not an alien but a plant of worldwide distribution. Remains found in ancient peat bogs indicate that it has existed on this continent for thousands of years. Experiments using non-persistent, biodegradable herbicides, combined with controlled burning, are now under way in Delaware in an effort to stop its spread and allow the original marsh plants to become re-established.

The fact is, far from being a source of diseased miasma, wetlands are actually vital to the health of our environment. Delmarva's marsh and estuarine ecosystems not only provide food and shelter for wildlife, they support, for at least part of their life cycle, up to two-thirds of the fish and shellfish caught by commercial and recreational fishermen. Healthy coastal marshes also absorb the energy of storms and reduce siltation in ports and river channels.

Freshwater wetlands are equally vital. Like coastal marshes, floodplains, river marshes and wooded swamps cushion the force of destructive floods and reduce the sediment load of rivers. Once all the peninsula's rivers were clear, but two hundred years of clearing and development have washed tons of sediment into the water and reduced the amount of light available to aquatic plants. Lately, the scope and pace of this erosion has accelerated so much that turbidity is now considered the single most serious problem affecting the quality of water in the Chesapeake Bay.

Wetlands are natural filters that can help solve this dilemma. Swamps and riverine floodplains trap both the dirt and surplus nutrients that wash off farmland, preventing the kind of over-enrichment of rivers and estuaries that robs aquatic organisms of oxygen. If not overloaded or despoiled beyond capacity, wetlands can even keep pesticides, heavy metals, and toxic substances from washing into river sediments.

Even though coastal marshes are now protected from flagrant abuse by legislative and regulatory programs, polluted run-off from urban streets and farmland, as well as the occasional oil spill, continue to threaten them. Legislation is currently being written to protect remaining interior wetlands as well.

Marshes

*There is a great marsh . . . which I passed in the night, thro the
middle of which runs [the] Elk.*
                                    —Alexander Hamilton, 1744

The waters of the Chesapeake and Delaware bays vary from fresh to brackish
to salt. As in most East Coast estuaries, the denser salt water moves to the
northeast, making the Chesapeake saltier on the Eastern Shore side, and the
Delaware Bay on the New Jersey side, a phenomenon that is believed to be
caused by the earth's rotation, or Coriolis force, the same force that in the
northern hemisphere causes water to run down drains in a clockwise direction.

In the Chesapeake the southern limit of fresh water is generally at the
mouth of the Sassafras River. In Delaware Bay it is somewhere between
Odessa and Woodland Beach. The water in the middle part of both estuaries
could best be described as dilute seawater. In the Chesapeake it is mildly brackish from the Sassafras to Kent Island, becomes slightly saltier in the middle bay
and is nearly as salty as seawater off the Eastern Shore of Virginia, approximate
delineations that shift to the north or to the south according to the rainfall. In
Delaware Bay, the salt line has been creeping northward in recent years because of increasing withdrawals of fresh water from the upper Delaware River.
At the same time there has been a rise in sea level causing more salt water to
flow into the mouth of both bays.

Most of the peninsula's marshes grow in brackish water, but there are
freshwater communities at the heads of the bays and up long rivers, like the
Nanticoke and Pocomoke, and true salt marshes on the lower peninsula and
behind the barrier islands that rim the Atlantic coast. Fresh, brackish, or salt,
virtually all are influenced by the tide. On Delmarva, the only non-tidal

marshes are at the edge of diked impoundments or along the edge of inland ponds, piedmont rivers, or Delmarva bays.

The species of plants in any wetland are selected by the level of standing water and the presence or absence of salt. In most Delmarva marshes, these factors are further complicated by river currents and the tide. Neither are constant. River currents shift in strength according to the rainfall, and twice a month, during the full and new moons, the spring tides may inundate the entire marsh and wash against the inland shore. When the moon is waxing or waning, however, the weaker neap tide barely changes the level of the creeks and rivers.

These constantly changing water levels favor emergents—grasses and herbs with roots that can grow in saturated soil, but, unlike floating plants, are not dependent on the water to support them. Yet marshes also have wet spots, dry spots, and areas that are intermittently or constantly flooded and each of these tend to select particular species as well.

For instance, in freshwater tidal marshes, a tall robust grass with a dense reddish-brown flowering cluster called Walter's millet, *Echinochloa walteri*, grows on the low ridge of sediment that builds along the banks of creeks. The seeds are relished by rails, teals, and red-winged blackbirds.

Behind these low levees is often a wet zone that is filled with river bulrush, *Scirpus fluviatilis*, a sedge with scaly brown flower clusters. It may be draped with tearthumbs, *Polygonum arifolium* and *P. sagittatum*, plants whose sharp, downward pointing barbs make them among the most inhospitable of marsh plants.

Sweet flag, *Acorus calamus*, and arrow arum, *Peltandra virginica*, are two marsh-growing members of the arum family, Araceae, that grow in areas intermittently flooded by the tide. The arum family, which also includes jack-in-the-pulpit and skunk cabbage, is characterized by a cylindrical inflorescence called a spadix. Pickerelweed, *Pontederia cordata*, is a favorite plant of ducks that also likes the intertidal zone.

Narrowleaf cattail, *Typha angustifolia*, and Olney three-square, *Scirpus olneyi*, grow in flooded depressions, sometimes mixing with mats of yellow waterlily or floating spatterdock, *Nuphar advena*. In recent decades, two species of beggar's ticks, *Bidens laevis* and *B. coronata*, have moved into these marshes from the Midwest. Both hide unobtrusively in the vegetation until late summer when their flowers suddenly paint the marsh a brilliant yellow. The wildcelery, *Vallisneria americana*, however, is almost gone, killed off by too much silt in the water. Wildcelery is a submerged aquatic that once attracted rafts of canvasbacks to the freshwater marshes of the northern Chesapeake.

Many plants that are found in tidal freshwater marshes also grow in nontidal ones. These include the bur-reed, *Sparganium* spp., broad-leaved arrowhead, *Sagittaria latifolia*, jewelweed, *Impatiens capensis*, and the dense thickets of razor-sharp rice cutgrass, *Leersia oryzoides*. If the water is both clear and clean, wild rice, *Zizania aquatica*, may occur in the wet spots. Wild rice has a distinctive feathery inflorescence in August, when the female flowers rise above the drooping staminate male flowers. The seed, which ripens in early September, is prized both by gourmets and sora rails, *Porzana carolina*. Wild rice occurs in the non-tidal freshwater marsh in Brandywine Creek State Park, but the largest stand on the peninsula is where Broad Creek meets the Nanticoke River.

Non-tidal freshwater marshes are also full of spectacular wetland wildflowers that include, among others, green-headed coneflower, *Rudbeckia laciniata*, New York ironweed, *Vernonia noveboracensis*, cardinal-flower, *Lobelia cardinalis,* and blue flag, *Iris versicolor*.

The marshes that grow in the brackish water in the middle reaches of the bays or downstream on coastal plain rivers are a complex mix of fresh- and saltwater species. Here, while spring rains normally swell the river currents and push the salt water downstream, by late summer the flow has slackened, allowing the salty tide to creep further upstream.

Less tolerant freshwater species like wild rice disappear, and are replaced by the more adaptable big cordgrass, *Spartina cynosuroides*. Cattails, arrowheads, and pickerelweed can all tolerate some salinity, however, and mix here with salt-marsh plants like smooth cordgrass, *Spartina alterniflora,* and saltmeadow cordgrass. Soft rush, *Juncus effusus*, arrow arum, water hemp, *Amaranthus canabinus,* and the tearthumbs and related smartweeds persist as well. The late summer tickseeds are not as common, but there are plenty of the enormous pink or white flowers of the rose-mallow, *Hibiscus palustris*.

Salt Marshes

The eastern side of the state is indented with a large number of creeks, or small rivers, which generally have a short course, numerous shoals and soft banks skirted with very extensive marshes.
— William Guthrie, 1795

Delmarva's salt marshes are broad, fluid plains of black mud and grass that rim the lower Chesapeake and Delaware bays and build behind offshore barrier islands along the Atlantic shore from Cape Henlopen to Cape Charles. They are fashioned of river silt and ocean sand that has been trapped by the roots of marsh grass, and they are slowly migrating inland over the peninsula's foundation of Pleistocene sand and gravel. The wooded hummocks that dot them like islands are, in fact, the exposed tops of prehistoric hills.

As the incoming tide gradually fills the creeks and floods into the grass, it brings with it minute invertebrates and the tiny drifting larvae of shellfish, annelids, and snails. As it slackens and begins to ebb, the eddying currents expose creek banks perforated with the holes of fiddler crabs, burrowing shrimp, and marine worms. Flats of rippled mud appear that are home to mollusks, crustaceans, and biting flies. Clapper rails creep softly out of the grass, waders stand like patient sentries, and flocks of crying shorebirds wheel in to feed.

Salt causes living cells to lose water by osmosis. A salt marsh, therefore, is a physiologically dry habitat for the organisms that live there. Without special adaptations, they would shrivel and die. Some of these adaptations are ingeniously complex. The salt-marsh grasses of the genus *Spartina,* for instance, have membranes on their roots that exclude salt, as well as glands on their leaves that excrete it. If the salinity level continues to increase, there are even cells that can allow the salt to concentrate in order to neutralize the osmotic pressure.

Each of the three species of *Spartina* that grow in Delmarva's salt marshes has evolved a particular relationship with the tide. The saltwater cordgrass, *S. alterniflora,* is the prevalent species in our marshes. It is also the pioneer. Cordgrass extends the marsh by trapping sand and silt with its strong underground stems as it colonizes low islands and rims the banks of tidal pools and creeks that are flooded daily by the tide.

Saltmeadow cordgrass, *S. patens,* is the fine, low-growing grass on which cattle grazed during the early days of settlement. It grows on the higher marsh where it can only be reached twice a month by the spring tides. The third species of *Spartina,* big cordgrass, *S. cynosuroides,* is found in less saline areas at the landward edge of the marsh, safely out of reach by all but the highest spring or storm tides.

While most salt-marsh grasses are in the genus *Spartina*, spike grass, *Distichlis spicata*, also grows in wet areas of the high marsh and there are two kinds of rushes, the delicate northern black rush, *Juncus gerardi*, and the coarser, more southern, black needlerush, *J. roemerianus*. Saltwort, *Salicornia*, is the only plant that can survive in the bare, muddy areas called salt pannes, where evaporation has caused the salt to concentrate. While most marsh plants moved onto the marsh to escape competition and became adapted to the salty environment, saltwort is a true halophyte, or salt-seeking plant that cannot grow anywhere else. Its cylindrical, fleshy stems are edible and were once used in salads and pickles.

Three species of woody plants rim the landward side of the marsh, or colonize high spots in the open that are only reached by occasional storm tides.

They are sweetgale or wax myrtle, *Myrica cerifera,* the southern species of bay-berry, the marsh elder, *Iva frutescens,* an awkward shrub with thick fleshy leaves, and groundsel tree, *Baccharis halimifolia.* Both marsh elder and ground-sel tree are collectively known as hightide bush. They are woody members of the Composite family. Groundsel tree is especially conspicuous in late summer when the seed heads look like hundreds of tiny white plumes. American holly, *Ilex opaca,* also thrives in the low woods bordering the marsh, along with its shrubby relatives, the inkberry, *I. glabra,* and winterberry, *I. verticillata.*

In all marshes, fresh, brackish, or salt, the nutrients carried in by the water are absorbed by the roots of marsh plants. When the emergent plants die at the end of the growing season, they are quickly decomposed by bacteria and other organisms and the resulting detritus washed back into the water where, in a reduced, soluble form, it is eventually consumed by the phytoplankton. The turnover is quick, compared to other ecosystems. Marsh plants renew them-selves every year, the algae are replaced in a matter of days and some kinds of bacteria are regenerated within a few hours.

The health of the marsh, as well as the rivers and estuaries, is intimately connected with the presence or absence of plankton. Plankton, which is further divided into phytoplankton (plants) and zooplankton (animals), are tiny organ-isms that are carried passively about on the tides and river currents. Plankton are heavily grazed by filter-feeding fish and shellfish that, in their turn, feed herons, snakes, and turtles as well as larger fish and, eventually, man.

Like the plants of dry land, phytoplankton contain chlorophyll and, through photosynthesis, use light to convert carbon dioxide into the carbohy-drates that are at the base of this food web. Oxygen is a by-product of this process. However, like plants anywhere, phytoplankton also *need* oxygen, as well as certain nutrients, to grow and survive. If nutrient levels in the water are adequate, a natural bloom of phytoplankton occurs every spring in Delmarva's rivers and estuaries. The principal species of this spring bloom are several mi-croscopic green algae called diatoms. There are freshwater diatoms and saltwa-ter diatoms, and they come in many shapes and sizes.

Phytoplankton also help keep the water clean by consuming excess nutri-ents introduced by decaying plants and organisms (as well as by municipal and industrial wastes). However, they can be easily killed by pesticides, excessive turbidity, and thermal pollution (the warming of the water by industrial cooling systems). Sewage or other organic pollution, on the other hand, may result in too much bloom, causing the phytoplankton to deplete the oxygen in the water to the point where it is uninhabitable for higher organisms. In other words, healthy rivers and estuaries have stable populations of many kinds of these organisms. Too much silt reduces light and production; organic pollution

113

causes certain species to explode and then crash; and toxicity reduces the numbers of species allowing the most tolerant to dominate.

The tiny floating animals called zooplankton are the next strand in the food web. Most of the zooplankton are made up of tiny crustaceans called copepods. Copepods are tiny torpedo- or bottle-shaped organisms that move erratically through the water in short spurts. There are both fresh- and saltwater species and they are so numerous that almost any scoop of pond or river water will contain some. In brackish estuaries and rivers, the zooplankton also includes the larvae of various crabs and oysters.

Next are the amphipods, mysids, and worms: tiny bottom-dwelling organisms that also come in both fresh- and saltwater species. Amphipods are the most numerous. They are small crustaceans; the familiar beach-dwelling sand flea is an amphipod. Mysids are delicate translucent little shrimps that feed on both kinds of plankton. Together, mysids and amphipods, plus various kinds of aquatic worms, make up a large part of the diet of many kinds of fish and crabs, both juvenile and adult.

Of shellfish, we have Oysters, Crabbs, Cockles, Mushels; some oysters six inches long, and one sort of cockle as big as the Stewing Oysters, they make a rich broth.

—William Penn, 1683

Numberless absurd little fiddler-crabs stood erect, waving each his one preposterously large claw at the intruder, or went popping into their holes that riddled the marsh.

—Howard Pyle, 1879

Clams, including razor (jackknife) clams, *Ensis directus*, soft-shelled clams, *Mya arenaria*, hard clams, *Mercenaria mercenaria*, small baltic macomas, *Macoma balthica*, and tiny gem clams, *Gemma gemma,* all tunnel beneath the intertidal mud flats in our bays and rivers, to escape extreme temperature and salinity changes. So do various kinds of mud and snapping shrimp and some twelve kinds of burrowing worms.

A squirt of water from a small round hole in the mud at the edge of the marsh betrays the presence of the soft-shelled clam. Soft-shelled clams live in both brackish and salt water. They have long siphons that reach through the mud to the water. Soft-shelled clams, also called manninose, are harvested in the Chesapeake by hydraulic dredges and shipped to restaurants all over the East. They also make good eating for whistling swan, diving ducks, and raccoons.

The world-famous Chesapeake Bay oyster, *Crassostrea virginica*, lives in deeper water, usually between eight and twenty-five feet down. Oyster larvae take two or three weeks to develop from fertilized eggs to eyed larvae. The larvae then form part of the zooplankton, floating idly on estuarine currents, grazing on phytoplankton, until they grow heavy enough to sink to the bottom. If they are lucky enough to land on a hard sandy surface or a pile of old shells, they will attach themselves and start on the next stage of growth. Oysters cannot survive on soft silt where they sink below the surface, and too much sediment coming in on river water can also smother them. There must, however, be enough movement of the water to bring in new supplies of planktonic food.

Adult oysters only spawn in salt water, but the spat and young oysters are safer from the attacks of oyster drills and mud crabs in water of lower salinity. In recent years, oysters in both the Chesapeake and Delaware bays have seriously declined due to a microscopic parasite called MSX. The letters stand for multinucleated spore, name unknown. It has now been officially named *Minchini nelsonii*. It is thought that this parasite has actually co-existed with oysters for thousands of years, but the general decline in water quality has destroyed the oyster's ability to resist it.

One spectacular denizen of the intertidal mud flat is the large mantis shrimp, *Squilla empusa*. Mantis shrimp are over eight inches long and look like flattened lobsters. They are colored a pale chartreuse green and have jackknife claws that somewhat resemble those of a praying mantis. Mantis shrimp are fierce predators, emerging at night to prey on other shrimp, fish, crabs, and even others of their own kind.

Most burrowing creatures of the mud flat, however, are mild-mannered creatures that feed on suspended plankton as well as organic material in the sediments. They have adapted to their intertidal life in a variety of ways. For instance, during heavy rains or increased river flow, a lugworm, *Arenicola* spp., can draw fresh water into its body to keep itself in osmotic equilibrium until the excess salt diffuses out. Should the salinity level suddenly rise, on the other hand, the lugworm withdraws into the wet sand to keep itself from shriveling.

Lugworms also retreat to a deeper level when the mud begins to dry at low tide. Although they can apparently get oxygen from either air or water, they will perish if water remains in their burrow at low tide long enough to become depleted of its oxygen.

Snails thrive in the upper marsh. The shell of *Melampus bidentatus*, the saltmarsh snail, is top-shaped and rather fragile. Having no operculum, the horny "door" that protects many snails from drying, it hides in the moist grass. Saltmarsh snails breathe air and climb up the stalks of grass as the tide comes in, although they can also submerge for short periods if necessary. While most land snails hatch from eggs as tiny snails, saltmarsh snails hatch as floating larvae. Each individual is both male and female yet no individual snail can mate with itself, thus insuring cross fertilization.

The marsh periwinkle, *Littorina irrorata*, is also found clinging to salt-marsh grasses, mingling with the mud dog whelk, *Nassarius obsoletus*. Both dot the surface of the mud at low tide, feeding on diatoms and organic debris.

Colonies of ribbed mussels, *Geukensia demissa*, half-bury themselves along the banks of creeks. Mussels are, in fact, very important to the health of a salt marsh. Their shells, which are bound into an aggregate with tough byssal threads, strengthen the marsh's leading edge, and provide a firm base for the roots of saltwater cordgrass. Mussels are filterfeeders. They strain all manner of particles from the water, swallowing the edibles and piling the inedibles, called pseudofeces, in tiny hummocks on the surface of the marsh mud.

Crabs are common in salt marshes. Hermit crabs, *Pagurus* spp., drag their borrowed shells about in the shallow water at the edge of marsh pools and guts. Having no shells of their own, they must commandeer those of dead snails. As one snail shell is outgrown, they switch to another and cling so tenaciously that it is almost impossible to pull one free.

Molting blue crabs, *Callinectes sapidus*, hide in the mud and marsh grass until their new shells harden. The adult female mates just after her final molt, while she is still in the soft-shell stage. Afterward, up to two million eggs will adhere to her underside in a spongy mass as she migrates toward the salty water of the lower bays. The eggs hatch into larvae that are carried into the ocean as part of the zooplankton and will be dispersed over the inner continental shelf for the five or six weeks that it takes for them to develop into the postlarval

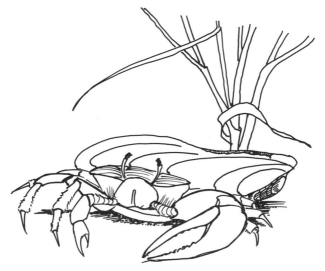

stage. The tiny crabs, which at this stage look more like crayfish, then float to the surface and are blown back into the estuaries. They migrate up the bays by swimming to the surface on the high tide and sinking to the bottom on the low tide, gradually moving into shallow brackish water where they stay until they develop into adult crabs. With such a chancy reproductive cycle, it is no wonder that the number of blue crabs found in the Delaware and Chesapeake bays varies widely from year to year.

In the salt marsh, small brown fiddler crabs dart between the *Spartina* stems at low tide. Their J-shaped burrows aerate the mud and help decompose organic matter and provide nutrients for the marsh grass. The name, fiddler crab, refers to the male's single large claw which superficially resembles a fiddle.

There are three species on Delmarva. The largest, *Uca minax*, has bright red joints on his fiddler claw and is found in brackish water marshes. The small one found in salt marshes is *U. pugnax*, and the last, *U. pugilator*, is known as the sand fiddler because it prefers sandy areas. The Latin names, *pugnax* and *pugilator*, refer to the male fiddler's pugnacious movements during breeding season when he waves his great claw like a boxer in an effort to entice a lady fiddler to his burrow. After laying her eggs, the female carries them about on her abdomen until they are ready to hatch.

Most crabs have gills, but the fiddler has a primitive lung under the edge of its shell and breathes air, although it can also withstand short periods without oxygen. Fiddlers feed on small dead animals and fermenting marsh plants at the edge of creeks and briny pools. In winter, they retreat into their burrows and wait out the cold weather in a state of slowed metabolism that resembles hibernation.

Marsh crabs, *Sesarma cinereum* and *S. reticulatum*, also dig burrows in the marsh mud at the edge of creeks. They mingle with the fiddlers but have heavier, square-shaped shells and no large claw. The marsh crab's larvae float in the water like its marine ancestors. The female carries her eggs to the water's edge and launches them on the current. While most will die, this system does insure the dispersion of the species.

High tide also brings fish into the marsh to feed, spawn, or hide from their enemies. Summer is the spawning time for killifish and sheepshead minnows, *Cyprinodon variegatus*. Killifish males put on their breeding colors, clasp the females, and spew eggs and milt into the water. The fish then sweep the sticky eggs toward the water's edge where they adhere to the stalks of *Spartina* until they hatch, about two weeks later.

The male four-spined stickleback, *Apeltes quadracus*, is the most solicitous of fish parents. He builds a nest of plant fragments stuck together with mucus. He then entices the female to spawn nearby, picks up the eggs and puts them into the nest, and stands guard until they hatch.

Insects of the Marshes and Swamps

The multitude of fireflys glittering in the dark upon the surface of the [Elk River] marsh makes it appear like a great plain scattered over with Spangles.
—*Alexander Hamilton, 1744*

The skeeters were so thick you could twirl a pint cup around your head and catch a quart every time.
—*Ralph C. Wilson, nineteenth century*

Wetlands are full of insects, and spiders spin shimmering webs in the marsh grass. Sapphire and emerald dragonflies and damselflies dance above the water, and fireflies wink their luminous green or yellow lights. Where insecticides are not a factor, grasshoppers, crickets, and plant hoppers also come into marshes to feed at low tide.

Butterflies are common. Those with host plants that grow in wet meadows and freshwater marshes include various kinds of skippers, the bronze copper, *Lycaena hyllus*, whose larvae feed on water dock, *Rumex orbiculatus*, and regal fritillaries that sip nectar from the swamp milkweed, *Asclepias incarnata*. Viceroys like inland swamps and ponds. The caterpillers eat willow and poplar leaves and the adults hover around late summer composites like Joe-Pye-weed, asters, and goldenrod. If turtleheads, *Chelone glabra*, grow in the marsh, there may also be a few Baltimores, *Euphydryas phaeton*, so named because their orange and black colors match those on Lord Calvert's heraldic shield.

Of the approximately fifty species of insects in the marsh, the ones most of us know best are the pests: the mosquitoes and midges, the blackflies, horseflies, deerflies, greenheads, and all the tiny biting insects known as no-see-ums.

Of these, the saltmarsh mosquito, *Aedes solicitans,* is the most notorious. It is not the only mosquito in the marsh, but it is the most widely travelled. The

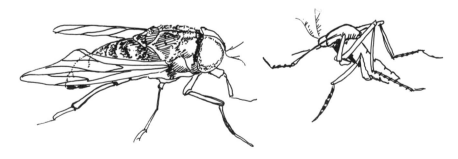

female may fly many miles inland for the blood meal she needs to produce eggs for the next generation. The male, on the other hand, is a harmless fellow who stays close to home and feeds on plant juices.

The female saltmarsh mosquito lays about 100 eggs during her two-month life expectancy, placing each one individually on the surface of the mud or attaching it to the stem of a marsh plant near the waterline. When a heavy rain or spring tide washes the eggs into the marsh pools, the larval wrigglers emerge by the thousands. They are consumed by minnows, ducks, and dragonflies, and collected by swallows to feed their nestlings, yet enough always survive to begin the next generation.

Female horseflies and deerflies, order Tabanidae, also need a protein-rich blood meal to develop eggs. Unlike humming mosquitoes, they land without a sound to deliver their painful bite. Greenheads, *Tabanus americanus,* are a type of horsefly with large emerald green eyes. While male greenheads, like male mosquitoes, are innocuous creatures that live quietly on flower nectar and pollen, a land breeze may carry scores of voracious females to nearby beaches.

Female greenheads deposit their eggs in masses on marsh vegetation overhanging the water. Upon hatching, the predacious larvae burrow into the mud where they remain for as long as one to two years before emerging as adults.

The triangular, yellow-brown deerfly, *Chrysops atlanticus,* is another ferocious biter. Deerflies lay clusters of shiny black eggs on the leaves of marsh plants just above the waterline. Like greenheads, the larvae pupate in the mud. While each individual takes several months to develop, adults continue to emerge at intervals throughout the summer.

Marshes are also full of tiny biting insects of the order Ceratopogonidae, known as no-see-ums: gnats, sandflies, and punkies. Some species bite only in bright sunlight, others at dusk or only on cloudy days, but all have a flight range of less than a mile. The females lay their eggs in the sandier parts of the marsh, where the larvae hide in debris for the six months it takes them to develop into adults. The summer populations peak twice, in May or early June, and again in August.

Marsh flies in the family Chloropidae are tiny and black with green eyes. Some are called eye gnats because of their habit of lighting on the moist skin around the eye. The larvae live in stems of grass and eat plant tissue.

Birds of the Marshes

There are infinite numbers of wild pidgeons, black birds, Turkeys, Swans, wild geese, ducks, teales, widgins, brants, herons, cranes, etc. of which there is so great abundance, as that the Rivers and creekes are covered with them in winter.
—Captain Thomas Yong, 1634

Some marsh birds prefer freshwater river marshes, others congregate in brackish and still others in salt, depending on their choice of food and nesting habitats. In Delmarva's freshwater marshes, song birds like red-winged blackbirds, bobolinks, and marsh wrens mingle with bitterns, coots, and gallinules. Swamp sparrows breed in fresh marshes in most of the northeast, although Delmarva's endemic subspecies, the coastal plain swamp sparrow, likes the brackish marsh.

The red-winged blackbird, *Agelaius phoeniceus*, is particularly fond of the cattail marshes that rim Delmarva ponds or border the freshwater streams. The males are the first to arrive in the spring, usually appearing sometime in March, often to seek out the same section of the same marsh where they have nested before. Balancing on a cattail stem, the birds defensively flash their bright red shoulder patches and fill the soft spring air with their liquid call of "konk-la-ree."

The females follow in April. An aggressive male red-winged who has staked out a claim on a choice bit of marsh may mate with as many as three females. Polygyny, as this behavior is called, is thought to occur only in prime territories that offer plenty to eat for the offspring; a latecomer in an inferior location usually must settle for a single mate. The red-winged's nest is built by the female bird who weaves it of grasses and reeds and suspends it neatly between the stems of marsh plants.

Red-wingeds, like many birds, molt in late summer. During this vulnerable time, they retreat into the marsh to feed quietly on the seeds of wild rice, dotted smartweed, tearthumbs, and Walter's millet, emerging in mid-September to join the huge flocks of red-wingeds, grackles, starlings, and cowbirds that descend on the peninsula's ripe cornfields like a horde of Biblical locusts. At this time, Delmarva's resident population of breeding birds is swelled by millions of migrants from all over the northeast.

Bobolinks were once hunted on the peninsula where they were known as reedbirds. Until nesting pairs were discovered in Delaware's Thousand Acre Marsh, they were thought to be here only in the fall, when the migrating flocks paused in Delmarva's freshwater marshes to rest and feed before continuing on their way to wintering grounds in Brazil. In spring, the male bobolink, *Dolichonyx oryzivorus*, whose Latin name means "long-clawed eater of rice," is a conspicuous black and white bird with a brilliant yellow patch on his head, but he loses this flamboyant plumage in the post-breeding molt. Thus, both the male and female bobolinks that come through Delmarva in the fall are inconspicuous birds, which look rather like large buff and brown sparrows.

The marsh wren, *Cistothorus palustris*, is as small, quick, and perky as its suburban cousins, the house and Carolina wrens. However, while the house and Carolina wrens nest in woodland cavities, the marsh wrens weave a compact, hollow grass ball, lashing it to the stems of cattails or cordgrass a few feet above high water. The entrance is at the side.

In spring, the low gutteral chatter of the male marsh wren often continues far into the night. The male arrives first, a week or so before the female, and for reasons known only to him, builds numerous dummy nests even though his efforts are but a poor imitation of the cozy, feather-lined chamber that is ultimately fashioned by the female. Each fall, Delmarva's breeding birds go south for the winter and are replaced here by northern migrants. So, even though marsh wrens are present on the peninsula all year they are not necessarily the same birds.

True to their name, sedge wrens, *C. platensis*, nest in stands of sedges in the drier sections of the marsh. They are smaller than marsh wrens and lack the latter's prominent white eye stripe. Sedge wrens are feisty and opportunistic birds that will destroy the eggs of other birds, including other sedge wrens, that encroach on their territory. Unlike most birds, who abandon their nests as soon as the young have fledged, both marsh and sedge wrens roost in them all season. They feed primarily on marsh insects and, like the red-winged blackbirds, are polygynous: in favorable habitats, the males will mate with several females.

Two sparrows are also found in Delmarva marshes. The coastal plain swamp sparrow, *Melospiza georgiana nigrescens*, is now considered a distinct subspecies of the more northern swamp sparrow, *M. georgiana*. It is endemic to the peninsula. Our coastal plain sparrow is grayer than the species and has more black on its head; thus, it can blend effectively against the surface of Delmarva's black marsh mud. It also has a stouter bill, perhaps to probe more successfully for the marsh invertebrates on which it feeds. These darker birds were first discovered nesting in stands of big cordgrass in the Nanticoke River marshes and later in the Great Marsh at Lewes, Delaware, and in shrubby brackish marshes along Delaware Bay. They build bulky nests in tussocks of marsh vegetation, usually close to open water.

Seaside and sharp-tailed sparrows, *Ammospiza maritima* and *A. caudacuta,* also nest in Delmarva's coastal salt marshes. The birds are quite similar and, where their breeding ranges overlap, have even been known to hybridize. The seaside sparrow is a drab olive-brown bird with a small yellow patch in front of the eye. It generally prefers the wetter portions of the marsh. The sharp-tailed has a gray ear patch that is completely surrounded by yellow. Sharp-taileds are shy wary birds that quickly drop into cover when flushed. They hide their cuplike nests deep in the marsh grass.

Now quite rare, the American bittern, *Botaurus lentiginosus,* can be found all the year round only on the Middle Atlantic coast, including Delmarva. Both the American bittern and its cousin the least bittern, *Ixobrychus exilis,* also winter in Central and South America, and have suffered from the widespread loss of wetlands on both continents.

The bittern, like other members of the heron family, Ardeidae, stalks its prey. It treads slowly through the marsh, spearing small fish or frogs with a lightning quick dart of the head. Also like herons and egrets, bitterns fold their necks in flight, although, except when migrating or indulging in their spectacular courtship flights, they would far rather hide than fly. If threatened, a bittern will stretch its neck vertically and point its bill toward the sky in a perfect imitation of the surrounding vegetation.

The American bittern is traditionally known as the stake driver, because of the booming, hammering clunk that is the male's peculiar territorial call. In spring, it may be heard for hours at a time. Unlike other herons, they are solitary nesters, piling a careless heap of dead grass on a tussock a few inches above high water. The young birds leave the nest when they are about two weeks old.

The least bittern is half the size of the American bittern and has dark patches on its back and head that are missing in the larger bird. Least bitterns are so secretive and solitary that only the low muted "coo" floating over the emergent grass confirms their presence in a marsh. While the American bittern booms, the least bittern claps. Like many marsh and meadow nesting birds, a bittern never flies directly to its nest but lands some distance away and walks quietly in.

Coots and gallinules are chicken-like birds related to the rails, Rallidae. They are not common on the peninsula, but of the three species known to be in our freshwater marshes, the common gallinule, or moorhen, *Gallinula chloropus,* is the most plentiful. Gallinules are brown and grey birds, with red bills, and cackling hen-like voices. Their nests are built of sun-dried aquatic plants that are anchored in clumps of vegetation, close to open water.

Purple gallinules, *Porphyrula martinica,* are rare even in the South where they are year-round residents, yet in 1975 and for several years afterward purple gallinules were reported nesting in the Dragon Run Marshes of New Castle County, Delaware—the first record of a breeding pair north of the Carolinas. Purple gallinules build their nests on islands of floating vegetation and step delicately across the marsh on waterlily pads.

The American coot, *Fulica americana,* is a slate-colored bird with a conspicuous white bill that is often seen feeding among flocks of ducks in winter. Coots typically fuss and fight among themselves and patter across the surface of the water when taking off. They resemble aquatic pigeons, but are actually related to the gallinules and, like gallinules, have fat lobes on their toes to help them swim.

Rails

On the least appearance of danger, [rails] lower the head, stretch out the neck, and move off with incomparable speed, always in perfect silence.
                                                    —John James Audubon, 1842

Rails are the secret agents of the marsh. They can slink through grass without a ripple and, if encountered on the water, will simply sink from view. Even their fibrous domed nests fade into the surrounding vegetation.

They fly only as a last resort. In fact, flying seems to be an effort for rails. Their legs dangle awkwardly and they drop quickly into the marsh at the first opportunity. Only their voices reveal their presence and that rarely, as many rails only call during the breeding season.

During a long spring twilight, a variety of peculiar grunts and whistles may be heard issuing from Delmarva's marshes. In freshwater river marshes it is the clear, wavering whistle of the sora, or the short "tid-ick, tid-ick" of the Virginia rail, while salt and brackish marshes ring with the accelerating bark of the clapper, or the grunts and burps of the king rail.

Rails belong to an ancient family of birds that date back some 70 million years. Of the six species found in North America, five are known to breed in the peninsula's marshes, and the sixth, the yellow rail, migrates through. As is true of so much of our wildlife, the ranges of the northern soras and Virginia rails overlap on Delmarva with those of the southern king, black, and clapper rails.

The clapper rail, *Rallus longirostris*, and the king rail, *R. elegans,* are the largest of the group, about the size of a small hen. The tiny mouselike black rail, *Laterallus jamaicenses,* is the smallest. He is only as big as a sparrow. In between are the sora, *Porzana carolina*, and the Virginia rail, *Rallus limicola*. Clapper, king, and Virginia rails all have long, slightly decurved bills, but the bills of black rails and soras are short.

The sora and the Virginia rails prefer freshwater marshes. The king rail likes brackish, the diminutive black rail, brackish or salt, and the clapper rail salt. King, clapper, and Virginia rails stay in the same marsh all winter, but our sora rails breed in the freshwater marshes of the upper bays and move down the peninsula in the cold season. The tiny black rail is so secretive that its range is largely unknown; it is thought to migrate to the Gulf Coast for the winter.

Sora rails build their nests in cattails that grow in fresh standing water and sometimes congregate on the silt levees that form at the edge of creeks. Virginia rails prefer the higher, drier parts of the freshwater marsh; their nest is a platform of coarse vegetation carefully hidden under a canopy of reeds and grasses.

King rails haunt brackish marshes filled with Olney three-square. Olney three-square is also attractive to muskrats and their trails make good hunting grounds for crayfish burrows, a favorite food of the king rail. These birds like to build their nests in the cradle-like base of the swamp rose-mallow, hidden beneath the plant's broad concealing leaves. The chicks of all rail birds can swim as soon as they are hatched. Most leave the nest within the hour and can forage for themselves by the second day.

The clapper rail is the salt-marsh version of the king rail. In areas where salt and brackish marshes overlap, they are even known to interbreed. The clapper is a grey-brown bird, about the size of a chicken. Local hunters call it a marsh hen and they call the first full-moon tide of September a marsh hen tide, because it floods the marsh and forces the birds to fly, making them easier to find. Clapper rails sneak out of the grass at low tide, silently probing the exposed mud along creek banks for worms and crustaceans. Both king and clapper rails also eat killifish, crayfish, fiddler crabs, and clams, regurgitating the shells in small pellets.

Clapper rails nest about the last week in May, building a cupped platform of dead grasses in a clump of *Spartina*. Even though the site is above the normal high tide, the nests are sometimes flooded out by spring or storm tides. Perhaps to compensate for this possibility, clappers may lay up to a dozen eggs. The eggs and chicks are tended by both parents.

The black rail prefers the brackish and salt tidal marshes on the Atlantic coast of the peninsula. Black rails are tiny birds that run along mouse runways deep in the grass. They sing only at night, but their insistent call of "ki-ki-kerrr" may be repeated for hours at a time during the spring breeding season. For such diminutive birds, black rails are reputed to be surprisingly aggressive; when displaying for the female, the males rattle and stamp their feet, spread their wings and hiss.

Geese and Swan

Of the water, the Swan, Goose, white and gray, Brands, Ducks, Teal, also the Snipe and Curloe and that in great numbers; but the duck and the Teal excel, nor so good have I ever eat in other Countries.
                                                                      —William Penn, 1683

Night-shooting with reflectors . . . somewhat like the headlight of a locomotive, is fixed in the bow of a light, flatbottomed boat . . . one paddles . . . while the other, holding his . . . double-barrel cocked and ready watches the patch of light . . . the startled birds gaze for a moment in stupid amazement . . . it is perhaps the surest way of killing swan.
                                                                      —Robert Wilson, 1876

At the time the peninsula was settled, migrating flocks of waterfowl were so plentiful on the Chesapeake and Delaware bays that the governor of New Sweden, Johan Rising, once requested "a bird-catcher who could capture geese and ducks in nets in the low places in spring and fall, since these birds come here by thousands."

Canada geese, tundra swan, pintails, mallards, and black ducks still winter in Delmarva's brackish water areas, even though hunting pressures, droughts, and the widespread draining of the birds' northern breeding sites have resulted in a serious decline in the populations of some species. A notable exception is the Canada goose, *Branta canadensis*, a species that has undergone a veritable population explosion over the last fifty years. Delmarva's fields and brackish marshes have now become the principal wintering ground of the so-called eastern race and we are now host to twenty times the number of Canada geese than were here in the 1940s. The increase is apparently due to the use of mechanical pickers to harvest soybeans, corn, wheat, and other grains. It is estimated that these machines leave up to 10 percent of the crop on the ground, a veritable bonanza for the geese. Besides crop grains, geese are also fond of Olney three-square, and vie with the muskrat population for its tasty rootstocks. Flocks foraging in marshes or stubble fields are always guarded by sentinel birds, non-feeding individuals who patiently stand and keep watch.

Although they winter in brackish water marshes, geese require a fresh-water habitat for nesting. In spring, the broken honking of migrating flocks of Canada geese once again fills the air over the peninsula and the thin undulating Vs set off for their breeding grounds in northeastern Canada. There they and their goslings are relatively safe from predators and find ample grazing on the luxuriant grasses and sedges that grow in the moist soils of the arctic tundra.

Nevertheless, each year more and more birds seem content to stay on the peninsula the year round, grazing on our grassy lawns, golf courses, and meadows and happily nesting at the edge of freshwater impoundments, farm ponds, and along the banks of freshwater streams.

Male Canada geese are slightly larger than females, but their plumage is identical. Their calls, however, are not. The gander's is a low, two syllable "a-honk, a-honk," while the female goose says "hink," on a higher note. Most of the time these two sounds blend so well that they sound like the call of a single bird.

Geese are monogamous and have a strong attachment to a particular nesting territory. Courting ganders stretch their necks and hiss. Both goose and gander also pump and bob their heads in a complicated series of courtship maneuvers after which the female literally builds a nest around herself. During the time she is sitting on the eggs, the gander is fiercely protective of the site, although it is immediately abandoned as soon as the goslings are hatched. Canada geese take good care of their young. The family stays together for many weeks, travelling over the water in a tightly knit group. The gander takes the lead, followed by a string of small goslings, while the female brings up the rear and keeps a sharp eye on her offspring.

Like many birds, Canada geese molt in mid-summer and are unable to fly for several weeks. At this time they retreat into the marsh with their half-grown goslings, re-emerging in early September. The whole family, newly feathered and able to fly, then join with other family groups to form the huge feeding flocks so common in Delmarva's fall and winter fields.

Snow geese are smaller and plumper than Canada geese. Young snow geese are greyish brown with dark bills, but the adults are white with black edges to their wings and have pink bills and feet. They fly into Delmarva's marshes in great spiralling flocks, changing color as they turn like plovers over a summer beach.

The greater snow geese, *Chen caerulescens atlanticus,* and the lesser snow geese, *A. caerulescens,* are geographical races of the same species that nest in different parts of the arctic tundra. (The blue goose is a color phase of the lesser snow goose.) Both come here in winter, but the lesser goes to the Chesapeake Bay and the greater to the Delaware Bay and Atlantic side of the peninsula where it used to feed on the vast beds of eelgrass, *Zostera marina*. The eelgrass died out in the 1930s, however, forcing the snow geese to turn to the rhizomes of smooth cordgrass for their primary food. They sometimes do considerable damage in the marshes at Bombay Hook, denuding large areas of marsh and leaving heaps of dead cordgrass stems in the beach wrack.

At one time, only the greater snow goose wintered on Delmarva; the lesser went down the Mississippi Valley to the Texas Gulf Coast. In recent years, however, more and more lesser snow geese are migrating down the Atlantic flyway. In late October, several thousands arrive at the Blackwater National Wildlife Refuge in Dorchester County, Maryland, to feed on cordgrass rhizomes and the rootstocks of Olney three-square. They also go into nearby farm fields for pasture grass and corn.

Brant, *Branta bernicla*, breed on islands in the Arctic Sea, but virtually the entire eastern population of these small black-necked geese now winters along the Atlantic shore from southern New Jersey to the Virginia–North Carolina border. They too once fed exclusively on eelgrass, and their numbers precipitously declined when the eelgrass disappeared. Recently, they have begun to compensate for the loss by shifting to a diet of sea lettuce, and in some cases, winter wheat.

It has been estimated that roughly a third of the nation's population of tundra swan, formerly known as the whistling swan, *Olor columbianus*, also spends the winter on Delmarva, particularly in brackish marshes between the Chester and Choptank rivers, on the Chesapeake side of the peninsula.

A few tundra swan have recently been reported as nesting in the Thousand Acre Marsh near Delaware City. Most, however, still breed on the arctic and subarctic tundra, as far away as Alaska. Swan are powerful flyers. Winging their way to wintering grounds on the peninsula, they may reach a height of over five thousand feet and cover up to a thousand miles without a rest. Like Canada geese, swan fly in a V formation and, with their swept back wings and long necks, they resemble miniature jet planes, even lifting their heads and lowering their black paddle feet like landing gear. Every March they leave the peninsula to begin their long migration flight to the north.

Seen on the water, tundra swan have longer necks than snow geese and are completely white except for their black bills. They hold their heads erect, without the S curve of the introduced European mute swan, *Cygnus olor*. They are beautiful birds, especially in the early morning or at twilight, when their white plumage appears a translucent pearly pink.

Swan feed on submerged aquatic plants and thin-shelled mollusks, particularly soft shell clams and Baltic macomas. In recent years, the gradual disappearance of the Bay's aquatic plants has forced flocks of them into the grassy fields and soybean stubble near the estuaries. To the dismay of Delmarva farmers, they are particularly fond of the young sprouts of winter wheat.

Marsh Ducks

The lordly canvas-back is for the wealthy alone, but "trash ducks," including many varieties which city gourmands relish, may be shot on almost any water-course.

Thousands of ducks were killed by swivels mounted in the bows of sail-boats and fired with terrible execution into the immense bed of fowl which could be readily approached at night . . . This method [was] used chiefly by "foreign gunners" and [was] in disfavor among the natives.

—Robert Wilson, 1876

Ducks, like geese and swan, have webbed feet and waterproof, insulated feathers. Ducks are much smaller, however, and fly considerably faster. Because their wings are small in relation to the weight of their bodies, ducks must also beat their wings continuously to stay aloft.

Marsh ducks are called dabblers because they dip their heads and tip up their tails when feeding, rather like a bobbing bathtub toy, a habit which is, incidentally, shared by feeding brant. When taking off, dabbling ducks do not patter across the surface of the water but leap directly into the air. They belong to the sub-family Anatinae, to differentiate them from diving ducks of the sub-family Aythyinae.

Black ducks, mallards, gadwalls, widgeon, green-winged teal, and northern shovelers all feed on the widgeon grass, *Ruppia maritima*, that is found in Delmarva's brackish marshes. They also like the seeds of Olney three-square, twig-rush, *Cladium mariscoides*, groundsel tree, and saltmarsh bulrush, *Scirpus robustus*. These vegetarian habits make marsh ducks extremely good eating. Before modern game laws restricted the practice, market gunners shipped them by the barrel to supply Philadelphia's food markets, particularly from Delaware's Thousand Acre Marsh.

Most marsh ducks breed in the prairie potholes of the northern Midwest and Canada and are only here in fall and winter. Only black ducks, mallards, gadwalls, and blue-winged teal nest on the peninsula.

The American black duck, *Anas rubripes*, is a dark, mottled brown, with a purple patch on the upper side of the wing and pink legs and feet. On the water, they are dark, squat, and rotund. The white lining to the wings is visible only in flight.

Black ducks feed primarily on marsh and aquatic plants, but they also eat snails, tiny clams, and occasional minnows. They breed all over the East, from Canada to North Carolina. In fact, they were once the most abundant duck breeding in the United States. They are still plentiful on Delmarva, nesting in tidal marshes, both brackish and salt, and inland on the edge of wooded ponds, yet Delmarva's wintering populations have declined by nearly 2 million birds in the last forty years, from an estimated 3.7 million birds in the 1950s to less than 2 million today. Discounting normal yearly fluctuations, this works out to a steady decline of about one to two percent a year.

The black duck's problems go beyond the all too familiar pressures of our troubled century. The principal reason for their disappearance seems to be that they are interbreeding with mallards. To some degree, of course, hybridization is a normal evolutionary tool for the production of new species and, like the greater and lesser snow goose, the mallard and the black duck are closely related. Also like snow geese, they were once separated by geography; the black duck was generally confined to the Atlantic flyway, and the mallard to the Mississippi flyway. However, the settlement of the continent and the opening of the land permitted mallards to move east; a natural migration that has been greatly increased by the release of pen-reared mallards by state wildlife agencies.

Male mallards are far more aggressive than male black ducks, and usually win in the competition for females. Because the resulting hybrids are fertile, back-crossing in succeeding generations tends to eliminate the black duck as a distinct species. The overharvesting of female black ducks has also been a factor. Hunters find it difficult to tell males from females on the wing and banding studies have shown that in some areas as much as 64 percent of the black ducks killed were young females.

The iridescent green head, white collar, and reddish-brown chest of the male mallard, *Anas platyrhynchos*, are unmistakable, but the female again looks like a black duck, especially from a distance when the mallard's lighter color and blue wing patches are not easily distinguished.

Mallards tend to be rather tame, especially those that congregate on inland ponds and busy harbors, so their mating behaviors, although brief, can be easily observed. Courting males raise themselves out of the water, stretch their necks, and shake their heads and tails. They may also dip their bills below the surface and flick water toward the female, or raise their wing tips briefly while stretching out their necks along the surface of the water.

A small number of gadwall, *Anas strepera*, also nest in the peninsula's brackish marshes, specifically at the Blackwater National Wildlife Refuge in

Wetlands

Dorchester County, Maryland, in the salt marshes of Somerset County, Maryland, and along the coast of Delaware Bay. Most, however, nest in the freshwater potholes of the northern plains states and prairie provinces of Canada.

On the water, male gadwalls appear as greyish-brown ducks with black rumps. In the air, they show a white belly and chestnut and black markings on their wings. Female gadwalls look very much like female mallards or black ducks. They have a white patch on the wing in the same location as the blue patch on the mallard and the purple on the black duck, but this difference is only visible at close range. Gadwalls feed in deeper water than mallards or black ducks and may even dive for their food occasionally.

Both blue- and green-winged teal, *Anas discors* and *A. crecca,* are found on the peninsula in winter. Neither were thought to breed here until nests of the blue-winged teal were found in the salt meadows of Somerset and Dorchester counties in the 1930s. Teal are smaller than other marsh ducks and fly in tight flocks. In the air, a flock of blue-wingeds shows dark undersides, the green-wingeds white. Teal are known to eat quantities of mosquito larvae as well as other insects.

Other marsh ducks that winter in Delmarva's brackish marshes include the American widgeon, *Anas americana*, also known as the baldpate for the male's conspicuous white crown, and the pintail, *A. acuta*. Pintails are slender, long necked ducks. The males have a conspicuous white breast and long pointed tail. The northern shoveler, *A. clypeata*, also spends the winter here, collecting in small groups on marsh pools and creeks. Shovelers are distinctive small ducks with long spoon shaped bills. Their bills have a comblike edge that is used to strain tiny crustaceans and plants from the water. All these birds breed in the prairie provinces of the north central United States and Canada. The shoveler also breeds in isolated spots in the East, but not on the peninsula.

The colorful wood duck, *Aix sponsa*, while not strictly a marsh duck, comes into Delmarva's freshwater marshes in late summer to feed on the seeds of arrow arum. They are the only species to do this. Arrow arum seeds contain calcium oxalate crystals and are repugnant to most waterfowl and marsh birds. Wood ducks are also the only ducks to roost in trees. They nest in tree cavities along the perimeters of inland ponds and streams. The newly hatched ducklings stay in the nest for only twenty-four hours before they climb up out of the hole and literally throw themselves to the ground.

Diving Ducks

The water grass, especially the Valisneria . . . gives its delicate flavor to the canvas-back.

—*Robert Wilson, 1876*

Diving ducks propel themselves underwater with large feet that are strategically placed far back on their bodies. With the exception of the lordly canvasback, *Aythya valisineria*, most are fish eaters that winter along the coast of the peninsula. The canvasback, however, is a vegetarian that once came into freshwater marshes of the northern Chesapeake by the hundreds of thousands to feed on underwater plants like wildcelery and eelgrass. When excessive turbidity killed off the wildcelery, the canvasbacks, too, began to disappear. They have learned to compensate somewhat by switching to macoma clams, a tiny mollusk that burrows into the muddy bottoms of quiet inlets and bays, but the populations are still declining. Like so many wintering ducks of the bay country, this large duck with a distinctive sloping profile breeds in potholes on the Midwestern prairies. As these continue to be drained for farming or dry up in recurring droughts the canvasback's vital nesting habitat is disappearing.

The mergansers are diving ducks, too, although their slender spikelike bills, and long, low silhouettes are quite different from those of the more familiar marsh ducks. Mergansers are fish eaters that nest near northern ponds and lakes. In winter, the hooded merganser, *Lophodytes cucullatus*, may be seen mingling with the dabblers in the peninsula's brackish marshes. The males have an unmistakable fan-shaped white crest on the head and a white breast.

The red-breasted merganser, *Mergus serrator*, spends the winter in saltier water near the coast where they feed on fish, crustaceans, and aquatic insects. The male has a green head with a conspicuous crest. When taking off, they run across the water. All mergansers fly with bill, head, neck, and body lined up on an exact horizontal plane.

Scoters appear heavy and black when seen off Delmarva's coast in winter. The white-winged scoter, *Melanitta fusca*, is the largest of the three species that come here. The white patch, for which it is named, is only visible when the bird is flying. The surf scoter, *M. perspicillata*, may be identified by a white patch on the head, and the black scoter, *M. nigra*, by a conspicuous orange bump on its bill.

The oldsquaw, *Clangula hyemalis*, is the peninsula's only sea duck with white on both its head and upper body. Oldsquaws fly in bunched, irregular flocks. They are very deep divers, plunging up to two hundred feet below the surface.

The greater and lesser scaups, *Aythya marila* and *A. affinis*, can be recognized by their dark heads and necks and the conspicuous patch of white on the trailing edge of the wing when in flight. The ruddy duck, *Oxyura jamaicensis*, is a small chubby duck that looks like a child's bathtub toy. Ruddy ducks feed by straining aquatic animals from soft muddy creek bottoms. They are so attuned to an aquatic environment that they are reputed to have difficulty walking on land.

Wetland Mammals

The musk-rat furnishes a savory dish for any one who will set a choke-snare in the nearest creek, and his skin will purchase the accompaniments to make up the meal.

—Robert Wilson, 1876

Raccoons, deer, meadow voles, rabbits, mice, and shrews are all common in wetlands, but the undisputed king of the marsh is the muskrat, *Ondatra zibethicus*. Muskrats have been trapped on the peninsula since the earliest days of settlement. The pelts, sold as "Hudson seal," were shipped in such numbers from Delaware that the town of Leipsic was named after the fur center of Germany. Muskrat meat, reputedly tender and sweet tasting, is sold as "marsh rabbit" on the peninsula where it is traditionally served with hominy.

The muskrat is a medium-sized rodent with a glossy waterproof coat and a naked, scaly tail that is flattened vertically like a rudder. It spends most of its time underwater, but occasionally one can be glimpsed swimming across a quiet pond or creek with his nose poking just above the surface of the water.

Muskrats are adaptable animals. In Delmarva's brackish marshes, they build dome-shaped lodges on the surface of the marsh, yet in the piedmont section of the peninsula, they burrow deep into the muddy banks of streams and ponds. The difference is in the soil.

Piedmont clay provides a strong support for an underground bank den, an elaborate system of tunnels, chambers, and ventilation holes that may be used for years by successive generations of muskrats. They excavate cozy sleeping or nursery chambers well out of reach of the pond water and line them with dried grass and other plant materials.

The fluctuating water levels in a tidal creek, however, would flood such an underground chamber, so the muskrats in Delmarva's tidal marshes build their houses above ground. Each lodge is about five to six feet in diameter and three to four feet high. They are constructed from the stems of cordgrass, cattails, and Olney three-square, and equipped with several underwater entrance tunnels cut through the underlying mat of decaying marsh vegetation. A muskrat lodge usually contains a central chamber and several grass-lined nests, each with its own escape hole and all carefully positioned above the level of normal high water.

Muskrats are also prolific. The male mates with any available female in estrus, each of which will produce two or more litters a year of five to six kits each. Only the female takes care of the young and she will evict those from earlier litters to make room for later ones. After they leave the parent nest, young muskrats often construct new lodges nearby, causing a colony to grow explosively until the food supply is exhausted.

The roots and stalks of cattails and Olney three-square are a muskrat's favorite food. By shredding them, he helps make the nutrients available to other organisms in the marsh. Muskrat tunnels may work havoc in the dam of a man-made pond, but their presence in a marsh is generally thought to be beneficial to other forms of wildlife. Brackish marshes on the peninsula that have been taken over by *Phragmites* often lack not only muskrats, but also the rice rats and voles that share their lodges and run along their surface trails. Foxes and raccoons break into muskrat houses to feed on the muskrat kits as well as other small animals found hiding from harsh weather or high tides. Turtles rest in muskrat tunnels and king, Virginia, and sora rails follow their paths through the grass. Even the muskrat "eat-outs" that result from over-population create scattered pools of arrowhead and arrow arum for migrating ducks and geese.

The mink, *Mustela vison*, another aquatic member of the weasel family, is also found in Delmarva's creeks and marshes. They are not nearly as numerous as muskrats, but their valuable, lustrous pelts make them a prime target of trappers. Mink are small, quick, and lithe, a little over half the size of a river otter, and have a bushy tail. They eat birds, frogs, or fish, but their chief quarry is the docile vegetarian muskrat, who, although larger, is no match for this fierce little predator. Like otters, mink are nocturnal and solitary, and spend much of their time in the water.

The peninsula's salt and brackish marshes are also full of rice rats, *Oryzomys palustris*, a small southern rodent that reaches the northern limit of its range on Delmarva and southern New Jersey. Rice rats are accomplished swimmers, and make extensive and well-defined runways in Delmarva's wet meadows and marshes. Since they are only active at night, they are seldom seen, but a floating mat of cut vegetation in the creek is a sure sign of their presence. Rice rats hide their nests under piles of marsh debris or weave them into the marsh plants a foot above the level of high tide. They are a favorite quarry of the northern harrier (marsh hawk), as well as of mink and weasels.

There are also a few nutria, *Myocaster coypus*, in the Blackwater marshes in Dorchester County, Maryland. Nutria are South American rodents about the size of a beaver that were released into Blackwater in the 1940s by the Fish and Wildlife Service, presumably to provide another source of furs for trappers. For a while, it was feared that they might drive out the peninsula's native muskrats, but luckily this has not proved to be the case.

> *The low grounds . . . [are] full of Beaver and Otter.*
> —*Captain Thomas Yong, 1634*

After an absence of nearly three hundred years, beavers, *Castor canadensis*, have returned to Delmarva and are once again building their lodges and dams in the freshwater streams and ponds of Delaware and the Eastern Shore of Maryland.

Beavers are large rodents, several times the size of muskrats. They have broad, horizontally flattened tails with which they slap the surface of the water if alarmed, a signal to every other beaver in the vicinity to dive. Beavers are strict vegetarians, dining on the twigs and leaves of trees and shrubs, the stems and roots of water plants, and the tender bark of young trees.

It is thought that the sound of rushing water stimulates beavers to build their dams. Apparently, they construct these barriers to raise the water level, thereby enabling them to feed more safely underwater. They can gnaw through small trees in a matter of minutes, leaving a stump like a sharpened pencil. The first saplings to be cut are dragged to the stream and planted firmly in the mud facing the current. Small logs, branches, and twigs are then piled on the top and the holes plugged with mud.

Beaver family life is close-knit and long-lived. The adults are monogamous and the young stay with their parents for at least two years. A single beaver lodge may harbor a whole colony of beaver families. It is also built on a frame of large branches and logs, filled in with smaller branches and plastered with mud and leaves.

The river otter, *Lutra canadensis*, is an aquatic member of the carnivorous weasel tribe. Otters have broad heads, small ears, stout necks, and heavy tapering tails. Their rich brown pelts are dense and waterproof. They have webbed toes and eyes that are set high on their heads to allow them to see above the surface when submerged. While they are most numerous near the headwaters of the peninsula's rivers, they are also found in brackish creeks and marshes where the water flows slowly and there is a good supply of small animals to eat. Otters are very sensitive to water quality, however, and disappear at the slightest sign of pollution. Still, even in the best habitats, they are rarely seen. Not only are they secretive and nocturnal, each adult otter may have a home territory that covers several square miles, although the young ones are thought to circulate within the ranges of several of their elders.

River otters are playful creatures. They build slides down muddy river banks and chase one another through the marsh, apparently for the sheer joy of it. They feed on crayfish, fish, crabs, and frogs, often poking their heads above water to swallow their catch. An otter trail through the marsh is typically strewn with fish scales, shells, and droppings.

Swamps and Bays

*About a mile from this house we began to enter one of the
most frightful labyrinths you can imagine. It was filled with tall
tangling shrubs thickly matted together almost impervious to
the light.*

—Thomas Nuttall, 1809

*In the southern flatlands the woods are mainly composed of trees
with needle-shaped leaves or pines . . . Chief among these is the
white-cedar . . . it is found in great numbers and of a beautiful
growth in all the forests . . . The great Cedar-Swamp seems
designed by nature for these trees to flourish in.*

—Donald H. Rolfe, 1799

Wooded Swamps

Wooded swamps are actually the peninsula's most common wetland. There are
almost twice as many acres of wooded swamps on the peninsula as there are
acres of marshland, although most are relatively shallow and tend to dry in
mid-summer. They occur on the floodplains of rivers and streams, in inland
depressions, or in low-lying areas at the edge of marshes. Many of these shallow swamps were once dominated by thick stands of Atlantic white cedar,
Chamaecyparis thyoides, a tree so intensively exploited by the early colonists
for its rot resistant wood that it was nearly extirpated from the peninsula. White
cedars, like many conifers, tend to be slow growing and do not sprout from
stumps, so when the stands were removed, fast-growing red maples and sweet
gums quickly moved in and altered the character of the swamp. Today red
maples and sweet gums dominate most of Delmarva's swamps, mixing on the

137

southern part of the peninsula with swamp tupelo, *Nyssa sylvatica* variety *bi-flora*, a subspecies of black gum, *N. sylvatica*. Black gum, or tupelo, is a common tree of sandy soils throughout the eastern seaboard, but swamp tupelo occurs almost exclusively in the wet bottomlands, ponds, and sloughs of the coastal plain. It has slightly narrower leaves than the species and a bulge at the base of the trunk. Such bulges are typical of many trees that grow in swampy soil.

Other trees found in the peninsula's shallow wooded swamps include green ash, *Fraxinus pennsylvanica*, river birch, *Betula nigra*, and various species of wetland oaks as well as the ubiquitous loblolly pine, a tree found in many kinds of habitat on the lower peninsula.

In swamps at the headwaters of certain Delmarva streams, there is a distinctive small tree called the seaside alder, *Alnus maritima*. The seaside alder resembles the common alder, *Alnus serrulata*, except for the fact that it flowers in the autumn. It is endemic to the peninsula, occurring only in Sussex County, Delaware, and in Dorchester, Wicomico, and Worcester counties, Maryland. There are also a few trees in a small area of south central Oklahoma: it is thought that they grew from seeds or plants carried west by the Lenni-Lenape Indians.

Delmarva's wooded wetlands are also full of winterberry, sweetbay magnolia, *Magnolia virginiana*, and sweet pepperbush, *Clethra alnifolia*. Greenbriers flourish; so does the magenta pink swamp rose, *Rosa palustris*.

Cypress Swamps

The Indian River Swamps, otherwise called the Cypress Swamps, are situated in Delaware and Maryland States, a little to the Southward of the True Cape Henlopen and distant from the sea about ten miles. They are full seven miles from East to West and ten or twelve from North to South, so that they must contain near fifty thousand acres of land . . . The whole of this immense Swamp is a high and level bason and consequently very wet; tho' undoubtedly the highest land between the sea and the bay, the waters descending from it in all directions . . . About one fifteenth part of this vast tract was once covered with the beautiful green cypress . . . whose regular and majestic height cast such a venerable shade that it kept every other tree of the forest at an awful distance and impressed the beholder with a religious solemnity.
—*A Citizen of Delaware, 1797*

Baldcypress, *Taxodium distichum*, is not a true cypress, but a southern tree that is related to the California redwoods. It is a deciduous conifer; the name bald refers to the fact that it drops its needles and twigs every autumn.

Extensive deposits of buried cypress have been found beneath the waters of the Chesapeake and in other locations on the peninsula, indicating that cypress swamps were once widespread on the peninsula. Presumably the sea level and climate changes that occurred in the remote past caused some to dry and others to flood. At present, the species reaches its northern limit in the Great Cypress Swamp in Sussex County, Delaware. There are also extensive stands on the upper Pocomoke River, along Nassawango Creek, and on the James Branch east of Records Pond. To canoe these areas is to drift back to primeval wilderness. Civilization seems remote.

Delmarva's cypress swamps are underlaid by a thick black muck that was originally laid down in Pleistocene and Miocene times. The ground is a wet sponge of sphagnum moss and the tannin-stained water the color of strong tea. While the peaty soil is permanently wet, it is only intermittently flooded, conditions that are perfectly suited to the baldcypress. In fact, while the towering cypress of Delaware's Trussum Pond—each surrounded by a supporting circle of "knees" and watery mats of waterlily, *Nymphaea odorata*, and spatterdock, *Nuphar advena*—fits the typical picture of a cypress swamp, there are troubling signs that the trees at Trussum's are gradually declining due to being constantly flooded. The pond, in fact, is man-made and most of the trees predate the hundred-year-old dam.

The knees for which cypress trees are famous are actually something of a mystery. The fact that they only develop on trees growing in saturated soil, leads some to think they provide oxygen to the roots, although no one has shown exactly how this is accomplished.

Till the year seventeen hundred and fifty-nine it lay in a measure unlocated, and was thought to be of little value: but since that period most of it has been surveyed for different proprietors.
—*A Citizen of Delaware, 1797*

The unfortunate history of Delaware's Great Cypress Swamp graphically illustrates the failure of our forebears to care for the rich natural resources of the peninsula. At the time of settlement, the swamp covered about 50,000 acres at the headwaters of the Pocomoke River. In 1758, a large tract of land adjacent to it was given to Captain John Dagworthy by Lord Baltimore for his services in the French and Indian War. He built a great plantation at the present site of Dagsboro, Delaware. Captain Dagworthy is thought to have been the first man to cut cypress in the swamp.

Cypress wood, like Atlantic white cedar, is extremely resistent to rot and Dagworthy was soon supplying markets throughout the peninsula and as far away as Trenton, New Jersey. Some of Delmarva's surviving eighteenth-century houses are still shingled with his cypress.

Quantities of cypress were cut from the swamp all through the eighteenth and nineteenth centuries, increasing the amount of sunlight reaching the ground and allowing the water to evaporate. The water level became lower, and the thick layer of peat began to dry. Dry peat, of course is extremely flammable.

> *[A] most terrible conflagration happened in June 1782; the swamp being at that time exceeding dry, by some means took fire and burnt for many weeks before much notice was taken of it . . . it was on the 20th of August, about two hours before sun-set, driven by a strong southwest wind, with such inconceivable fury, that it mowed or otherwise destroyed, at least three thousand acres of these venerable cedars in less than twelve hours . . . The smoak was so thick that we could not see a yard before us, and to prevent suffocation, were obliged to keep our mouths close to the ground; . . . the trees falling, the fire roaring, the atmosphere full of live coals at an amazing height like flaming meteors . . . The light of this fire was seen seventy miles off. The extent then of the horizone illuminated by it, must have been upwards of four hundred and twenty miles. Large quantities of coals were found on the sea shore, fourteen miles from the place where the fire then raged.*
>
> *—A Citizen of Delaware, 1797*

This fire, like the many that followed, apparently smoldered in the dried peat for many weeks before flaring up. Such creeping turf fires still occur in the swamp. They burn the roots of trees until they topple and send up eerie columns of smoke through what appears to be a blackened field of miniature volcanoes. Sussex County has many grisly tales of fugitives who fled to the swamp only to be surrounded and killed by these fires.

During the drought years of the 1930s, another great fire broke out in the swamp that was to burn for eight months. Periodically it seemed to subside only to creep underground and flare up in another location. It was said that the smoke was so thick that it made people's eyes water as far away as Wilmington. Not only standing trees, but also buried cypress logs were all burned to a cinder, killing off what little remained of the shingle business. (Ancient logs preserved in the peat had been traditionally mined by local people as a lucrative source of income.) When the great fire of the 1930s finally died, the peat had burned down to sand and the swamp had earned itself a new name: "The Burnt."

The loss of the peat allowed the water to flood in and turn the swamp into a river. With no cypress left, the swamp had no economic value, so, with the help of the federal government, local farmers drained much of the land for agriculture, gouging out long ditches with a huge machine called "the digger." Soon, red maple, sweet gum, and pine moved in, crowding out what was left of the cypress.

While little remains of the original cypress swamp, it is still an impressive expanse of uninhabited land. Delicate pink rose pogonias, *Pogonia ophioglossoides,* and white and yellow fringed orchids, *Habenaria blephariglottis* and *H. ciliaris*, grow in the remaining bogs. Wood ducks and eagles nest in the forest, otters slide into the ditches, and turkeys once again roam the woods. Over 11,000 acres are now owned by Delaware Wildlands, Inc., a private organization that is attempting to restore at least a part of the swamp to its original grandeur. In 1979 the Nature Conservancy also bought 539 acres on the Maryland side of the border near the headwaters of the Pocomoke River. It will not be an easy task, but perhaps in another century or two, much of what was so carelessly lost may be regained.

Swamp Warblers

The flamboyant prothonotary, *Protonotaria citrea*, with his lovely golden yellow head and breast, is one of several southern warblers that nest in Delmarva's wooded swamps. The others are the shy Swainson's warbler, *Limnothlypis swainsonii*, the yellow-throated warbler, *Dendroica dominica*, the worm-eating warbler, *Helmitheros vermivorus,* and the hooded warbler, *Wilsonia citrina.*

The prothonotary is our only cavity nesting warbler. In the East, it is found only as far north as the Pine Barrens of New Jersey. Every spring, the returning male picks several possible nesting sites by stuffing old woodpecker holes with moss, usually in willows about five to ten feet above the water. The female then chooses the site she likes and finishes the male's nest with a lining of grass and feathers.

The Swainson's warbler is normally found only as far north as the Great Dismal Swamp near Norfolk, Virginia, yet a small, disjunct population also nests in Delaware's Great Cypress Swamp and along the banks of the Pocomoke River. The Swainson's is a modest, brown bird that blends perfectly with the leaf litter as it probes the sodden soil for insects.

Swainson's warblers arrive on the peninsula about the third week in April, often returning to the same territory where they have nested before. The nests are relatively large and bulky and are usually built in damp, dense sections of the swamp, where there is a thick undergrowth of sweet pepperbush and greenbrier. Oddly enough, Swainson's warblers lay white unmarked eggs, only one of two species of warbler to do so. Most birds that nest in the open lay eggs that are camouflaged by blotches and spots; white unmarked eggs are usually only laid by species that hide them in dark cavities, like woodpeckers, owls, bank swallows, or kingfishers.

The male Swainson's has a distinctive, five-note territorial song; the first two notes slur downwards, the second two are low, and the last one high. They are timid about defending their nesting sites, however, and have been driven off by tapes played by overzealous birders in an effort to coax them out of hiding.

The worm-eating warbler likes the drier sections of the swamp. It looks very much like the Swainson's with only its black head-stripes to distinguish it. Its song, however, is quite different: a thin dry rattle somewhat like that of a chipping sparrow. Worm-eating warblers nest on the ground beneath dense shrubs and briars.

The eastern race of the yellow-throated warbler is a bird of the coastal plain. It reaches the northern limit of its range on Delmarva and Cape May, New Jersey. Yellow-throated warblers nest in cypress trees and evergreens. The bird climbs trees like a brown creeper, using its relatively long bill to forage for insects among bark crevices and fissures.

The hooded warbler looks like a prothonotary with a black cowl on its head. It builds a neat, compact nest a few feet off the ground in thick brushy undergrowth. Male and female hooded warblers have been shown to have different feeding habits. The males capture insects on the wing or glean them from the foliage but the females feed on the ground.

Despite its name, the Louisiana waterthrush, *Seiurus motacilla*, is not a thrush but a warbler. It also nests deep in Delmarva's wooded swamps. The waterthrush is a small brownish bird with pink legs; it resembles the ovenbird of our upland woods, except the waterthrush spends most of its time walking along the streambank or wading in shallow water. It bobs its tail like a spotted sandpiper. The birds flip over or pull leaves from the water, looking for small invertebrates and insects. They build wet leafy pathways to their nests, which are usually placed in a hole or nestled among the roots of a streamside tree.

Raptors of the Marshes and Swamps

The islands . . . are edged with gaunt, ragged oaks, bearing the immense nests of the fishing hawk and bald eagle, the latter . . . perched upon some projecting limb or sailing . . . in the blue ether, his silver head and tail flashing in the sunlight.

The bald eagle is rarely absent from the landscape—in summer cruising with piratical designs against the industrious fish-hawks, in winter watching from his perch . . . for a chance to make a raid on the waterfowl which swarm on the flats.
—Robert Wilson, 1876

In the early 1900s, a collector could buy a clutch of bald eagle eggs for ten dollars. Collecting any bird's eggs, particularly an eagle's, is unthinkable now, but at that time it was a popular hobby. The bald eagle, *Haliaeetus leuco-cephalus*, was also very common in the 1900s. It is said that, before World War II, there was an eagle's nest about every three miles along the convoluted Chesapeake shoreline.

DDT changed all that. In the 1950s and 1960s, eagle's eggs became so thin and fragile that reproduction virtually stopped. Suddenly, America's proud national bird began to slide toward extinction. Fortunately, the bald eagle is a powerful national symbol and its plight soon became a rallying point for the outlawing of DDT and its related compounds in this country. Unfortunately, DDT is still causing serious problems worldwide.

Nor are the eagle's pesticide problems behind him. In 1988, an insecticide called carbofuran, which is used extensively on potato and soybean fields, was suspected of killing more than a dozen eagles in the Chesapeake Bay region. Carbofuran is deadly to any small songbird who picks up the granules, and a scavenging eagle who feeds on a dead bird also ingests the poison. Carbofuran has also been found to leach into groundwater; at this writing it is under review by the EPA.

Nevertheless, the eagle is showing encouraging signs of recovery, although the majority of nesting pairs are still in only four locations: the Chesapeake Bay region, Maine, the Great Lakes, and in the Pacific Northwest. Our Delmarva eagles are principally found in the vicinity of the Blackwater National Wildlife

Refuge in Dorchester County, Maryland, although recently several nests have been identified along the upper Bay. There are also a few in Delaware and on the Eastern Shore of Virginia, and one pair is in the Great Cypress Swamp.

A breeding pair of eagles needs about a square mile of territory. Like many birds of prey, they are philopatrian, that is, the young birds return to nest in the place where they were raised. So, while it is true that the nation's four relic populations are steadily growing, the birds have not even begun to occupy the full scope of their original range. Wildlife biologists are trying to help them do so by a technique called hacking, a procedure in which eagle eggs are selectively removed from the nest and hatched in incubators. The young eaglets are fed by dummy parents, to avoid imprintation on humans, and released in a new territory when they are ready to fly, in the hope that they will return there when ready to breed themselves. So far, several new nesting territories have been established in this way.

The sight of a bald eagle is unforgettable. In active flight, the birds seem to throw themselves across the sky, but most of the time they wheel and soar on motionless outstretched wings, their white heads and tails shining in the sunlight.

Immature eagles lack the white head and tail of the adult, but have indistinct splotches of white on the underside of their wings and tail. They are often larger and heavier than their parents, like indulged overfed children.

Fish is the main staple of the eagle's diet, but he is also a shameless scavenger of ducks and geese that have been shot by hunters and will even steal muskrats from traps, habits that Benjamin Franklin thought made him unworthy to be our national bird.

Blackwater's eagles usually return to the peninsula from the Gulf Coast sometime in December. Before breeding, the pairs indulge in spectacular courtship flights, sometimes locking talons and executing a series of descending somersaults. One to three eggs are laid and hatched sequentially, beginning at the end of February. The nest, or eyrie, is a huge pile of sticks, cornstalks, and cattails that are stuck together with clumps of sod and lined with marsh grass. The birds also drop leftover fish heads, bones, and animal skulls into the interior of the nest. Every year more material is added until the eyrie may reach ten feet in diameter and weigh hundreds of pounds. Such a construction obviously requires a huge tree. At Blackwater, the pairs usually choose an old loblolly pine or oak near open water or at the edge of the marsh.

A few golden eagles, *Aquila chrysaetos*, also winter on the peninsula. They, too, ride the air currents on flat extended wings, but lack the bald eagle's white head and tail. When seen from below, an adult golden eagle looks much like an immature bald except for the bold circle of white near the outer edge of each wing: the white on an immature bald eagle's wing is less defined and closer to the bird's body.

A fishing eagle swoops close to the surface to snatch a fish from the water with his talons. An osprey, *Pandion haliaetus*, on the other hand, stalls in mid-air, hovering like a sparrow hawk over an inland meadow, before plunging into the water feet first. The bird often sinks briefly beneath the surface before reappearing with his prize held firmly in his talons. Slow motion films show that the osprey actually flies out of the water. When returning to his perch, he holds one foot ahead of the other in order to carry the fish in an aerodynamically efficient position. Ospreys also drag their feet in the water occasionally, apparently to cause small fish near the surface to jump.

Ospreys nest in loose colonies, building their nests about fifty yards apart. Studies done on an osprey colony in Nova Scotia have shown that the birds actually exchange information about good fishing grounds and even discriminate between fish species. An osprey returning with an alewife, for instance, will cause other birds to take to the air and retrace his flight path, yet one returning with a flounder will not. The birds seem to know that, because alewives move in large schools, they have a good chance of getting a fish for themselves. Catching a bottom fish like a flounder, on the other hand, is a random occurrence, not likely to be repeated.

Like eagles, ospreys mate for life and are devoted parents. The male feeds the female all during courtship and egg laying, and, even after the eggs have hatched, he continues to bring food for her to feed to the young. Ospreys build their nests near open water, on the top of telephone poles, channel markers, or dead snags. They also use sticks and sod for building materials, as well as anything else they can find, including trash, cow dung, or eelgrass. The birds return to the same nest each year, spending a total of about four months repairing it, incubating the eggs, and feeding the nestlings. Young ospreys can fly at two months but return to the nest to be fed by their parents until they can successfully fish on their own.

Banding studies have shown that Delmarva's ospreys winter in Brazil, Colombia, and Venezuela, returning to the peninsula about the middle of March. The Chesapeake Bay area has the largest population of nesting ospreys in the United States and most of our birds, helped by the Bay's diverse convoluted shoreline and plentiful supply of fish, continued to produce young successfully in the 1960s and 1970s when other U. S. populations were seriously declining. Ospreys return to Delmarva every year around St. Patrick's Day and, no matter what the weather, their high keening call is a sign that spring has arrived.

Wetlands

Whereas the eagle soars and the osprey hovers, the marsh hawk, now called the northern harrier, *Circus cyaneus,* glides. Harriers wheel a few feet above the grass, systematically quartering the marsh in search of small rodents, showing a conspicuous white rump as they tilt their wings and swiftly change direction.

Harriers build flimsy nests of sticks and grass directly on the ground in the higher, drier sections of the marsh. Except in spring when they indulge in exuberant courtship flights, they are low-flying birds that rarely perch above the level of a fencepost. A courting pair of harriers, on the other hand, bounces high in the sky, while the male executes a series of fanciful stalls and barrel loops.

The number of harriers in any particular area normally depends on the supply of the small rodents on which they feed. Like all predators, however, they are extremely vulnerable to concentrations of pesticides in the food chain and are not as plentiful on the peninsula as they once were. Delaware reported only two breeding pairs in 1987.

The rough-legged hawk, *Buteo lagopus*, occasionally winters on the Delaware Bay side of the peninsula. It is considerably larger than a harrier and, instead of a white rump, has a white tail banded with black. Rough-legged hawks also hover on beating wings and when seen from below have a dark belly and a black patch on each wing.

Both the saw-whet owl, *Aegolius acadicus*, and the short-eared owl, *Asio flammeus*, are seen occasionally on peninsula marshes in the fall and winter. The saw-whet is a tiny earless owl, smaller than a screech owl, with blotchy brown streaks on its breast. It breeds in the coniferous forest of the north and at high elevations in the Appalachian Mountains.

The short-eared owl also breeds in the far north. It is larger than the saw-whet and is streaked on its back as well as its breast. During migration, short-eared owls sometimes gather in large flocks to hunt rodents in Delmarva's marsh grass.

Periodically a snowy owl, *Nyctea scandiaca*, appears on the peninsula in a state of near starvation. Snowy owls are huge white birds, as big or bigger than the great horned owl. Their staple food is the arctic lemming, a species notorious for its cyclical population explosions and crashes. In years when the lemmings are scarce, the birds are forced south to find other small rodents.

The peninsula's hardwood swamps are the domain of the barred owl, *Strix varia*, also called the swamp owl on Delmarva. Barred owls frequently hunt over marshes and pine woods, but they nest deep in the swamp, possibly because our pine woods have few trees old enough to provide them with the cavities they need.

146

Barred owls are large, puffy-headed, streaked, gray-brown owls. They do not have ear tufts. Most owls have yellow eyes, but barred owls, like barn owls, have brown ones. They call "Who cooks for you? Who cooks for you-all?" in the deep woodland night.

The barred owl is the nocturnal equivalent of the red-shouldered hawk, *Buteo lineatus*. They enjoy the same ecological relationship in the hardwood swamp as the great horned owl and the red-tailed hawk in upland woods, nesting close together and hunting the same prey. Eggs of both species have even been found mixed together in neighboring nests, with the hawk incubating one clutch and the owl the other.

Like the red-tailed, the red-shouldered hawk is a buteo, but instead of the red tail, it has conspicuous black and white bands across its tail and a breast as red as a robin's. The red shoulders are not usually visible from below. Like many of their fellow species, red-shouldered hawks use the same nest year after year and indulge in acrobatic mating flights in the breeding season. A courting pair will spiral upwards a thousand feet or more before diving or side-slipping toward the nesting territory. The numbers of red-shouldered hawks have declined in recent years. Not only are they vulnerable to pesticide concentrations, they must have mature forested swamps in order to reproduce successfully.

Delmarva Bays

A band of several hundred Delmarva bays, also known as sinkholes, whale wallows, round ponds, black bottoms, or loblollies, were once spread diagonally across the peninsula in a southwesterly direction from Delaware's southern New Castle County into Caroline County, Maryland. Many no longer exist, having been drained or filled for agriculture. Those that remain range in size from a quarter of an acre to two acres or larger and are up to four feet deep in the wettest season. Some of the smaller shallower bays become merely soggy in mid-summer, but others have standing water all year.

These circular ponds or depressions seem to occur where the water table is high and Miocene-aged clays lie close to the surface. They are rimmed like a crater and drain from the center like a giant puddle. While not visibly linked, they may, in fact, be connected underground. Their origin is unknown although a number of fanciful theories, including stranded whales and ancient meteorite showers, have been suggested.

These peculiar ponds occur on some of Delmarva's highest land, the upland backbone of the peninsula, yet their vegetation resembles that of acidic bogs. Sphagnum moss is abundant where the soil is saturated, and buttonbush, *Cephalanthus occidentalis*, fills the flooded centers, often surrounded by mats of fragrant waterlilies, *Nymphaea odorata*. Sweet pepperbush, winterberry, blueberries, and deerberries, *Vaccinium* spp., crowd the banks. Trees on the perimeter include swamp cottonwoods, sweet gum, black gum, and red maple. There are also white oaks, swamp white oaks, *Quercus bicolor*, willow oaks, and persimmon, *Diospyros virginiana,* all growing in locations that may be periodically or continually flooded.

Wet Meadows

Wet meadows are another enigma. They occur on poorly drained soil over a high water table, and are filled with sedges, grasses, and extremely rare plants. Some of these meadows actually flood in wet seasons, but most are merely saturated the year round. They apparently occur on old pond basins or on low-lying farmland. Some lie between certain shallow marshes and adjacent upland.

One in particular in Sussex County, Delaware, has been a favorite hunting spot for botanists since the 1870s. Detailed floristic records are available for this small poorly drained field which lies between a public road and an old railroad track. When the records were compiled and updated in 1979 by the Society of Natural History of Delaware, this spot was found to contain no less than 50 of the state's official list of 449 rare plants. Rare is defined as having three or fewer known populations in the state. Over half the plants there are, in fact, endemic to Delaware or are at the extreme limit of their geographic range. Many exist only on this one rather unprepossessing site.

Reptiles and Amphibians of the Wetlands

Few people seem to disbelieve the fascinating power of snakes, mention only the subject, and every one is ready to tell something wonderful about it.
—A Citizen of Delaware, 1797

The northern water snake, *Natrix s. sipedon*, is the most common aquatic snake found in still and slow-moving waters of the peninsula's creeks, river marshes, and swamps. Northern water snakes come in a bewildering variety of colors and markings, but any large mottled snake seen in the water is usually this species. Water snakes swim with their head just breaking the surface, leaving a long V-shaped wake behind them.

The redbelly water snake, *Natrix erythrogaster*, is a large southern species of swamps and marshes that reaches the northern limit of its range in Delaware's Great Cypress Swamp. Young redbelly water snakes may be boldly blotched, but the adults are a plain chocolate or red-brown color. They are classified as aquatic snakes even though they leave the water in hot, humid, summer weather.

The rare queen snake, *Natrix septemvittata*, hides in brushy thickets near the piedmont streams of northern Delmarva. It is a slender mud-brown snake with a longitudinal beige stripe that likes to stretch out along a low branch near the stream bank where it blends perfectly with its surroundings. A hunting queen snake can stay underwater for long periods, bumping against underwater rocks. It is looking for crayfish that have recently shed their shells, a delicacy which is thought to be their only food.

The poor man [must] content himself with the mud turtle and "snapper."
—Robert Wilson, 1876

Turtles are common in all of Delmarva's freshwater wetlands. The Eastern painted turtle, *Chrysemys picta*, feeds on aquatic vegetation, insects, crayfish, and small mollusks. It is found in every swamp, pond, or shallow freshwater marsh with a soft muddy bottom. On sunny afternoons, groups of painted turtles like to bask on submerged logs or floating vegetation, slipping softly into the water at the least disturbance. Painted turtles have bright yellow streaks on either side of the head and red spots around the edge of their smooth dark shells.

The red-bellied turtle, *Pseudemys rubriventris*, is also common in Delmarva's coastal plain ponds. It is the only large basking turtle in its rather limited range; red-bellied turtles are only found on coastal plain New Jersey and the Chesapeake Bay region south to eastern North Carolina. Although much larger than the painted turtle, the red-bellied also likes to sun itself on logs. Its color and markings are very variable. Males have red stripes up the side of their shells, although some turtles are so dark, you must wet the shell to see them. The female's red markings are less defined, but both males and females have a wash of red or pink on the undershell or plastron.

Spotted turtles, *Clemmys guttata*, are small dark turtles with conspicuous yellow dots on their head and shells. They, too, like muddy, slow-moving water and are common in Delmarva's freshwater swamps and wet meadows.

All these turtles are harmless, gentle creatures. The snapping turtle, *Chelydra serpentina,* is anything but. Snapping turtles are common in all our freshwater wetlands, as well as in brackish river marshes. With its large head, too-small shell, and long saw-toothed tail, it looks like a prehistoric survivor from the age of the dinosaurs. Snapping turtles grow to enormous sizes: thirty-five pounds is not unusual for a mature adult. They are considered legal game on Delmarva.

Snapping turtles rarely bask like other turtles, but may be encountered in early summer when they travel overland in search of a place to lay their eggs. If you should meet one, give it a wide berth. A snapping turtle can snap like lightning in all directions, even over the back of its shell. Yet, while they have ferocious dispositions on land, they tend to be secretive underwater, burying themselves in the mud with only their eyes showing. As a rule, they eat fish, plants, carrion, and other reptiles but will also pull under and drown young ducklings or mammals if they get the chance.

Like the snapper, the eastern mud turtle, *Kinosternon subrubrum*, can also tolerate brackish water. Mud turtles are small (three to four inches long), smooth, and brown. Their heads are spotted or streaked with yellow. They can be distinguished from a stinkpot, *Sternotherus odoratus*, another small, mud-colored turtle, by the stinkpot's narrow, too-small plastron that provides scant protection for its underside. Stinkpots are bottom crawlers. They leisurely patrol the bottom of ponds and swamps in search of food. Their inelegant name refers to a musky secretion that is exuded from glandular openings on either side of the body. Stinkpots only leave the water to lay eggs, but they sometimes bask in shallow water with the top of their shells above the surface. They are the only musk turtles found outside the Deep South.

The bog turtle, formerly called the Muhlenberg bog turtle, *Clemmys muhlenbergi*, is one of the rarest reptiles in the eastern United States. Although officially listed as endangered, it can still be found in boggy, wet sedge meadows in northern Delaware, where a clear, slow-moving stream provides a constant supply of cool water. The bog turtle is small and secretive with a dark shell and a conspicuous orange blotch on either side of the head.

Frogs

Delmarva's freshwater wetlands are full of frogs. Even rare species are plentiful here. The low woodlands and flooded Delmarva Bays of Delaware's Blackbird State Forest provide such ideal frog living conditions that fourteen of the peninsula's sixteen species can be found in this one location.

Frogs are amphibians. The adults breathe oxygen and can hop about on dry land, yet they must mate and lay their eggs in the water. The tadpoles, of course, live entirely underwater, breathing through gills like a fish.

Every spring, choruses of male frogs serenade the females, and each species has its own unique song. Male frogs always substantially outnumber female frogs. The female lays hundreds of eggs (singly, in clumps, or in long strands, depending on the species) while the male clings to her back and fertilizes them as they are released. Each tiny egg will hatch into a tadpole from five to forty days later. Some species of tadpoles develop into adult frogs in a matter of weeks. Others take up to two years.

Many of our most familiar frogs belong to the family Ranidae, or true frogs. They include the bullfrog, the green frog, the southern leopard, and pickerel frogs. The carpenter frog is the rarest member of this group. The wood frog, mentioned in the section on woods, is also a Ranidae.

The bullfrog, *Rana catesbeiana*, is the largest and most well known Ranidae species. Bullfrogs are found in every freshwater habitat, on the peninsula and elsewhere, and their "jug-o-rum" breeding call is a familiar spring sound around ponds, swamps, and the sluggish portions of freshwater streams. Bullfrogs are the only amphibian considered a game species on Delmarva, where hunting for bullfrogs, called gigging, takes place between May and September.

The green frog, *Rana clamitans melanota*, is another abundant species. Green frogs are smaller than bullfrogs, but are found in the same habitats. A calling green frog sounds like the plucking of a loose banjo string.

Wetlands

The pickerel frog, *Rana palustris*, and the southern leopard frog, *R. sphenocephala*, are both green-brown frogs with conspicuous spots on their legs and back. The pickerel frog is common throughout the peninsula, but the southern leopard frog is found only on the coastal plain. Except in the breeding season, both these species may be found in open fields and meadows many yards from water.

The carpenter frog, *R. virgatipes*, is a southern species only found on the coastal plain between southern New Jersey and Georgia. It is known as the bog frog because it prefers the sphagnum wetlands of the peninsula's cypress swamps and Delmarva bays.

The treefrog family, Hylidae, has seven species on the peninsula, of which five are true treefrogs of the genus *Hyla*. They are the northern spring peeper, *H. c. crucifer*, the gray and the Cope's gray treefrogs, *H. versicolor* and *H. chrysoscelis*, and the green and the barking treefrogs, *H. cinerea* and *H. gratiosa*. Treefrogs are well adapted for living in bushes and trees. Their relatively long toes end in tiny adhesive discs that cling to twigs and bark.

While the musical trill of the spring peeper can be heard in nearly every damp lowland in early spring, the actual frog is secretive and rarely seen. Peepers are very small, only about an inch long, gray or olive-brown. A conspicuous X on their backs gives them their specific name, *crucifer*, which is Latin for cross. After the breeding season, peepers hide in brushy second-growth woods and feed on insects.

The gray and Cope's gray treefrogs are slightly larger than the spring peeper, about one and one-half inches, but the two species resemble each other so closely that few people can tell them apart. The call of the Cope's gray is said to be faster and shorter in duration, but it is a distinction only clear to the expert.

Gray treefrogs are plentiful in the Delmarva bays of Delaware's Blackbird State Forest where, every spring, the males sing from the bushes and trees a few inches above the water surface. At dusk on a May evening they look like tiny silver bumps in the light of a flashlight beam. Gray treefrogs are easily approached and, when picked up, cling to the hand with their tiny disc toes.

The peninsula's rarest frog, the barking treefrog, is also found in the Delmarva bays of Delaware's Blackbird State Forest and adjacent Maryland. Male barking treefrogs that are attempting to entice females to their breeding pond sound exactly like a distant pack of hounds. The male stimulates the female to lay eggs and then fertilizes them externally as they sink into the water. The eggs hatch quickly into tiny tadpoles and metamorphose into adult frogs in a matter of weeks.

Barking treefrogs are more than twice the size of the gray treefrog. They are a blotched green-brown color with a white line on the side of the body and

hind legs. Like other treefrogs, they climb into trees and bushes, but they also bury themselves in the mud in hot dry weather. They will blow themselves up like a small balloon if alarmed. Barking treefrogs seem to prefer temporary fishless ponds and moist woodlands. Until 1984, when they were unexpectedly found thriving in Blackbird State Forest, the nearest population was thought to be in Virginia, on the western shore of the Chesapeake Bay.

The green treefrog is another southern species that reaches the northern limit of its range on Delmarva. In the south, green treefrogs are called rain frogs because they sing loudest before a rainstorm. They also are found near the coast and are, in fact, one of the few frogs that can tolerate mildly brackish water. Because a frog's skin is porous, the osmotic pressure of salty water tends to draw out its vital body fluids.

Two non-arboreal frogs in the family Hylidae are the northern cricket frog and the New Jersey chorus frog.

Cricket frogs, *Acris crepitans*, are tiny little creatures, between half an inch to a little over an inch long, with a dark stripe on the thigh. Their loud call sounds like marbles hitting each other. They do not climb trees, but hide in the grass at the edge of the water.

Chorus frogs, like peepers, are often heard but almost never seen. They sing day and night in the cool days of early spring, especially when it rains, and sound rather like someone running a fingernail over the teeth of a pocket comb.

Wetlands

While chorus frogs require shallow bodies of water for breeding and for the development of tadpoles, they live in a wide variety of habitats at other times of the year, including farm fields. The New Jersey chorus frog, *Pseudacris triseriata kalmi*, is a geographical subspecies of the western chorus frog, *P. t. triseriata*. It is found only on the Atlantic coast from Staten Island to the southern tip of Delmarva.

The tiger salamander, *Ambystoma tigrinum*, is also an amphibian, as well as another unique species of the peninsula Delmarva bays. Tiger salamanders are about six inches long. They are fat, smooth, and mud-colored with scattered spots, and only breed in fishless ponds. The peninsula's Delmarva bays perfectly fill the bill and are the only place where these creatures can be found in abundance.

The Atlantic Coast

Beaches and Barrier Islands

These hillocks [of sand] . . . are continually shifting their position, moving ever inland and southward, destroying every thing in their way.

—Howard Pyle, 1879

A shifting land of salt air, sand, shells, and screaming gulls that is continually swept by the wind and shaped by the tide: this is Delmarva's Atlantic coast. It is a linear string of sandy spits and islands, backed by salt marshes and interrupted by shallow estuaries, that stretches all the way from Cape Henlopen, Delaware, to Cape Charles, Virginia.

These sandy beaches and islands are, in fact, only the most recently exposed edge of the continental shelf. The sea, as we have said, is rising. In geologic terms one could say it is advancing rapidly across the entire coastal plain. Immediately after the last Ice Age, about twenty thousand years ago, the rate of rise was about three feet per century, slowing to about six inches per century in the last eight to ten thousand years. It was this latter, more gradual rise that flooded the Chesapeake and Delaware estuaries and created Delmarva's coastal marshes.

Now the advance is picking up speed once again, possibly because the quantities of carbon dioxide that are released into the atmosphere by the burning of fossil fuels act to trap the sun's warmth and accelerate the melting of the ice caps—the so-called greenhouse effect. At the same time, the land is sinking due to the compaction of soft coastal sediments and a certain settling of the earth that geologists call tectonic subsidence.

If the melting continues unabated until the ice caps disappear, the sea will rise several feet and most of the peninsula will be underwater. It will not be the

157

first time; Delmarva has already been inundated about eight times in the past one and a half million years. In fact capes and barrier islands have changed dramatically in the relatively short time since the peninsula was settled. Between 1784, when the old Cape Henlopen Lighthouse was built, and 1926, when it fell into the sea during a storm, the cape lost as much as twelve feet a year to erosion. When the storm hit, the lighthouse, which had originally stood some 600 yards from the shoreline, had already been seriously undermined. A three-day northeaster hit the same area in 1960, exposing at the edge of the surf the remains of a pine forest that, three hundred years before, had stood on the back of a barrier island.

All beaches move in this way, continually shifted about by currents that run parallel to the shore, a phenomenon known as littoral drift. Grain by grain, these currents are capable of transporting thousands of tons of sand over the course of a single year.

Somewhere offshore of Ocean City, Maryland, the underwater topography causes these offshore currents to diverge. Above this point, they sweep the sand to the north and below it, to the south. This configuration has added about four miles of new land to the southern tip of Assateague, while removing it from Ocean City where some buildings now stand a mere fifty feet above the high tide line. Littoral currents also wash an average of two to three feet of sand off the beach at Rehoboth and Bethany every year and drop it into deep water off Cape Henlopen.

Barrier islands like Fenwick, Assateague, and those off the coast of the Eastern Shore of Virginia are all in a similar state of flux. Most of these islands are less that five thousand years old. Between eight and eleven thousand years ago, according to drill samples, the sea was well to the east of our present coastline, and marshes covered the area where the islands are now. Apparently, they were once part of an older, now submerged, lagoon and barrier system.

Until recently, barrier islands were thought to have originated as offshore sandbars. The sand, so the theory went, was first piled up by the surf and then gradually elongated by littoral drift. However, evidence like the buried pine forest at Cape Henlopen, combined with the ancient shells of estuarine mollusks that have been found buried in the marsh mud, have convinced geologists that these islands are in fact the tops of sand dunes that once lined the shore to the east. When the sea flooded into the lowlands surrounding the dunes, they became islands.

Viewed in cross section, a barrier island is shaped rather like a teardrop, short and round on the ocean side yet spread across the floor of a shallow lagoon on the landward side. This configuration is the result of rollover, a phenomenon that occurs when storm tides wash over and through the oceanfront dunes, sweeping the sand into the lagoon and depositing it in overwash fans. Rollovers enable a whole island to migrate, and thus to survive in an era of rising seas, by continually reshaping the dunes and creating new marshes and intertidal flats on the shoreward side. At the time it occurs, it seems as if the whole island is being destroyed, yet rollovers replenish ecosystems that would otherwise be drowned.

Varying currents and wave action result in different patterns of island migration. Among the barrier islands off the Eastern Shore of Virginia there are three such patterns. Those in the northernmost group, Assawoman, Metompkin, and Cedar, are gradually moving to the west in a course that is roughly parallel to the shore. Parramore, Hog, Cobb, and Wreck islands, on the other hand, are gradually rotating as sand is deposited at their northeastern tips and eroded from their southern ends. Littoral drift is also causing most of the islands in these two groups to shrink while those to their south, Myrtle, Ship, Shoal, Smith, and Fisherman islands are growing larger as southerly currents sweep sediment in their direction. Fisherman Island, the most southerly island of the chain, is also the youngest.

The changes can be dramatic indeed. Early in this century the town of Broadwater lay on the southern end of Hog Island. In the 1920s, faced with the inevitable inundation of their town, the citizens of Broadwater loaded many of their houses on barges and moved them to the mainland. The site where it stood is now under the sea somewhere to the east of the present island.

One can travel between ocean and sound, the whole distance to Chincoteague Inlet, finding habitation about once in a dozen miles.
—Bayard Taylor, 1871

Mankind has always been drawn by the sea. In 1865, Dr. Joseph Leidy, a professor of anatomy at the University of Pennsylvania Medical School, was sailing off Delaware's coast when he noticed what appeared to be enormous heaps of shells sparkling in the sun along the shore between Lewes and Henlopen. Closer inspection revealed the piles to be oyster and clam shells mixed with charcoal and ashes and interspersed with pottery fragments, clay pipes, jasper arrowheads, animal bones, and even fragments of human skeletons. These piles were, in fact, the peninsula's first landfills, the accumulation of thousands of years of trash generated by Indian fishing encampments.

Because none of the piles contained European artifacts, they are thought to pre-date European settlement. In fact, Delmarva's Atlantic shoreline was the last part of the peninsula to be settled. With the exception of twenty-five colonists who lived on Hog Island for a brief period in the 1670s, the coastal islands were used principally for grazing livestock. Some of these colonial herds subsequently gave rise to hardy feral populations. In the 1980s, a roundup staged by the Nature Conservancy on Hog Island netted sixty cows and two hundred sheep, all of which were moved to the mainland.

By the mid-nineteenth century, there were small, scattered villages on several of Virginia's islands, populated, for the most part, by the families of the men who tended the life-saving stations. Yet there were no houses within four or five miles of Rehoboth Beach until the 1870s, when the more accessible summer resorts along the shore of Delaware Bay became too polluted for swimming, and for the first time the railroads made it possible for vacationers to travel easily to the more distant ocean beaches of the peninsula.

By the 1890s, Virginia's islands had also become dotted with summer houses, hotels, and hunting lodges, as the railroad brought many of the nation's business and political leaders to shoot waterfowl and shorebirds. Most of the buildings on the islands were destroyed by a hurricane in 1933. Still, even coastal resort towns like Rehoboth Beach, Delaware, and Ocean City, Maryland, remained relatively small until the construction of the Chesapeake Bay and Delaware River bridges in the 1950s. Since that time, development has soared. Scores of vacation houses, condominiums, hotels, and marinas have been built, most with little thought of accommodating the natural dynamics of the coast.

By 1962, Assateague was undergoing the same type of development. Builders had paved access roads, installed electric lines, and sold thousands of house lots when a powerful northeaster slammed into the coast, blowing all of the development away. Congress, which had been studying the idea since 1935, finally became convinced that development was neither feasible nor desirable for the island and, in 1965, the Assateague National Seashore was born.

South of Assateague, the Nature Conservancy bought some 35,000 acres on the ocean side of the Eastern Shore of Virginia, including thirteen barrier islands, and a 1,400-acre tract on the mainland consisting of marshes, forests, and agricultural fields. Five more of these Virginia islands are also owned by state and federal agencies. As a result, Delmarva now has the largest area of unspoiled, protected barrier island coastline in the nation, stretching from Assateague to Cape Charles, Virginia.

Shall be likened unto a foolish man which built his house upon the sand: and the rain descended, and the floods came and the winds blew, and beat upon that house; and it fell: and great was the fall of it.
—Matthew 7:26-27

Overdevelopment, however, is a serious problem on other parts of the shoreline. Many popular Delmarva beaches must now be periodically replenished with sand trucked in from other parts of the peninsula and some have had temporary closings because of the presence of coliform bacteria in the water. Pollution also threatens the fish and shellfish populations in many of the small estuaries known as inland bays.

Quite apart from the inherent value of natural ecosystems, when over-building occurs on beaches and islands, the mainland's first line of defense against hurricanes is also destroyed. Left to its own devices, a sand dune can readily absorb the punch of 120-mile-per-hour winds and wind-driven storm surges. Hurricanes of this magnitude may be few and far between, but smaller destructive storms are frequent. Northeasters periodically slam into Del-marva's coast with enough force to undermine buildings, break power lines, and wash out roads and bridges. Even normal winter winds repeatedly cause damage to beachfront structures.

Virtually all of Delmarva's public beaches have been altered in a way that interferes with forces like littoral drift and the natural migration of barrier is-lands. Even seemingly innocuous structures like beach groins interrupt the nor-mal flow of sand by depriving beaches downstream from natural accumulation. During a storm, groins may cause the sand to disappear altogether, leaving only a thin ribbon of grit where the beach used to be.

Jetties can also have far-reaching effects. Before the 1933 hurricane, As-sateague Island was attached to the mainland at its northern end, part of forty-eight miles of continuous barrier beach. When the hurricane cut an inlet south of Ocean City, Maryland, dividing Fenwick Island from Assateague, it was decided to keep the channel open artificially by fortifying the banks of the inlet, to establish permanent access for boats into Assawoman and Sinepuxent bays. While this has provided recreation for hundreds of fishermen, it has also re-moved over a thousand feet of land from the northern end of Assateague.

To provide mooring and access for boats, stone jetties were built on either side of the Indian River Inlet. This stopped the periodic opening and closing of the channel by storm surges and littoral drift. The jetties provide permanent access to Rehoboth Bay, but have caused the strip of beach to the north to erode to the point where it must be continually and expensively replenished.

These conflicts are not easily solved. It is estimated that up to ninety thou-sand people now visit Rehoboth and Dewey beaches on a typical summer hol-iday weekend, and these are only two of Delmarva's popular coastal resort towns. While this represents a large slice of the area's economy, the number of visitors also poses a threat to the long-term health of the beaches and inland bays that they come to enjoy. There have already been fish kills and beach closings: nonpoint-source pollution represents a growing danger to the health of the inland bays. It seems clear that more and stricter controls will have to be imposed—controls that will ultimately affect everyone that visits, lives, or earns their living at the beach.

Some of these controls are already in place, and others are on the horizon. For instance, federal money is no longer available for the construction of roads, bridges, or sewers in coastal areas and, in 1987, several of Delmarva's more popular inland bays were accepted as part of the National Estuary Program, a federally funded program developed to help states improve troubled estuaries. A few states have even passed laws that restrict all building, as well as re-building, within a certain distance from the water. Although they may prove difficult to enforce politically, such laws are necessary to preserve the coastline from further degradation.

> *The beach . . . rises but a few feet above sea level. The sand, which is like velvet to the feet, has a gradual slope . . . the huge waves . . . subside rather than break violently.*
>
> *—Bayard Taylor, 1871*

Peninsula beaches, like others along the mid-Atlantic Coast, are what geologists call depositing shores. When laden river currents collide with ocean waves they lose their carrying power. The heavy quartz particles that make up sand are then dropped to mix with shell fragments on the beach while the silt, which consists of light clay particles and organic fragments, remains suspended and is carried offshore. The fine sand that gives Delmarva's beaches their soft velvet quality is due to the gradual slope of her beaches—the gentler the slope, the finer the grains of sand.

Once deposited on the beach, the sand is then constantly rearranged, not only by waves and currents, but also by the wind. A wind speed of more than fourteen feet per second stirs up a veil of swirling sand a few inches above the surface of the beach; any plant or piece of driftwood large enough to slow its speed will begin to collect sand on its lee side and may eventually build into a dune.

Undisturbed ocean beaches, such as those on Virginia's barrier islands, are usually broad, sandy plains that slope gently upward toward a wide, undulating rim of dunes. Behind these primary dunes is a line of older dunes, now covered with thickets and woods. Salt marshes rim the inland, bayside of the island. Brackish marshes, or even freshwater ponds, may occur in mid-island swales as rainwater seeping through the sandy soil forms a lens that floats on the salt water beneath the island.

All kinds of factors determine which plants and animals are found at the seashore—the distance from the sea, the nature of the soil, the amount of exposure, and the available food. Chance also plays a part since seeds, eggs, and larvae are carried from one beach to another by coastal currents.

Water moderates the temperature of the air, keeping beaches and barrier islands cooler in summer and warmer in winter than the adjacent mainland. There is less rain and snow, but fog is common and the humidity high. Salt spray, the invisible vapor that forms when air bubbles rise to the surface of the sea and burst, is pervasive, carried inland by onshore winds. Along with shifting sands, lack of shade, and the constant threat of storms and overwash, salt spray contributes to the harshness of the coastal environment for the organisms that live there.

Dunes

In some places the sand-hills were eighty feet high, covering every vestige of trees they have buried, except at the sloping sides, where the occasional skeleton top of some dead pine protrudes.

—*Howard Pyle, 1879*

The sun, reflecting off bare sand, can raise the temperature in a dune hollow as high as 150°F, and dry the sand to a depth not reached by most plant roots. The wind is constant, and, laden with salt spray and abrasive blowing sand, it buries plants on the leeward side of a dune while undercutting those to windward. Rain, washing through the porous dune, prevents much of the salt from accumulating, but it leaches most of the nutrients in the process.

In sum, a sand dune is one of the harshest environments on earth for plants. Dune grass, *Ammophila breviligulata*, is one of the few species able to thrive there. In fact, dune grass is uniquely fitted for life on a dune. It forms a mat of tangled roots called rhizomes a few inches below the surface, effectively binding the unstable sand. Every few feet along their length, penetrating roots descend into the dune and clumps of waving grass ascend to carpet the landward slope, growing over the crest to a point just beyond the reach of storm waves. Parallel ridges along the inner side of each blade of grass clamp together in hot, dry weather, reducing surface transpiration. A waxy coating on their surface also helps conserve moisture while the grass's inherent flexibility keeps it from breaking in the wind.

A healthy stand of grass stabilizes the dune, moderates the force of the wind, and cools the surface of the sand. The grass clumps may have to pierce through a yard of sand to the light. Being buried by blowing sand actually

163

stimulates their growth; dune grass declines on beaches that have been artificially stabilized.

Sea oats, *Uniola paniculata*, the primary dune binder on more southern beaches, also occurs in scattered locations on the Virginia barrier islands. Sea oats is a tall, picturesque plant that responds to burying by sending up rhizomes with new plants at the tips.

Once the dune has been stabilized, clumps of other grasses may appear, like the blue-green bitter panic grass, *Panicum amarum*, the graceful switch-grass, *Panicum virgatum*, or the prickly seeded sandbur, *Cenchrus tribuloides*.

Dune plants adapt to their environment in a variety of ways. Most have deep questing roots that range far beyond their tops. Others, like beach (false) heather, *Hudsonia tomentosa*, have needlelike leaves that hug the stems like scales. Still others are fat and succulent. The thick leaves of the seaside golden-rod, *Solidago sempervirens*, are as smooth and shiny as plastic, while the silvery leaves of the seabeach evening primrose, *Oenothera humifusa*, are covered with fine hairs to retard evaporation. Plants like the diminutive, low-growing seaside spurge, *Euphorbia polygonifolia*, hug the sand to avoid the wind. Others, like the prickly pear, store moisture in fat fleshy stems and turn their surfaces away from the midday sun. The prickly pear, *Opuntia compressa*, is a true cactus—it has no leaves. Photosynthesis takes place in the joints of the stems.

Dense stands of wax myrtle grow in the shrubby thickets on the back side of the dunes, interwoven with vines like trumpet-creeper, *Campsis radicans*, poison ivy, and greenbrier. Dry soil trees like red cedar are also common, but only a few barrier islands, notably Parramore, Revel's, and Smith, could be said to have true maritime forests. The trees there are mostly young loblolly pines, red maple, and black cherry, but there are also a few plants of the southern redbay, *Persea borbonia,* in low swales.

The woods on Smith Island also contain live oak, *Quercus virginiana*, at the northernmost edge of its range, for like so much else on the peninsula, Delmarva's islands south of Assateague are a transition zone between the north and the south. Besides sea oats, redbay, and live oak, a southern species of holly called yaupon occurs in thickets on Parramore, Revel's, and Smith Islands.

The beach . . . rises but a few feet above sea level.
                                                    —Bayard Taylor, 1871

Plants of the upper beach, between the face of the dune and the high tide line, must also be strong to survive. Some are succulents, like sandwort, *Arenaria peploides*, a plant that forms fat clumps of rubbery leaves, and sea kale, *Cakile edentula*, a succulent member of the mustard family. Others are prickly, like saltwort, *Salsola kali*, and beach clotburr, *Xanthium strumarium*.

This higher part of the beach is flooded only when storm surges come in beyond the normal high tide. The invading water swirls the sand into new patterns and litters the beach. Shells, crabs, fish, and the egg cases of whelks and skates collect in lines of dry seaweed, providing valuable shelter and breeding places for beach fleas.

Beach fleas, *Talorchestia* spp., are so named because they pop out of the wrack like fleas. They are actually segmented amphipods. The word amphipod means having feet on both sides. At night, beach fleas are attracted to light like moths. They spend the day buried in the sand above the high tide line, coming out only after dark to feed on decaying plants and animals.

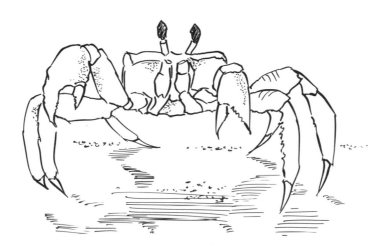

The large round holes that riddle the upper beach are the burrows of the ghost crab, *Ocypode quadrata*, a beach-dwelling cousin of the fiddler crab. Ghost crabs are well named. They seem to appear from nowhere, dash sideways across the beach, and vanish into their holes. Their light tan color makes them all but invisible against the sand. Ghost crabs are said to turn and face a full moon. They have large eyestalks, relatively thin shells and long hairy legs. They feed on beach fleas, springing on them like a cat, and dead fish. In turn, they are eaten by raccoons and occasionally by birds.

A ghost crab burrow descends vertically into the sand for up to three feet. Holes on the upper beach, near the toe of the foredune, are those of older crabs. The younger ones burrow just above the high tide line, apparently because they must wet their gills from time to time. Ghost crab larvae float in the water as part of the zooplankton. They are a southern species, found only as far north as Delaware Bay.

Bleached keyhole urchins, *Melitta quinquiesperforata*, tiny rainbow-colored coquinas, slipper shells, *Crepidula fornicata*, and jingle shells, *Anomia simplex*, also litter these beaches. Shells of both the knobbed and channeled whelks, *Busycon carica* and *B. canaliculatum*, are also common. So are their egg cases, strings of parchment-like pouches, usually empty, but sometimes containing perfect miniature whelks. With the exception of the coquinas, *Donax variabilis*, a species that burrows in the wet sand washed by waves, all these animals live below the low tide line.

The black devil's purse (or mermaid's purse) found in the wrack is the egg case of a skate, *Raja* spp. Skates are bizarre flat fish that "fly" through the water by flapping their winglike pectoral fins. Sand collars, too, are sometimes found on these beaches. They are smooth, perfectly rounded rings of sand that are the egg cases of moon snails, *Polinices duplicatus*. Moon snails are carnivorous, digging through the sand for clams and other bivalves which they kill by piercing the shell.

The Atlantic . . . growing gray in the sunset, rolled in, and broke in long, heavy, lazy swells.
— Bayard Taylor, 1871

While most marine animals live between the upper limit of the high tide and the underwater limit of light penetration, the lower limit for most crabs, shellfish, sea turtles, and horseshoe crabs is the depth to which waves affect the bottom.

Some marine species spend their whole life at one depth, while others migrate back and forth between deep and shallow water, and still others spend their early life in one habitat and the rest of their life in another. Because life near the beach is chancy at best, most have an extremely high rate of reproduction.

The animals that inhabit the turbulent swash zone between the tides must cope with turbulent water, shifting sands, and alternating submersion and exposure. One of the most numerous is the mole crab, *Emerita talpoida*. Unlike most crabs, mole crabs do not have pincers. In fact, they do not look much like crabs at all. Female mole crabs are inch-long, stout, ovoid creatures, with hairy antennae and tails that fold underneath their bodies. The males are about one-half their size. At high tide, large groups of these creatures advance and retreat with the waves, facing up the slope of the beach in order to trap tiny animals and organic matter from the backwash. As the tide ebbs, they burrow into the sand to wait for the next flood. Mole crabs are eaten by blue crabs, shorebirds, and fish.

166

The purple speckled lady crab, *Ovalipes ocellatus*, also dines on mole crabs. It pokes its large claw into the sand, runs in a circle and pulls up a mole crab like a cork out of a bottle. Despite their genteel name, lady crabs are fierce predators, as quick and ill-tempered as blue crabs. They inhabit shallow water, digging into the sand until only their eye stalks are exposed. They also are found in the saltiest parts of the Chesapeake and Delaware bays.

Sea spiders . . . are as large as turtles, have hard shells over themselves like turtles . . . they have many feet like crab feet, [they] have tails about an ell in length [shaped] like a tooth edged saw with which one can saw off the hardest wood. And when the wind lies from the sea into the mouth then large quantities of them are driven ashore.

—*Captain Thomas Yong, 1634*

One member of the benthos, or bottom dwelling animals, that is particularly at home along the coast of Delmarva is the horseshoe crab, *Limulus polyphemus*. Delaware Bay, in fact, has the largest concentration of them in the entire world. Once a year they are driven ashore in large quantities, not by a sea wind but by the urge to reproduce. In so doing, they render a valuable ecological service to a large segment of the world's shorebirds.

Horseshoe crabs, like blue crabs, are arthropods, but they are more closely related to spiders and scorpions than to crustaceans. They have book gills, made like the pages of a book, that closely resemble the book lungs of terrestrial arachnids, a fact that leads some scientists to theorize that both species are descended from a common ancestor. In any case, the horseshoe crab's resemblance to fossil trilobites tells us that he has scarcely changed in three million years.

An adult female horseshoe crab may be two feet long including her carapace and tail. The males are smaller and have appendages that look like boxing gloves, called pedipalps. They are designed to grasp the carapace of the female during mating.

Horseshoe crabs spend the winter buried in the mud at the bottom of Delmarva's bays and estuaries, where they dine on soft-shelled mollusks and worms. In March they begin to stir; one can imagine them pulled out of the mud by some ancient primordial urge. Then on a moonlit night in early May, millions of male horseshoe crabs appear on Delmarva's beaches. They come in on the extra high spring tide, and line the water's edge in a band up to twenty feet wide and one to two crabs deep, as many as ten thousand on one-half mile strip of beach. Then, as the tide turns, female crabs rise out of the water behind them. The males scramble after them waving their tails like sticks in the surf.

When a male attaches himself to a female, they inch up the beach together. The female digs a hole in the sand and lays her eggs while the male fertilizes them. They then cover the egg mass with sand and return to the water. That is, if they are lucky; many crabs are flipped by the surf and cannot right themselves. They die on the sand before they can be rescued by the next incoming tide.

Each female horseshoe crab lays up to eighty thousand transparent, olive-green eggs and buries them in clumps two to eight inches below the surface of the sand. At the height of the season, horseshoe crab eggs are all over the place. There may be as many as fifty nests per square yard of beach near the high tide line where converging waves pile them into small heaps.

The embryos develop rapidly and are ready to break free of the eggs by the next spring tide, just two weeks after they were laid. The tiny crabs then shed their shells several times during the first year, and about once a year thereafter. It takes them from nine to eleven years to fully mature and some live as long as fifteen years. When a horseshoe crab molts, the entire ventral margin of the shell splits open, allowing the animal in his new shell to wiggle free. Empty shells often wash up on the beach.

In the nineteenth and early twentieth centuries many tons of horseshoe crabs were collected on Delmarva during the spawning season for pig feed or to be ground up as fertilizer—so many that by the 1940s their numbers had seriously dwindled. Luckily, laws forbidding the taking of live crabs allowed populations to recover: the horseshoe crab has been around a long time.

> While the world-renowned "diamond-back" terrapin is reserved for the rich man's table, it is the poor man who catches and sells him at twelve and twenty-four dollars per dozen, and contents himself with the mud turtle and "snapper."

> [Oystermen take terrapin on a] calm morning . . . after a hard frost . . . provided ice has not formed on the river. One man paddles, while another stands at the bow armed with a pair of "terrapin-paws" (long handled tongs). As the boat moves slowly along the tongman peers into the water, which in such weather is clear enough for the bottom to be distinctly visible at . . . seven or eight feet. A little swell in the soft mud catches his eye, and the paws are plunged down and closed upon a terrapin.
> —Robert Wilson, 1876

In the first days of settlement, diamondbacks, *Malaclemys t. terrapin*, were so plentiful on the peninsula they were an annoyance to fishermen and so cheap they were fed to slaves. In fact, slaves grew so tired of eating terrapin meat that in 1797 an ordinance was issued that prevented owners or masters from giving it to them more than three times a week.

By 1900, however, terrapin had become so scarce that they were selling for about seven dollars an inch of shell. Only changing fads and protective legislation saved them from being hunted to extinction. Terrapin are still caught on the peninsula by proggers who use baited traps or walk the black mud of stream banks at ebb tide looking for tell-tale air bubbles.

Diamondbacks are saltwater reptiles of coastal marshes and barrier islands. They have concentric grooves and ridges on their shells and flecked or spotted heads and legs. The females are nearly twice the size of the males, about eight inches for her to five inches for him.

The diamondback eats a fastidious diet of fresh snails, crabs, worms, and the occasional green plant. Any pollution in the water will cause it to disappear. The female lays her eggs in the warm sand above the high tide line in May or June, digging a hole with her hind feet. At that time, her tracks are clearly visible crossing the sandy beach in a wavering line. After ninety days, if the eggs have not been eaten by skunks or raccoons, tiny turtles with shells only a little more than an inch long emerge, leaving the empty shells scattered on the sand like shriveled pieces of old rubber.

The Atlantic loggerhead turtle, *Caretta caretta*, is a true seagoing turtle that normally only nests as far north as the Outer Banks of North Carolina. They, too, lay their eggs in the sand, a fact that has put them on the endangered list in this era of widespread beach development. Dead loggerheads occasionally wash up on Delmarva's barrier beaches, however, and it is hoped that they will eventually breed on our protected barrier islands. With this in mind, officials at the Chincoteague National Wildlife Refuge are transplanting eggs in an effort to coax them to extend their breeding range north.

Birds of the Beach and Coastal Islands

Also the snipe and Curloe, and that in great numbers.
— *William Penn, 1683*

In one of those elegant relationships common in nature, just as the horseshoe crabs are strewing their eggs over Delmarva's beaches, huge flocks of migrating shorebirds arrive for a few weeks of food and rest on their way to their nesting grounds in the Arctic. They fly in from Brazil, Patagonia, and Tierra del Fuego, from the beaches off Chile and Peru, and from mud flats in Suriname, Venezuela, and Guyanas. By early May, when the horseshoe crabs are at the height of their breeding season, literally millions of these birds crowd onto the peninsula's sandy rim, especially along the beaches of lower Delaware Bay where up to a hundred thousand birds may collect on a strip of beach only a few hundred yards long.

The principal spring flocks on Delmarva, in order of abundance, consist of semipalmated sandpipers, *Calidris pusilla*, red knots, *C. canutus*, ruddy turnstones, *Arenaria interpres*, and sanderlings, *Calidris alba*. There are also shortbilled dowitchers, *Limnodromus griseus*, dunlins, *Calidris alpina*, and various others, such as whimbrels, *Numenius phaeopus*, least and white-rumped sandpipers, *Calidris minutilla* and *C. fuscicollis*, semipalmated plovers, *Charadrius semipalmatus*, black-bellied plovers, *Pluvialis squatarola*, and willets, *Cataoptrophorus semipalmatus*. The birds descend in a frenzied crowd, squabbling among themselves as they probe beneath the sand or pluck floating eggs out of the surf. At dusk they leave the beaches to rest in coastal salt marshes. Oddly, those in Delaware Bay fly across New Jersey to the sea, apparently not satisfied with the marshes that line the lower estuary.

By the time they arrive on Delmarva, the birds have completed roughly half their journey. Each has also lost about one-half its body weight. It has been estimated that a red knot must eat one horseshoe crab egg every five seconds, twenty-four hours a day for two weeks, in order to gain back enough weight to continue its flight to the Arctic. Delaware Bay, with its huge population of breeding horseshoe crabs, is the only place where they can do this, and the lower bay is the largest spring staging area for shorebirds in all of eastern North America. In recognition of this fact, Delaware and New Jersey have recently made these beaches part of an international Shorebird Reserve Network. It is sobering to think that an oil spill in the wrong place at the wrong time could wipe out as much as 80 percent of the entire world population of some of these species.

The birds must leave by the end of May in order to reach their destination in time to breed and successfully raise their young in the brief Arctic summer. Only the willet stays behind, the only coastal sandpiper to nest on Delmarva. By June, its plaintive cry of "pull will willet" can be heard over the peninsula's coastal marshes and dunes as courting birds drop in and out of the grass and flash their black and white wing patches. Oddly enough, willet mothers leave both their mates and offspring a mere two to three weeks after the young birds hatch, leaving the male to attend the brood for two more weeks before he, too, flies off to his wintering grounds. The young birds must then follow on their own.

By mid-summer, other species of shorebirds again begin to appear on our beaches, this time on their way south. Whimbrels arrive around the middle of July and are soon followed by groups of red knots (called robin snipe on the islands), dunlins, and others. They do not come in huge numbers as they do in spring, but singly or in small flocks. By August, returning sanderlings are dashing about the beach like mechanical toys, probing the sand for mole crabs, beach fleas, and flies, while semipalmated sandpipers run up and down in the swash zone and black-bellied plovers and ruddy turnstones search for beach fleas in the driftline.

> With the exception of a few species . . . every gull and tern common to the Atlantic coast may be seen.
> —Robert Wilson, 1876

In addition to the periodic visits of the shorebirds, the strategic geographic location of Delmarva's undeveloped coastal islands also attracts nesting colonies of nearly every species of bird that breeds along the East Coast of the United States.

At first glance, these sandy or marshy islands, some of which lie only inches above high water, do not seem an ideal place to raise a family, yet it is their very lack of diversity, as well as their isolation, that makes them so attractive to birds. Islands lack the predatory snakes, foxes, or raccoons of more diverse and accessible locations, although they do pose other problems. An early season storm can inundate an island and wipe out an entire nesting colony. Voracious fish crows and gulls attack both the eggs and young of many birds and, even in the best of times, eggs laid on a hot, sandy beach or a pile of shells will soon cook if left unprotected.

The most numerous of the beach nesters on these islands is the black skimmer, *Rynchops niger*, surely one of the most distinctive birds found along the East Coast. This slim, graceful, black and white bird flies just above the water, breaking the surface with its lower mandible and snapping it shut the moment the bird feels the pressure of a fish. The bill is red with a black tip; the lower mandible, which is a third longer than the upper one, has a flexible hinge that allows it to spring open without injury if the bird encounters an obstacle in the water.

On Virginia's barrier islands, colonies of these "flood tide birds" often mingle with those of the common tern. The young skimmers, whose white color blends with the sand, hide from predators by scratching themselves into a hole and kicking sand over their backs. They are fed by their parents until their lower mandibles elongate enough to allow them to fish for themselves.

Seven species of terns are found on these islands. Most also nest here, depositing their eggs in a simple scrape on the beach or atop a pile of oyster shells in the marsh. Our largest tern, the Caspian, *Sterna caspia*, however, rarely breeds here, usually occurring only as a migrant. A Caspian tern is almost as large as a herring gull and has a stout red bill.

The royal tern, *S. maxima*, is only slightly smaller, and far more numerous: up to ten thousand nest on Delmarva's coastal islands. Royal terns congregate in dense colonies on the upper beach, each female laying her eggs just far enough from her neighbor so the incubating birds do not touch. After hatching, royal tern chicks travel about in a tight group called a creche. It is a mystery how the adult bird recognizes its own offspring, yet it is common to see a royal tern hover briefly over a colony before dropping in to feed its own chicks. The peninsula is as far north as the royal tern nests. The birds winter in Florida, the Bahamas, Cuba, and Costa Rica.

The common tern, *S. hirundo,* the sandwich tern, *S. sandvicensis*, and the diminutive little tern, *S. albifrons*, also nest on the beach. Nesting sandwich terns are found in small groups among the colonies of royals. In fact, the two species are so closely allied that it is rare to find one without the other. The sandwich tern is considerably smaller, however, and has a black bill with a yellow tip as opposed to the royal's large orange bill. Like all terns, both species have a short black crest on the back of the head and a white forehead for much of the year.

Beyond the breakers, a common tern plunges headfirst into the water, sinking well below the surface before reappearing with its catch. It is chasing quick silvery schools of fry and small fish like the pipefish, *Syngnathus fuscus*, or the American sand lance, *Ammodytes americanus*. A large flock of hovering terns usually means these fish are being chased to the surface by marauding bluefish. Common terns are not as common as they once were. Much of their beach habitat has been lost to development and their nesting colonies are often preyed upon by herring gulls.

The situation for the little tern is even worse. Little terns, formally called least terns, are our smallest species of tern, slightly larger than a swallow. There are still thought to be several thousand little terns nesting on Virginia's barrier islands, but their numbers have precipitously declined elsewhere on the peninsula and along much of the East Coast. These graceful little birds, who were once killed by the hundred thousands and stuffed to decorate women's hats, are now threatened by beach goers, dogs, and ORVs.

Each female little tern lays two eggs in a shallow depression in the sand, not far above the line of the highest tide. On hot summer days, it is common to see an incubating bird leave its nest, plunge into the water and return to shake water onto its eggs. The trouble is, if something happens to their clutch, little terns do not re-nest like other birds. They also tend to return to the same area year after year despite encroaching development. However, they can be lured by decoys to new nesting sites and will also use dredge spoil sites—two hopeful signs for the future.

The Forster's tern, *Sterna forsteri*, is a medium-sized species that looks much like the common tern. Both species have a black tip to their orange bills, but the Forster's tern is a slightly larger, lighter-colored bird, with white wing tips. Both the Forster's and the larger gull-billed tern, *Gelochelidon nilotica*, nest on piles of oyster shells in the marsh.

> *The nest . . . of the Willet [is] on the ground beneath an overshadowing knot of grass, the gull's upon a few sticks or drift, open to the air.*
> —*Howard Pyle, 1879*

Gulls thrive on human garbage. Until recently, only the laughing gull, *Larus atricilla*, nested on Delmarva; the ring-billed gull, *L. delawarensis*, the herring gull, *L. argentatus*, and the greater black-backed gull, *L. marinus*, were here only in winter. While this is still true of the ring-billed gull, our landfills have caused populations of herring and greater black-backed gulls to explode to the point that they now nest on grassy offshore islands and salt marshes far to the south of their former range.

Herring and greater black-backed gulls usually fish just beyond the line of breakers or forage in the swash zone of the beach. In spring, they follow farm tractors across newly plowed fields picking up worms and grubs. These birds are also scavengers, picking up dead animals and birds, as well as aggressive predators that regularly steal the eggs and young of other birds.

The laughing gull is both smaller and slightly better mannered. It feeds principally on marine invertebrates and fish, and less often on seabird eggs and chicks. Adult laughing gulls have conspicuous black heads and slim wings with black tips. They nest in the cordgrass at the edge of tidal guts.

Two plovers, the piping plover, *Charadrius melodus*, and the Wilson's plover, *C. wilsonia,* also nest on Delmarva's beaches. The piping plover, which is now officially listed as an endangered species, is a gentle bird, as pale as a ghost crab, with a plaintive flutelike whistle. It lays its eggs in a hollow in the sand that is rimmed with bits of broken shells. Piping plovers are not colony nesters: each brooding female sits more than a hundred feet from her neighbor. Banding studies have shown that the birds tend to keep the same mate and return to the same beach every year, a habit that has threatened their survival in the face of intensive beach development.

The Wilson's plover is a southern bird, larger than the more common migrant, the semipalmated plover, with a heavy black bill and a wide neck band. Because it, too, breeds on East Coast beaches, it also has suffered from widespread development. While both these plovers have found a safe haven on Delmarva's protected barrier islands, their numbers are now so alarmingly small that it will take a strong effort to protect nesting habitats along the entire Atlantic seaboard to save them.

One of our most endearing beach nesters is the American oystercatcher, *Haematopus palliatus*, a thick-set black-headed bird with a long, heavy, red-orange bill and bright orange eyes. Oystercatchers, with their noisy habits and bobbing manner of walking, resemble children's pull-toys. Their tough bills are used to pry open or break the shells of bivalves, particularly ribbed mussels and oysters. They often tear these shellfish loose from their beds and carry them home to a cache before consuming them.

Studies have shown that individual oystercatchers use one of two learned techniques to break the bivalves open: they hammer or they stab. A stabber waits until the mussel has opened its shell slightly to feed and thrusts its bill into the gap, breaking the adductor muscle. A hammerer, on the other hand, loosens the mussel from its moorings and inflicts rapid well-directed blows until the shell breaks. If the bird breaks its own bill in the process, he can grow a new one in two to three weeks.

Young oystercatchers learn one of these two techniques from their parents. Until they do, they exist on marine worms and crabs, which they also consume by hammering on the underside of the shell.

Oystercatchers are adaptable birds. If nesting sites are unavailable on the beach, they use piles of shells in the marsh. They are also expanding their range to the north and are now found on Cape Cod. Both their eggs and young are extremely well camouflaged. Young oystercatchers hide from intruders by flattening themselves against the sand.

A few of Delmarva's more southern islands also support the stick nests of the brown pelican, *Pelecanus occidentalis,* in thickets of wax myrtle and cedar. Pelicans are awkward, comical birds, with large bills and pouches that quiver in hot weather like a fat man's wattles. The pouch acts like a fishnet. As the bird surfaces from a dive it first dips its bill to drain the water out before raising it skyward and swallowing the fish. Like the royal terns, young brown pelicans also travel about in a tight group called a creche.

In the 1960s, pesticides and the widespread loss of their nesting habitats nearly caused these birds to disappear altogether from the East Coast. By 1970, there was only one viable population left and it was in Florida. Since DDT was banned, however, they have recovered fairly well, although they will continue to need protected nesting sites.

Fish crows, *Corvus ossifragus,* also nest in trees along the coast and scavenge for food on Delmarva's beaches and barrier islands. Fish crows are slightly smaller than the common crow of inland fields, but the difference is so small that they would be virtually indistinguishable if it weren't for their voice; a nasal "ca" instead of the raucous "caw" of the common crow. Fish crows eat marine invertebrates, berries, and seeds. They also prey on the eggs of herons, gulls, and terns, and will even eat young birds if they can get them.

The boat-tailed grackle, *Quiscalus major,* is another large black bird of Delmarva's beaches and islands. The male is an iridescent black color with a conspicuous long tail. The female is both browner and smaller. Boat-tailed grackles nest in coastal salt marshes south of New Jersey, where they often mingle with egrets and snow geese. They wade into shallow water to spear fish like a heron and are also one of the few birds that eat toads.

Nighthawks, *Chordeiles minor,* and horned larks, *Eremophila alpestris,* both nest on Delmarva's coastal sand dunes as well as in inland fields. The horned lark lines a shallow depression in the sand with roots and grass, but the nighthawk simply deposits its eggs beneath a clump of sheltering dune grass. Both species will perform distraction displays if threatened.

Waders

There are . . . herons, cranes, etc.

—Captain Thomas Yong, 1634

As it requires about four birds to make an ounce of plumes [for the millinery trade] these sales meant 193,960 herons killed at their nests, and from two to three times that number of young or eggs destroyed. Is it, then, any wonder that these species are on the verge of extinction?

—Herbert Job, 1903

The peninsula's heronries are surely among its most unique natural features. On certain uninhabited islands, or at the edge of a remote marsh, hundreds of nesting pairs of great blue, little blue, and tricolored (Louisiana) herons, black-crowned and yellow-crowned night herons, snowy, great, and cattle egrets, and glossy ibis come together in large noisy gatherings every spring. There are mixed species heronries on Virginia's Atlantic barrier islands, and in Tangier Sound in the lower Chesapeake, yet one of the largest colonies on the entire East Coast is on Pea Patch Island in Delaware Bay.

The Pea Patch Island heronry, which can be observed through binoculars from a public overlook, is on fill that was dredged from the shipping channel early in this century and dumped on the north end of the island. The nests number in the thousands. They are, for the most part, flimsy platforms of sticks, lodged in the crotch of a tree or balanced on top of a dense shrub, with as many as twelve nests in a single tree. The female does all the nest building while the male bird brings her sticks, although both sexes help incubate the eggs.

With the exception of the great blue heron, *Ardea herodias*, which also has its own heronries, most large wading birds only breed in these mixed colonies. To avoid competition for sites, each species keeps to a particular level. The great blue herons build large twiggy nests at the tops of the highest trees, among the slightly less bulky constructions of the great egret, *Casmerodius albus*, while the nests of the other seven species cluster beneath, about twelve feet off the ground or below. Birds of a similar size seem to mingle together, like the great blue heron and the great egret, or the little blue heron, *Florida caerulea*, and the snowy egret, *Egretta thula*.

At the end of the breeding season, the birds leave the colony and spend the rest of the summer feeding in marshes and swamps all over the peninsula, including, as in the case of the great blue heron, farm ponds some distance from the coast. Some great blues spend the winter here as well, although many also go with the other heron species to Central and South America.

Heronries are busy, smelly places. The parent birds fly in and out continuously while the stench of guano and regurgitated fish permeates the air. Many of the nesting trees seem to be dying, apparently because of the accumulated guano which increases the alkalinity of the soil, and dead nestlings occasionally litter the ground. Perhaps they fell from the nest or were killed by a marauding fish crow, raccoon, starling, owl, or gull, all of which prey on the eggs and young. In 1976 the heronry at Pea Patch Island was also attacked by a nematode infection transmitted through a small fish called the mummichog. Only the cattle egrets, who do not feed on fish, escaped.

Partly because of this setback, cattle egrets, *Bubulcus ibis*, are now the most abundant species nesting at Pea Patch Island. Cattle egrets are small, stocky white birds, with bright orange bills and legs, and buff plumes during the breeding season. They are a relatively recent import to this country. Flocks of cattle egrets came to South America from Africa at the end of the last century, and spread northward into the United States in the 1940s and 1950s. They are now a common sight in Delmarva's fields, where they follow farm tractors or feed among herds of grazing cattle.

Herons and egrets have long legs that are well suited for wading in shallow water and their long necks and sharp bills are formidable weapons for spearing the fish, frogs, and aquatic insects on which they feed. The birds preen periodically to keep their feathers clean and waterproof, using a secretion from oil glands and a waxy substance from certain patches of feathers known as powder down.

Next to the cattle egrets, the great blue heron is our most familiar heron. It is a tall greyish-blue bird that waits motionless in shallow water for a passing fish. The great blue's long flexible neck has unequal length vertebrae, a fact which apparently allows the bird to strike with lightning speed.

Little blue herons are also slate blue, but they are only about half the size of the great blue and lack the latter's dark crest. Immature little blues are white, causing them to be easily confused with the snowy egret. Snowy egrets have "golden slippers," however, conspicuous yellow feet that are obvious when the bird walks or flies. A snowy egret feeds by stirring up the water with his foot to flush out tiny shrimp and aquatic insects. They grow handsome plumes in the breeding season, and were once a prime target of the millinery trade.

The Louisiana heron, *Egretta tricolor*, walks through the marsh using his feet to flush out aquatic organisms from the mud. Tricolored herons sometimes raise one wing and peer beneath it, then turn and raise the other. It is not clear why they do this; perhaps the shadow attracts prey or perhaps it just helps the bird to see into the water.

We also have two species of night herons: the black-crowned, *Nycticorax nycticorix,* and the yellow-crowned, *Nyctanassa violacea*. Night herons are squat, relatively short-legged birds that stand hunched in the marsh for most of the day and do their feeding at night. Of these, the black-crowned is the most numerous and the most gregarious, although the yellow-crowned seems to be on the increase in many of Delmarva's nesting colonies. The black-crowned night heron also has the most northerly range of all the birds in Delmarva's heronries.

The glossy ibis, *Plegadis falcinellus,* nests among the herons but is a member of a different family. Herons, night herons, and egrets, as well as the bitterns, all belong to the family Ardeidae whereas ibis are in the family Threskiornithidae with the tropical spoonbills. They are dark brown birds with long decurved bills that fly with their neck extended instead of tucked into an S position.

The crow-sized green heron, *Butorides striatus*, is also common on Delmarva. It does not breed in heronries, but nests by itself in the wooded edges of ponds and marshes. It is a small, stout, dark bird with conspicuous orange legs in the breeding season. It hides in the emergent vegetation, craning its neck and peering into the shallows for aquatic invertebrates and fish. If alarmed, green herons fly up with a loud squawk.

Mammals of the Beach and Barrier Islands

This is the breeding-place of a race of ponies, which run wild, feeding on the strong beach grass.
— Bayard Taylor, 1871

Many of Delmarva's mammals are as much at home on barrier beaches and islands as in more inland habitats. Deer readily swim from island to island and marshy guts and creeks near the beach provide plenty to eat for the raccoon, muskrat, and rice rat. Even the elusive river otter and mink are occasionally found on the larger Virginia islands. There are probably as many meadow voles on grassy islands as in fields. Bats, too, have been observed and probably nest in the trees on larger islands, although there is little information about them. Assateague has Delmarva fox squirrels and opossums, as well as such human imports as house mice and Norway rats.

Island animals must have swum across a channel at low tide or serendipitously hitched a ride on a boat or floating debris, so it is not surprising that shrews or moles have not been recorded, and reluctant swimmers like rabbits, squirrels, and foxes are rare.

Harbor seals, *Phoca vitulina*, are seen off Delmarva's beaches and islands in winter and bottlenose dolphins, *Tursiops truncatus*, often congregate off Smith Island, Virginia, in April and May. They are occasionally seen offshore in summer as well. There have also been strandings of the Atlantic white-sided dolphin, *Lagenorhyncus acutus,* and the grampus dolphin, *Grampus griseus*, on Assateague Island, and saddleback dolphins, *Delphinus delphis*, have come ashore on Cobb and Parramore islands.

Whales, too, occasionally strand themselves on Delmarva's beaches. Pilot whales, *Globicephala melaena*, here at the southern limit of its range, have been found on Parramore and Smith islands. A short-finned pilot whale, *G. macrorhyncha*, has also come ashore on Parramore, and finback whales, *Balaenoptera physalus*, and goosebeak whales, *Ziphius cavrostris,* have been reported on Cedar and Cobb. Judging from strandings to the north and south of Delmarva, various other species are probably off our shores as well.

Delmarva's most famous island mammals, however, are not natives at all. They are the diminutive Japanese sika deer, *Cenus nippon*, and the wild ponies of Assateague. The delicate, tame sika deer that wander the edge of the road and lurk in thickets of greenbrier are favorites of tourists. They were originally released on the island in the 1920s and are more closely related to elk than to our native white-tailed deer.

Some say the wild ponies are descended from horses that escaped from a Spanish ship that was wrecked off Pope's Island just north of the Maryland line. Others say the vessel was wrecked on the south end of the island and the crew rescued by the Indians. Still others claim the ponies were put ashore by pirates while cynics claim they are merely descendents of colonial livestock.

The most detailed account of the shipwreck I have ever read is the tale of a Cuban navigator named Pedro Murphy who told a Spanish tribunal in 1821 that he was the only human survivor of the wreck of the armed merchantman *San Lorenzo*. He said the ship, which was bound for Spain in the early 1800s with a cargo of gold and silver from Peru, ran aground on Assateague after breaking up in a gale. Also on board were one hundred small draft horses that had been used by the Spaniards in Panamanian mines. The horses, bred to be small in order to work in mine tunnels, had been blinded by the Spaniards to make them easier to handle underground. The mines had been shut down after conflicts with Indian rebels and the horses were being returned to Spain.

According to the navigator's story, he and a companion and some of the blind horses escaped through the surf to the island. His companion died, but Don Pedro was eventually rescued by fishermen and made his way to Philadelphia where he boarded another ship to Spain. This story is from *Abercrombie: Walks and Rambles on Delmarva Peninsula*. In corroboration of this story is an 1826 report of an American fishing rights commissioner that mentions finding 45 tiny horses, some of which were blind.

If the tale is true, the Spanish ponies undoubtedly bred with horses already on the island, for we know that Assateague, as well as other coastal islands, was used for grazing livestock by farmers wishing to avoid mainland taxes and fencing requirements. In 1691, free-roaming horses were so plentiful that Maryland passed a law forbidding the import of any more, claiming that the free-roaming animals were destroying farm crops. Wild horses were also said to be hunted with dogs for sport on the lower peninsula.

Whatever their origin, the ponies wander the island in small herds consisting of a stallion, four or five mares, and their foals. While they have become used to visitors, they are quite wild, subsisting on marsh and dune grasses and water from the island's freshwater impoundments and natural ponds. A fence separates the Maryland ponies, which are managed by the National Park Service, from the Virginia herd, which is managed by the Chincoteague Volunteer Fire Company. Each year, the Virginia ponies are rounded up and some of the foals sold at the Pony Penning and Auction that takes place at Chincoteague on the last Wednesday and Thursday in July.

Epilogue

"Captain Hooper, when were you last on the old Peninsula?"
"Never, Madame, since I left it thirty-five years ago." "Why, sir,
from your frequent mention of the place, I should think you would
want to slip over there at lest once every session of Congress."
"Never, Madame! I never wish to see it again; for I might be
disappointed. I always want to remember it as it appeared to me
last in the days of my youth: the most beautiful spot under the
eyes of Providence."
—George Alfred Townsend, 1872

We live in a troubled century, a time when the entire natural world seems doomed, spinning ever closer to destruction by global forces beyond our control. We are all afraid to return to the lands of our youth, lest we, too, are disappointed.

Yet, at the same time, we now know what must be done to protect vital natural resources, so they can be used in a way that sustains the complex interactions of ecological communities. Surely, if each of us works to preserve, protect, and restore what we can, Delmarva's magnificent woods, marshes, and estuaries, with all their rich beauty and abundant life, can once again prevail.

Nature Areas Open to the Public

Abbott's Mill Nature Center—Milford, DE

Ashland Nature Center—off Route 82 near Wilmington, DE

Brandywine Creek State Park—near Rockland, DE

Bellevue State Park—Carr Road, off Route 95, near Wilmington, DE

Walter S. Carpenter State Park—near Newark, DE

Elk Neck State Park—near Elkton, MD

Iron Hill—near Newark, DE

Pea Patch Island—off Delaware City, DE

Lums Pond State Park—near Kirkwood, DE

Chesapeake and Delaware Canal—near St. Georges, DE

Eastern Neck Island National Wildlife Refuge—near Rock Hall, MD

Tuckahoe State Park—near Denton, MD

Martinak State Park—near Denton, MD

Idylwild Wildlife Management Area—near Federalsburg, MD

Seth Demonstration Forest—near Easton, MD

Redden State Forest—near Georgetown, DE

Trap Pond State Park—near Laurel, DE

Blackwater National Wildlife Refuge—near Cambridge, MD

Wicomico State Forest—near Salisbury, MD

Pocomoke State Forest—near Snow Hill, MD

Janes Island State Park—near Princess Anne, MD

Blackbird State Forest—near Blackbird, DE

Bombay Hook National Wildlife Refuge—near Smyrna, DE

Norman G. Wilder Wildlife Area—Canterbury, near Dover, DE

Killen Pond State Park—near Felton, DE

Prime Hook National Wildlife Refuge—near Milton, DE

Cape Henlopen State Park—near Lewes, DE

Delaware Seashore State Park—near Rehoboth Beach, DE

Between Ocean and Bay

Fenwick Island State Park—near Bethany Beach, DE
Fishermans Island National Wildlife Refuge—near tip of peninsula
Chincoteague National Wildlife Refuge, Chincoteague, VA
Assateague Island National Seashore—near Berlin, MD

Nature tours are also available through:

Abbott's Mill, R. D. 4, Box 207, Milford, DE 19963
The Chesapeake Bay Foundation, 162 Prince George St., Annapolis, MD
    21401
The Delaware Nature Society, Ashland Nature Center, Hockessin, DE 19707
The Nature Conservancy,
    Virginia Coast Reserve, Brownsville, Nassawaddox, VA 23413
    Delaware Field Office, P. O. Box 1324, Dover, DE 19903
The Society of Natural History of Delaware, Delaware State College,
    Dover, DE 19901-2275

Bibliography

Abercrombie, Jay. *Walks and Rambles on the Delmarva Peninsula: A Guide for Hikers and Naturalists.* Woodstock: Backcountry Publications, 1985.

Amos, William H. "Exploring the Bottom of Delaware Bay." *Delaware Conservationist* Summer 1957.

Amos, William H., and Amos, Stephen H. *Atlantic and Gulf Coasts.* New York: Knopf, 1985.

Baird, Donald, and Galton, Peter M. "Pterosaur Bones from the Upper Cretaceous of Delaware." *Journal of Vertebrate Paleontology* 1 (June 1981): 67-71.

Biggs, R. B., Sharp, J. H., Church, T. M., and Tramontiano, J. M. "Optical Properties, Suspended Sediments and Chemistry Associated with Turbidity Maxima of the Delaware Estuary." *Canadian Journal of Fisheries and Aquatic Sciences* 40, supp. 1 (1983): 172-179.

Burger, George. "Agriculture and Wildlife," in Brokaw, Howard P., ed. *Wildlife and America.* Washington: Council of Environmental Quality, 1978.

Burt, William, H. *A Field Guide to the Mammals.* 3rd ed. Boston: Houghton Mifflin, 1976.

Brown, Lauren. *Grasses: An Identification Guide.* Boston: Houghton Mifflin, 1979.

Carter, Jane Lewis. "The Down River People of the Lenni-Lenape Indians." Reprint from *Edmont, The Story of a Township.* Kennett Square, Pa.: KNA, 1976.

Chambers, Kenneth, A. *A Country-Lover's Guide to Wildlife.* Baltimore: Johns Hopkins U P, 1979.

Cole, Gerald L. "History of Agricultural Exportation from Delaware." *Transactions of the Delaware Academy of Science* 2 (1971): 149-156.

Conant, Roger. *Reptiles and Amphibians of Eastern and Central North America.* Boston: Houghton Mifflin, 1958.

Cronon, William. *Changes in the Land: Indians, Colonists, and the Ecology of New England.* New York: Hill and Wang, 1983.

Custer, Jay F. "Cultural Diversity in the Middle Atlantic." *Woodland Cultures.* Newark: U of Delaware P, 1986.

———. *Delaware Prehistoric Archaeology.* Newark: U of Delaware P, 1984.

Custer, Jay F., and Griffith, Daniel R. "Late Woodland Cultures of the Middle and Lower Delmarva Peninsula." *Late Woodland Cultures of the Middle Atlantic Region.* Newark: U of Delaware P, 1986.

"Delaware: Its Rocks, Minerals and Fossils." Delaware Geological Survey. U of Delaware, May 1980.

Dennis, John V. "The Bald Cypress in the Chesapeake Bay Region." *Atlantic Naturalist.* 36 (1986): 5-7.

Eckholm, Eric. "Slight Bird Sets Flight Record." *New York Times,* 2 Sept. 1987.

Ehrlich, Paul R., Dobkin, David S., and Wheye, Darryl. *The Birder's Handbook: A Field Guide to the Natural History of North American Birds.* New York: Simon & Schuster, 1988.

Elias, Thomas. *Complete Trees of North America: Field Guide and Natural History.* New York: Crown Publishers, 1980.

Federal Writers Program. *Maryland, A Guide to the Old Line State.* New York: n.p., 1940.

———. *Delaware, A Guide to the First State.* New York: Middle Atlantic Press, 1938.

Fleming, Lorraine. *Delaware's Outstanding Natural Areas and Their Preservation.* Hockessin, Del.: n.p., 1978.

Godfrey, Michael A. *A Sierra Club Naturalist's Guide to the Piedmont of Eastern North America.* San Francisco: Sierra Club Books, 1980.

Gosner, Kenneth. *A Field Guide to the Atlantic Seashore.* Boston: Houghton Mifflin, 1979.

Goss-Custard, John D. "Hard Times on Mussel Beach." *Natural History* Mar. 1987: 64-70.

Griffith, Daniel R. "Ecological Studies of Prehistory." *Transactions of the Delaware Academy of Science* 5 (1974): 63-81.

Hancock, Harold. "The Sense of the Times: Colonial Delaware." *Transactions of the Delaware Academy of Science* 6 (1975): 143-162.

———. *Delaware Two Hundred Years Ago, 1780-1800.* Wilmington: n. p., 1987.

Harrison, Hal H. *A Field Guide to Birds' Nests.* Boston: Houghton Mifflin, 1975.

Jordan, Robert R. "The Impact of Geology in Delaware: Past Present and Future." *Transactions of the Delaware Academy of Science* 7 (1976): 11-30.

Karinen, Arthur E. "Numerical and Distributional Aspects of Maryland Population, 1631-1840: Part Two." *Maryland Historical Society* 60, no. 2 (1963): 139-160.

Kraft, John C. "Geological Reconstruction of Ancient Coastal Environments in the Vicinity of the Island Field Archaeological Site, Kent County, Delaware." *Transactions of the Delaware Academy of Science* 5 (1974): 83-118.

———. "The Coastal Environment." *Transactions of the Delaware Academy of Science* 7 (1976): 31-65.

Kricher, John C. *Field Guide to Eastern Forests.* Boston: Houghton Mifflin, 1988.

Lauginiger, Edward M., and Hartstein, Eugene F. "Delaware Fossils." Delaware Mineralogical Society. 1981.

Lawrence, Susannah. *The Audubon Society Field Guide to the Natural Places of the Mid-Atlantic States.* Vol. 1, *Coastal.* New York: Knopf, 1984.

Layton, Charles. "They Hope to Save Great Swamp." *Philadelphia Inquirer* 26 (Jan. 1975).

Lippson, Alice Jane, and Lippson, Robert L. *Life in the Chesapeake Bay.* Baltimore: Johns Hopkins U P, 1984.

Lund, Bruce, et al. *Massachusetts Field Guide to Inland Wetland Plants.* Massachusetts Audubon Society and Massachusetts Division of Water Resources: n.d.

Maits, Buckley. *The Natural Resources of Delaware.* Delaware State Soil and Water Conservation Commission: Jan. 1966.

Meanley, Brooke. *Blackwater.* Cambridge, Md.: Tidewater Publishers, 1978.

———. *Birds and Marshes of the Chesapeake Bay Country.* Centreville, Md.: Tidewater Publishers, 1975.

Middleton, Arthur P. *Tobacco Coast: A Maritime History of Chesapeake Bay in the Colonial Era.* Newport News, Va.: The Mariners Museum, 1953.

Milne, Lorus, and Milne, Margery. *The Audubon Society Field Guide to North American Insects and Spiders.* New York: Knopf, 1980.

Mulinax, Gary. "Cypress Swamp Returns to Roots." *Sunday News Journal,* 17 June 1982.

Munroe, John A. *Colonial Delaware: A History.* New York: Kraus International Publications, 1978.

Myers, J. P., et al. "Conservation Strategy for Migratory Species." *American Scientist* 75, no. 1 (1987): 19-26.

Newcomb, Lawrence. *Newcomb's Wildflower Guide: An Ingenious New Key System for Quick, Positive Field Identification of Wildflowers, Shrubs and Vines.* Boston: Little, Brown, 1977.

Niering, William. *Wetlands.* New York: Knopf, 1985.

Passmore, Joan O. *Three Centuries of Delaware Agriculture.* Delaware State Grange and Delaware American Revolution Bicentennial Commission, 1978.

Perry, Bill. *A Sierra Club Naturalist's Guide to the Middle Atlantic Coast: Cape Hatteras to Cape Cod.* San Francisco: Sierra Club Books, 1985.

Peterson, Roger Tory. *A Field Guide to the Birds.* Boston: Houghton Mifflin, 1980.

Peterson, Roger Tory, and McKenny, Margaret. *A Field Guide to Wildflowers of Northeastern and North-Central North America.* Boston: Houghton Mifflin, 1975.

Pickett, Thomas E. "Guide to Common Cretaceous Fossils of Delaware." Delaware Geological Survey. U of Delaware, 1972.

———. "Generalized Geologic Map of Delaware." Delaware Geological Survey. U of Delaware, Apr., 1976.

Pomfret, John E., and Shumway, Floyd M. *Founding the American Colonies: 1583-1660.* New York: n.p., 1970.

Preston, Dickson J. *Talbot County: A History.* Centreville, Md.: Tidewater Publishers, 1983.

Pyle, Robert Michael. *The Audubon Society Field Guide to North American Butterflies.* New York: Knopf, 1981.

Rutman, Darrett B. *The Morning of America.* Boston: Norton, 1971.

Scharf, J. Thomas. *History of Maryland from the Earliest Period to the Present Day.* Baltimore: John B. Piet, 1879.

Scott, Jane. *Botany in the Field.* New York: Prentice Hall, 1984.

Sharp, Jonathan H., ed. *The Delaware Estuary Research as Background for Estuarine Management and Development.* Lewes: U of Delaware, College of Marine Studies, and New Jersey Marine Sciences Consortium, 1983.

Silberhorn, Gene M. *Common Plants of the Mid-Atlantic Coast: A Field Guide.* Baltimore: Johns Hopkins U P, 1982.

Simons, Ted, et al. "Restoring the Bald Eagle." *American Scientist* May-June 1988, 253-259.

Stokes, Donald W., and Stokes, Lillian Q. *A Guide to Animal Tracking and Behavior.* Boston: Little, Brown, 1986.

Sutton, Ann, and Sutton, Myron. *Eastern Forests.* New York: Knopf, 1986.

Taylor, Ronald A. "The Case of the Vanishing Beaches." *US News and World Report* 22 (June 1987).

Teal, Ronald A., and Teal, Mildred. *Life and Death of the Salt Marsh.* Boston: Ballantine Books, 1969.

The Governor's Task Force on Marine and Coastal Affairs. *The Coastal Zone of Delaware.* Newark, Del.: College of Marine Studies, Apr.-Oct. 1970-71.

Tyler, David Budlong. *The Bay and River Delaware.* Cambridge, Md.: Cornell Maritime Press, 1955.

Weeks, Christopher. *Where Land and Water Intertwine: An Architectural History of Talbot County, Maryland.* Baltimore: Johns Hopkins U P, 1984.

Weslager, C.A. *Delaware's Buried Past.* New Brunswick, N. J.: Rutgers U P, 1944.

———. *Red Men on the Brandywine.* Wilmington: Middle Atlantic Press, 1953.

White, Christopher. *Chesapeake Bay: Nature of the Estuary, A Field Guide.* Centreville, Md.: Tidewater Publishers, 1989.

———. *Endangered and Threatened Wildlife of the Chesapeake Bay Region: Delaware, Maryland, and Virginia.* Centreville, Md.: Tidewater Pubishers, 1982.

White, Jim. "Jeepers, Creepers." *Delaware Conservationist* 22, no. 1 (1989): 15-19.

Wright, Louis B. *Cultural Life of the American Colonies: 1607-1763.* New York: n.p., 1957.

Whittendale, Tom. "Is the Black Duck Really in Trouble?" *Delaware Conservationist* 22, no. 4 (Winter 1986-1987): 19-21.

Index

Diatoms, 113

Dicentra cucullaria, 49

Didelphis virginiana, 74

Digitaria sanguinalis, 78

Dinosaurs, 6, 9

Diptera, 53, 84

Distichlis spicata, 112

Ditching, of marshes and swamps, 106-107

Dogbane, 85

Dogwood, 39, 49, 51, 78

Dolichonyx oryzivorus, 120

Dolphins: Atlantic white-sided, 178; bottlenose, 178; grampus, 178; saddleback, 178

Donax variabilis, 166

Dove, 6

Dowitchers, short-billed, 170

Dragonflies, 6, 118

Dragon Run Marsh, 122

Dryocopus pileatus, 59

Dumetella carolinensis, 97

Dunlin, 170, 171

DuPont Company, xiv, 39

Dutch elm disease, 40

Dutchman's breeches, 49

Dutch settlers, xiv, 24, 25, 36

E

Eagles: bald, 36, 42, 141, 143-144; golden, 36, 141, 144-145

Eastern meadowlark, 85, 86

Echinochloa walteri, 110

Ecotones, 95

Eelgrass, 127, 131

Egret: cattle, 176, 177; great, 176; snowy, 176, 177

Egretta thula, 176; *E. tricolor*, 177

Elaphe guttata, 67; *E. o. obsoleta*, 66

Elk, eastern, 69

Elk River, 24, 35

Emerita talpoida, 166

English grass, 36

English settlers, xiv, 25, 26, 31

Ensis directus, 114

Eocene epoch, 8, 9

Epigaea repens, 50, 51

Eptesicus fuscus, 76

Erigeron canadensis, 78; *E. annuus*, 78

Erythronium americanum, 49

Eumeces fasciatus, 68; *E. laticeps*, 68

Euphorbia polygonifolia, 164

Euphydryas phaeton, 118

Eurytides marcellus, 53, 85

F

Fagaceae, 48

Fagus grandifolia, 48

Falco sparverius, 88

Fall line, 3

Farming, effect of early clearing, 34

Felis concolor couguar, 70

Fenwick Island, 158, 161

Fern, 50; Christmas, 49

Festuca spp., 81

Finch: house, 100; purple, 100

Finns, 24, 25

Fire, as selector, 51; in swamp, 140

Fireflies, 118

Fish, ancient, 9

Fisherman Island, 159

Flickers, 59

Flies, 6, 84; blackflies, 118; deerflies, 118, 119; horseflies, 118, 119; marsh flies, 119

Florida caerulea, 176

Flycatcher, great crested, 99

Forest: ancient boreal, 14; coastal plain, 46; ecology, 46; mixed-mesic, 15; original, 45; piedmont, 46

Magnolia, sweet bay, 7, 50, 51, 138

Magnoliaceae, 7

Magnolia virginiana, 7, 51, 138

"Magothy Formation," 7

Malaclemys t. terrapin, 168

Mallard, 125, 128, 129, 130

Mammals, ancient, 9

Man, first appearance on peninsula, xiv

Manninose, 114

Manokin River, 28

Mantids, 84

Maple, red, 32, 48, 50, 80, 137, 141, 148, 164

Marine worms, 112, 114

Marmota monax, 92

Marsh elder, 113

Maryland, Eastern Shore of, xi, xiii, 33

Matawan group, 8

Mayapple, 50

Medicago sativa, 83

Melanerpes carolinus, 59; *M. erythrocephalus*, 59

Melanitta fusca, 131; *M. nigra*, 131; *M. perspicillata*, 131

Meleagris gallopavo, 64

Melitta quinquiesperforata, 166

Melospiza georgiana, 121; *M. georgiana nigrescens*, 121; *M. melodia*, 82, 99

Mephitis mephitis, 93

Mercantilism, 31

Mercenaria mercenaria, 114

Merchant mills, 35

Merganser: hooded, 131; red-breasted, 131

Mergus serrator, 131

Mesozoic era, 6, 7

Metompkin Island, 159

Mice, 46, 101

Michini nelsonii, 115

Microtus pennsylvanicus, 90

Middletown, DE, 37, 38, 39

Midpeninsular divide, 13

Milkweed, 85; swamp, 118

Mimus polyglottos, 97

Mink, 133-134, 178

Minnow, sheepshead, 117

Minquas Creek, 24

Miocene epoch, 9, 10

Miocene soils, 139, 148

Mispillion River, 32

Mississippian epoch, 6

Misumena spp., 84

Mitchella repens, 50

Mniotilta varia, 57

Mockingbird, 97

Moles, 90, 178; eastern, 90; northern star-nosed, 90

Molothrus ater, 54

Monmouth group, 8

Monoculture, effects of, 35

Moorhen, 122

Mosquitoes, 107, 108; saltmarsh, 118-119

Mourning dove, 98

Mouse, white-footed, 70

MSX, 115

Mullein, 78

Multiflora rose, 78, 79, 80

Mummichog, 176

Murderkill River, 32

Murphy, Pedro, 179-180

Muskrat, 124, 125, 132-133, 178

Mussels, ribbed, 116

Mustela frenata, 101; *M. vison*, 133

Mya arenaria, 114

Myiarchus crinitus, 99

Myocaster coypus, 134

Myotis lucifugus, 76

Myrica cerifera, 51

Springtails, 52

Squash, 16

Squids, ancient, 6

Squilla empusa, 115

Squirrel, 47, 51, 178; Delmarva fox 40, 71, 73, 178; eastern fox, 73; gray, 71, 72; red, 71, 73; southern flying, 71

Stake driver, 122

Starlings, 40

Steinkern, 8

Sterna albifrons, 172; *S. caspia*, 172; *S. forsteri*, 173; *S. hirundo*, 172; *S. maxima*, 172; *S. sandvicensis*, 172

Sternotherus odoratus, 150

Stewartia malacodendron, 51

Stickleback, four-spined, 117

Storeria d. dekayi, 100; *S. o. occipitomaculata*, 67

Strawberries, 39

Strix varia, 146

Sturnella magna, 85

Sumac, 78, 79

Susquehanna River, 11, 13, 14, 15, 22

Susquehannock Indians, 18, 19, 24, 25, 26

Swan: mute, 127; tundra, 125, 127-128, whistling, 80

Swanendael, 24

Swedish settlers, xiv, 24, 25

Sweet flag, 110

Sweet pepperbush, 138, 148

Sycamore, 50

Sylvilagus floridanus, 91

Symplocarpus foetides, 49

Syngnathus fuscus, 172

T

Tabanidae, 119

Tabanus americanus, 119

Talorchestia spp., 165

Tamiasciurus hudsonicus, 71

Tamias striatus, 71

Tanager, 54; scarlet, 58; summer, 58

Tangier Sound, 176

Taraxacum officinale, 78

Taxodium distichum, 32, 138

Teal: blue-winged, 128, 130; green-winged, 128, 130

Tearthumb, 110, 111, 120

Tectonic subsidence, 157

Tent caterpillars, 100

Terns: Caspian, 172; common, 172; Forster's, 173; gull-billed, 173; little, 172, 173; royal, 172, 175; sandwich, 172

Terrapene carolina, 69

Terrapin, 168-169

Tertiary period, 9, 11

Thamnophis s. sirtalis, 66

Third Haven Meeting House, 34

Thistle, 81, 85; bull, 82; Canada, 82; field, 82; nodding, 82; pasture, 82; tall, 82

Thousand Acre Marsh, 120, 127, 128

Threskiornithidae, 177

Thrush, wood, 55

Tick, 96; deer, 53; wood, 53

Tipularia discolor, 50

Titmice, 54

Toads: American, 89; Fowler's, 89

Tobacco, 27, 33, 35, 37

Toothwort, 49

Towhee, rufous-sided, 99

Toxostoma rufum, 97

Trailing arbutus, 50, 51

Tree ferns, 6

Treefrogs: barking, 152; Cope's gray, 152; gray, 152; green, 152, 153; northern spring peeper, 152